Advance Praise for
Executing Your Strategy

"There is nothing more frustrating than to see a great strategic opportunity being destroyed with poor execution; in this book the authors make execution leadership come to life with great examples from their deep experience. Read it. Then do it—again and again until it becomes habit."
   —*Carl Spetzler*, CEO, Strategic Decisions Group

"The methods described in *Executing Your Strategy* helped us accelerate our transformation during the course of our journey to becoming a solutions company."
   —*Rob Johnson*, President, North America, APC-MGE Companies

"Why do strategies fail, and can we do better? Morgan, Levitt, and Malek develop a practical road map complete with modern examples of six imperatives; integration of these imperatives is the key for doing the right thing and doing it right. To bring it home, they give us metrics and worksheets that are directly useful for executive MBA students—and executives."
   —*Rich Burton*, Professor of Strategy, The Fuqua School of Business, Duke University

EXECUTING YOUR STRATEGY

EXECUTING YOUR STRATEGY

How to Break It Down and Get It Done

Mark Morgan

Raymond E. Levitt

William Malek

Harvard Business School Press

Boston, Massachusetts

Library of Congress Cataloging-in-Publication Data

Morgan, Mark, 1954–
    Executing your strategy : how to break it down and get it done / Mark Morgan,
Raymond E. Levitt, William Malek.
        p. cm.
    ISBN-13: 978-1-59139-956-8 (hardcover : alk. paper)
    ISBN-10: 1-59139-956-4
    1. Strategic planning. 2. Project management. 3. Organizational effectiveness.
4. Leadership. I. Levitt, Raymond E. II. Malek, William III. Title.

    HD30.28.M6473 2007
    658.4'012—dc22

                                                                        2007021450

Contents

Acknowledgments   vii

Introduction   1
Why Strategic Execution Is So Difficult—
and What You Can Do About It

Part I   Strategy-Making Imperatives

One   Ideation Imperative   27
Clarify and Communicate Identity, Purpose,
and Long-Range Intention

Two   Vision Imperative   61
Translate Intention into Strategy, Goals, and Metrics

Three   Nature Imperative   91
Align Strategy, Culture, and Structure

Part II   Project Leadership Imperatives

Four   Engagement Imperative   141
Engage Strategy Through the Project Investment Stream

Five   Synthesis Imperative   181
        Monitor and Align Project Work

Six   Transition Imperative   213
        Move Project Outputs into the Mainstream

        Conclusion   239
        Executing Strategy by Doing the Right Things Right

        Notes   263
        Index   271
        About the Authors   289

Acknowledgments

In the summer of 1998 Ray Levitt had a fateful conversation with Bill Kern, who was then CEO of IPS Associates (now IPSolutions [IPS]) and a fellow board member of Vité Corporation. This conversation spawned the idea of launching a collaboration between Stanford and IPS to develop the Stanford Advanced Project Management Program (SAPM), in which the Strategic Execution Framework and Six Domains of Strategic Execution described in this book were conceived, tested, and refined. To Bill Kern and Ernie Nielsen, the first IPS program director of SAPM, we offer our profound thanks for conceiving the idea of SAPM and helping in uncountable ways to get the program launched.

Andy DiPaolo, associate dean of engineering and director of the Stanford Center for Professional Development (SCPD), and Paul Marca, head of professional education in SCPD, agreed in 1999 to experiment with a new kind of university-industry partnership to deliver professional education in advanced project management. Since 1999 SCPD and IPS staff members, including Julia Harms, Carissa Little, Ritu Chandra, Tim Wasserman, Holly Lewin, and Joyce Rice, along with many others, have provided phenomenal marketing and logistical support for delivering SAPM. It has been a joy to collaborate with all of you in creating and growing the award-winning SAPM executive education program that was the prime inspiration for this book. We thank all of you for your creativity in addressing innumerable challenges and for your dedication to making the SAPM program a world-class learning experience for its graduates.

The more than twenty-five hundred graduates of SAPM since 1999 have played a crucial role in shaping and enriching our understanding of the Six Domains by questioning and challenging our assumptions in class and afterward, and providing rich narratives from their own companies to illustrate and refine our framework. Many of your stories enrich this book.

Ann Bundy of IPS had the vision and capacity to help develop the "Project Management Manual" originally published by HBS Press in 1996. The enduring nature of this accomplishment sparked the reconnection to Harvard in 2003 that resulted in this book.

Stephanie Cerra of IPS put enormous effort into editing, document preparation, end notes, and citations. Your contributions greatly accelerated and enhanced the project of writing this book.

Phil Mason of IPS set up the collaborative workspace for the authors and editors to work in a version-controlled environment. The writing and editing processes of coproducing multiple versions of this book from locations around the globe were greatly facilitated by your foresight and efforts to create what we have come to know as the DMZ or document management zone. Thanks for taking the initiative.

Several anonymous reviewers selected by HBS Press pored over and tore apart two earlier drafts of the manuscript. We thank you for your detailed and constructive critique of our ideas and their expression, which helped to align our book more closely to the needs of HBS Press's readers.

Dr. Gideon Kunda of Tel Aviv University, wizard of organizational culture and our spirited coinstructor in SAPM, read and commented on early drafts of several chapters from this book. We benefited greatly from your incisive critique.

Rich Grimes of Capital Tower Group (formerly of AT&T Wireless) and Paul Holland of Hewlett-Packard provided specific feedback on two of the cases discussed in the book. Our special thanks are due to both of you.

As first time HBS Press authors we are more than usually indebted to Kirsten Sandberg, our editor there. Kirsten's tough, but always constructive, critique of our work was crucial in shaping the book into its present form. We thank you for being the sponsor of this writing project at the Press, for holding firm to your high standards, and for helping us, time after time, to swallow our pride and take yet another run at the reorganization of the content.

Colleen Kaftan, our inordinately talented, infinitely patient, and absolutely tireless developmental editor, was much more than an editor. You were the project manager of our strategic book execution project. You listened, heard, improved, integrated, and played back our dissonant voices to produce a coherent end product, always with incredible grace and a wry sense of humor. Your prior experience working with the editors at Harvard Business School Press kept the wheels of this project rolling smoothly on both sides. We express our unbounded appreciation and affection to you for your pivotal role in bringing this book project to fruition.

Acknowledgments by Mark Morgan and William Malek

Many IPSolutions colleagues and clients have contributed to the development of this book. We would especially like to acknowledge the contributions of:

- Kimm Ronberg, KC Anderson, and Barba Kandarian, for developing the client relationships that ultimately led to many of the experiences and insights documented in this book.

- Tom Geoghan and Darrell Blackburn, for long-term contributions in portfolio management, workshops, consulting practices, course development, and education services that helped us formulate our understanding of the overall organizational issues of strategy execution at the program and project level. Tom's work at IPS, eBay, and PayPal are leading examples of strategy execution. Thank you.

- Nigel and Patricia Yorwerth, for expert advice on how to write the original book proposal and architect the book. Your insight provided a critical view of the path forward toward writing this book.

- John Warren and Janet Ellison, for creating capabilities in benefits realization, soft skills courses, and many other facets of the SAPM program and the IPS business. Thank you for your hard work and dedication to our business, our clients, and our staff over the last decade of service.

- Andrew Cole, Rob Johnson, Amy DeCastro, Dave Johnson, Neil Rassmussen, and Bill Kabai from American Power Conversion, who have collaborated with us in pioneering applications of our teaching and consulting. Your spirit of collaboration and unstoppable drive provided a proving ground for many of our concepts, and your support has been truly a pleasure of a lifetime.

,owledgments by Raymond Levitt

.y approach to consulting, teaching, and writing about advanced project management has been inspired and informed by two remarkable scholars of organizations whose paths I was fortunate to cross early in my academic career: James G. March and W. Richard Scott. Jim March's brilliant lectures, loaded with insights that bridged across psychology, economics, sociology, and political science, inspired me with the vision that managers might one day be able to model and simulate their organizations well enough to "engineer" their work processes and structures in the way engineers design their bridges and buildings; Dick's patient tutelage over the past decade has led me to begin to understand how deeply societal institutions shape and regularize human activities and interactions.

John Kunz and Yan Jin are two other special colleagues and friends who have enriched both my life and my work. John's insights about applying non-numerical computing to difficult, fuzzy problems and Yan's brilliance and doggedness in developing the original Virtual Design Team agent-based simulation of project teams have been key foundations of my work. May we all live long enough to watch Stanford play in another Rose Bowl game together!

I have had the good fortune to work with more than sixty superb doctoral students at MIT and Stanford during my career to date. Let me assure every one of you that you have been my teachers as much as my students. Your past and ongoing work products are a continuing source of immense satisfaction and joy.

Finally, to Kathleen Adele Sullivan Levitt, my spouse and friend of more than thirty-three years: Only you can ever know how much your unconditional love, friendship—and your occasional "editorial" interventions—have enabled and enriched my personal and professional life, and improved this book. Thank you, and *Sláinte!*

Introduction

Why Strategic Execution Is So Difficult—and What You Can Do About It

There may be a thousand little choices in a day.
All of them count.

—Shad Helmstetter

THE GLOBAL BUSINESS landscape is littered with expensive, well-intended strategies that failed in the execution phase. Some make the front pages and the evening news. Many more die quietly or simply disappear into desk drawers and forgotten PowerPoint presentations. All represent a significant drain on resources that could have been used more profitably elsewhere. The spectacular flameouts of Carly Fiorina at HP, John Akers at IBM, John Sculley at Apple, and Pehr Gyllenhammar at Volvo are merely a few high-profile examples among thousands of CEOs whose strategies fail every year because of poor execution.

Corporations spend about $100 billion a year on management consulting and training, most of it aimed at creating brilliant strategy.[1] Business schools unleash throngs of aspiring strategists and big-picture thinkers into the corporate world every year. Yet studies have found that less than 10 percent of effectively formulated strategies carry through to successful implementation.[2] So something like 90 percent of companies consistently fail to execute strategies effectively.

1

Nevertheless, senior executives regularly retreat to their corner offices, to their boardrooms, or to elegant conference centers where they plan the Next Big Thing, leaving the grunt work of execution to the lower echelons. And that is precisely where strategy goes awry. When strategy makers neglect the critical connections between words and deeds—between ideas and action—they are almost guaranteed to fail.

Many executives understand this instinctively, but they lack a systematic approach for identifying and implementing the *right* array of actions to deliver on their promises. Worse, they ignore their own responsibilities toward the people at the execution level of the company. Over and over, they make broad—and mistaken—assumptions about how well the strategy they have in mind converts into understandable work at all levels of the organization, and whether the organization is capable of making the changes that are needed to implement the latest strategic vision. When executives think of the people who will implement strategy as mere lines and boxes on an organization chart, they inevitably fail to tap the full power of the enterprise.

In the midst of fast-changing technologies and increasingly competitive global markets, senior executives face extreme pressure from customers, competitors, market analysts, shareholders, boards of directors, and employees. All of these forces place a premium on the executives' ability to articulate strategy clearly and provide adequate resources for middle managers and workers to implement it within the context of the corporate structure, culture, attitudes, goals, measurement and reward systems, and ongoing operations. Often this requires reshaping the organization, developing new systems, learning new behaviors, and creating new types of interactions.

One of top management's biggest blind spots is the failure to recognize that any significant shift in strategy requires changes in day-to-day activities throughout the organization. Small shifts may require only minor changes. Significant shifts require significant changes—from subtle to sweeping—that can only be successful if implemented systematically. And people at all levels can either help or hinder the transition.

Strategy and Action: How Do You Know Where Your Organization Will Be Two Years from Now?

Executives regularly find themselves responding to a simple, almost formulaic question: Where do you expect to take your organization in two years' time? Like Akers, Sculley, and Fiorina, most executives answer by pulling out their strategy documents and launching into their official presentations.

A more important question, in our view, is, How do you know you will get there? Corporate leaders would come much closer to describing where their organization will be in two years' time by describing their current *investments*—the array of projects, programs, and activities where they have chosen to apply the scarce resources of time, money, energy, and attention. Put another way, the best indicator of strategic direction and future outcomes is an enterprise-wide look at what the company is *doing* rather than what it is *saying*—what the strategy makers are empowering people at the execution level to accomplish.

Don't believe it? Just go back two years and look at the major activities that have been completed in any given company. Compare that record with the strategy the company was espousing two years ago (if anyone can remember it). Chances are that the list of completed actions (initiatives, projects, programs, or work packages), along with another list of failed or aborted actions and those that were never undertaken, will offer a better explanation of the company's current position than its two-year-old strategy documents.

What a company is *doing*—its de facto strategy—can be summed up by identifying the group of projects in which it invests. In fact, for the espoused strategy to become a reality, it must be converted into the packets of work we call *projects*. Projects are the temporary initiatives that companies put into place alongside their ongoing operations to achieve specific goals. They are clearly defined packages of work, bound by deadlines and endowed with resources including budgets, people, and facilities.

The project—the lowly project—is the true traction point for strategic execution. It is the project that builds new products, new services, new systems, new skills, new alliances, or new delivery mechanisms for internal or external customers. A company's project portfolio drives its future value.[3] New businesses, new services, new channels, and new markets are opened by projects. The project portfolio—the array of investments in projects and programs a company chooses to pursue—is the agent of change, and the success of change initiatives depends on the ability to select and manage the projects that deliver the change.

Successful strategic execution requires tightly aligning the project portfolio to the corporate strategy, as shown in figure I-1. We call this the *engagement domain*, where the objectives of strategy meet the constraints of resources. It is the fundamental responsibility of executives to ensure that

FIGURE I-1

Strategic engagement: Translating the strategy into the project portfolio

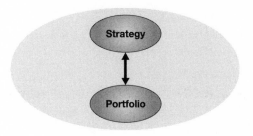

the corporation engages itself continuously in the right projects, invests project resources in the right amounts, and establishes the right priorities in an evolving competitive environment. It is also one of the most difficult challenges that leaders face.

The engagement domain, which requires companies to *engage the strategy via the project investment stream*, is the most central of the six domains of strategic execution. Executives have a tendency to think of this kind of work as being too "tactical" to take up their precious time. Nothing could be further from the truth—and this attitude can signal the unraveling of an organization. Some executives really get this, but too many don't.[4]

Every project investment either contributes to successful strategic execution or sucks resources away from successful strategic execution. Only by continuously reviewing the project portfolio, carefully allocating available resources, and consciously realigning the organization can a company bring its espoused strategy to life. Only through effective engagement in the strategic project portfolio will every working moment of every person's time, every dollar invested, and every activity undertaken align with the overall strategy rather than work against it.

Strategy makers can only align the engagement domain by working with and through project leaders at the execution level.

The Great Executive Blind Spot: The Strategic Role of Project Portfolio Management

Effective strategy consists of choosing to do the right things. Effective execution means doing those things right. Strategic execution results from executing the right set of strategic projects in the right way. It lies at the crossroads of corporate leadership and project portfolio management—the place where an organization's purpose, vision, and culture translate into performance and results. There is simply no path to executing strategy other than the one that runs through project portfolio management.

Project portfolio management is *always on*, whether executives at the top of the corporation recognize it or not. Everywhere in the organization, people must make thousands of small project investment decisions every day. The most subtle—and perhaps the most elusive—of such decisions are how to spend each working moment of every person's time. If the firm's leaders fail to engage actively in strategic portfolio management, those small but critical daily portfolio management decisions get delegated—by default—to the lowest level of the organization.

Without clear leadership that aligns each activity and every project investment to the espoused strategy, individuals will use other decision rules in choosing what to work on: first in, first out; last in, first out; loudest demand; squeakiest wheel; boss's whim; least risk; easiest; best guess as to what the organization needs; most likely to lead to raises and promotion; most politically correct; wild guess—or whatever they feel like at the time. Portfolio management still takes place, but it is not necessarily aligned with strategy, and it occurs at the wrong level of the organization.

The importance of portfolio management is not a new idea. Robert Simons and Antonio Davila, in their classic *Harvard Business Review* article, "How High Is Your Return on Management?" cite two cases that underscore the difference between passive project portfolio management and a more active, strategic, *engaged* approach.[5]

In the first case, Automation Consulting Services, a small Boston-based consulting firm, originally embarked on a strategy to differentiate itself by delivering state-of-the-art solutions to companies in industrial technology. The firm grew quickly to four locations, but after seven years of operation, it suffered a meltdown when the organization as a whole lost focus. Individual offices were taking their own directions, and the company was coming undone. Managers were trying to accomplish too many diverse projects, and their results suffered. Everyone was working harder and producing less. This has become almost epidemic in today's organizations. Lack of strategic clarity coupled with a "do it all" mentality chokes the organization, reduces output, decimates scarce resources, and leads to employee burnout.

No matter what the mission statement said at Automation Consulting Services, no matter what the strategy document said, no matter what the status reports described in quarterly reviews, the company lost its grip on project investments related to strategy. The talk of the organization became irrelevant to the walk of the organization, with each office walking in a different direction.

In contrast, Simons and Davila describe Automatic Data Processing (ADP) as an example of how company performance can be sustained over a long period of time: at the time of writing, ADP had registered 143 consecutive quarters (35 years) of double-digit earnings-per-share growth. This is a record unmatched by any other company on the New York Stock Exchange. How did it happen? Simons and Davila contend that ADP's stellar performance resulted from using a strict set of criteria with which to judge the alignment of projects with company strategy, and clearly communicating priorities to the organization. In their words:

> What separates these two organizations is plain: at ADP, managerial energy is riveted on specific, crystal clear strategic priorities only for the time it takes to get results. Certainly, the managers at both companies are aware that the world is teeming with business opportunities, but at ADP, managers also know there are only so many hours in a day and only so many managers to go around . . . Instead of trying to capture every flag like Automation Consulting Services tried to do, they make hard choices about where they will commit their energy and, more important, where they won't. This clarity of purpose transforms all energy into productive energy and propels strategy from the boardroom to the marketplace.[6]

These examples highlight the conversion of a strategic thought or direction from the boardroom to a product that makes it to a customer in the marketplace. Notice that the journey from boardroom to marketplace must pass through project management.

Simon and Davila argue that one measure of ADP's success is the ratio of management energy required to create productive energy in the organization. They call this measure *return on management*, or ROM, a powerful concept that shows how laser focus on the right strategic projects yields superior performance that is sustainable year after year.

The same disciplined approach can enlighten investment decisions for every kind of scarce resource. Any organization can enjoy excellent returns on all its investments—in terms of time, talent, funds, and facilities as well as managerial energy—if it carefully and continuously aligns its portfolio of projects and programs with a clearly articulated strategy. Both of these firms—like most organizations—are presented with more potential projects than they have the resources to execute. So doing the right projects means *actively deciding not to undertake the wrong projects*, which Automation Consulting Services failed to do.

Many executives fail to understand how crucial it is to determine the degree of alignment between investments and strategy. All one need do is look at the project portfolio to see whether the project work of the organization is aligned with the strategy or not. As Simon and Davila point out, ADP management did this religiously. But many executives today do not. With few exceptions, there remains a significant divide between strategic thinking and effective execution. Part of this problem springs from a human tendency to conceptualize much more quickly than to operationalize. Some of it may come from business school training that emphasizes theory over action.[7] Whatever the cause, competent and well-meaning executives routinely fail to integrate and align the work of the organization with the strategic vision of the organization.

The Hidden Language Barrier: Translating Strategy-Speak into Project Parlance

There is simply no way for senior management to accomplish a strategic transformation without getting deeply engaged in project management, the organizational systems that surround it, and the behaviors and terminology required to lead it. In some cases, particularly for radically new or transformative strategies, the senior executives themselves must become the project leaders.

Unfortunately, most executives and strategic thinkers have not yet learned the language of project management. Even thought leaders who emphasize the importance of strategic action or activities invariably fail to take the next step by recognizing that the most important—indeed, the *only*—actions and activities that serve to execute strategy are the projects and programs that will bring the organization from its current state to its desired future state.

We do not claim that this is a new idea. However, in our experience, what has been missing is a systematic framework within which to apply decades of important contributions on the subject. Consider Michael Porter's seminal piece, first published in 1996, "What Is Strategy?"[8] In it, Porter notes, "The essence of strategy is in the activities—choosing to perform activities differently or to perform different activities than rivals. Otherwise, a strategy is nothing more than a marketing slogan that will not withstand competition."[9] Activities, or processes, are created and changed through projects. So a strategy that requires new processes or activities requires projects to design and implement them. Yet this crucial role for projects is lost in almost all writing on the subject of strategy.

More recently, Lawrence Hrebiniak writes:

Execution is a process. It is not the result of a single decision or action. It is the result of a series of integrated decisions or actions over time.

This helps explain why sound execution confers competitive advantage. Firms will try to benchmark a successful execution of strategy. However, if execution involves a series of internally consistent, integrated activities, activity systems, or processes, imitation will be extremely difficult, if not impossible.[10]

Hrebiniak comes tantalizingly close to writing the word *project* but instead dances around it with words like *integrated activities*, *activity systems*, *processes*. Like Porter and others before him, Hrebiniak seems reluctant to recognize—or perhaps he simply ignores—the critical role of project management in strategic execution. It is as if that word—the lowly word *project*—simply cannot be uttered in the lofty language of strategy-speak. Therein, we believe, lies one of the difficulties in converting strategy into action.

This hidden language barrier prevents many senior executives from communicating effectively with the people who will actually bring the strategy to life. Executives speak of high-level strategic *outcomes* rather than specific *project outputs*, and too often they fail to link the two. The converse is also true: project and program managers rarely have the opportunity or inclination to think about the strategic implications of their work. They focus (and are rewarded) on *project outputs* rather than *strategic outcomes.*

To counteract this dangerous disconnect, corporate executives and strategy makers must eradicate the idea that the nuts and bolts of project and program management are beneath them. (A program is a cluster of interconnected projects.) Likewise, project and program leaders must take responsibility for understanding and internalizing strategy.

The language of strategy formulation covers high-level concepts such as the company's identity, intention, and purpose. It connects this collective who, what, and why with the corporate culture and the appropriate structure, and with the goals and metrics that will be used to measure strategic success. The language of the project portfolio covers the specifics of getting things done—who, how, when, and with which resources. It links the strategic project investments with ongoing operations and supports the transfer of new capabilities to the line.

In the human brain, the corpus callosum links the two brain hemispheres to align a person's actions with her visions and intentions. Research has shown that when the corpus callosum is severed, people are unable to translate their plans and desires into coordinated actions.[11] Similarly, *engagement* serves as the corpus callosum of strategic execution. If it is severed or malfunctions—if the project portfolio becomes disengaged from strategy—a lethal disconnect is created. Actions do not align with one another or with strategic visions and intentions, and the strategy has no hope of execution.

Two Types of Disconnect

A couple of vignettes from the mobile telephone industry illustrate two important ways in which faulty translation in the engagement domain can undercut execution. In essence, one company executed flawlessly, but its leaders failed to notice that they were investing in the wrong projects. The other company failed to invest the resources necessary to manage a crucial project well.

In the first case, the low-Earth-orbit satellite telephone service known as Iridium grew out of a complex development program that met all of its extremely aggressive technical and schedule targets within its original cost parameters. However, somewhere in its eleven-year duration, the program's initial strategic goals became irrelevant, as convenient and inexpensive cell phone technologies rose up to replace Iridium's value for customers.

In contrast, the program code-named Odyssey at AT&T Wireless represents a different kind of failure. The Odyssey number portability program was strategically critical when it was launched, with an immutable external deadline imposed by the FCC. The program remained crucial throughout its life cycle, but it failed catastrophically in execution. Within months of this dismal outcome, the Wireless division was absorbed by Cingular, at a considerable loss of value to AT&T.[12]

What Went Wrong in the Execution of These Endeavors?

No matter how well or how frequently the organization selects and updates a portfolio of strategic programs and projects, success in execution ultimately depends on two things: whether the planned objectives for each program and project remain relevant and feasible, given dynamic changes in the organization's competitive environment, and whether each of the strategic programs and projects is managed well enough to achieve the objectives that justified it at the time it was selected for investment. In other words:

- Do the right projects and programs! Executives must continually ask themselves tough questions about the market considerations and strategic rationale for all the work in the portfolio. What has changed since the last replanning session? Are the desired *strategic outcomes* still relevant in the evolving environment? Should some specific work be redirected or even canceled? Does the strategy require investment in systems and structures that goes well beyond the central investment in products and services?

- Do the projects and programs right! Is the work on plan? How do we know? Can we view the aggregate status of all work and utilization of all resources across projects? Are the targeted *project outputs* still relevant and feasible? Do people understand the strategic purpose and priorities of each project? Are they making all the necessary connections so that their work can transfer to the ongoing operations? Do they have access to all the resources they need? How are they managing changes?

Great execution in the absence of reasonable strategy is no better than great strategy with poor execution. Combine either one with poor ongoing portfolio management and you get the exact mixture needed for failure. The only antidote, as we argue throughout this book, is to think systemically in linking the evolving strategy to the project investments that will bring it to life.

Strategic Execution Requires Systemic Thinking

Strategic execution requires a systemwide approach that consistently drives organizations to do the right things—and to do those things right. Such an approach helps identify, map out, and prioritize the necessary project investments so that everyone understands what they must do and how they should interact with others to execute strategy. It also revisits the investment decisions regularly to make sure they stay on track.

American Power Conversion: A Major Strategy Shift

Consider a major strategy shift the leaders at American Power Conversion (APC) undertook in 2005. Founded in 1988 by three talented electronic power engineers from MIT Lincoln Laboratory, the Rhode Island–based company has led the pack in power conditioning technology throughout its history. APC's products, sold to consumers through retail channels, provide continuous and appropriate power levels, reducing the risk to equipment, especially electronics, that is sensitive to power events like lightning strikes, surges, or blackouts.

Outstanding product design capabilities and operational excellence in controlling production costs at distant factories translated to consistently high and growing profitability. By 2005 APC was a publicly traded company with about $2 billion in growing annual sales. The success of its longtime strategy, to create a constant stream of new power conditioning products and expand consumer sales to global markets, attracted a large number of strong competitors to challenge its core business.

Enter the inevitable: a shift in the marketplace that required an entirely new corporate configuration. In this case, the change came from APC itself, in the form of a new strategic initiative to combat the trend toward low-margin commoditization by offering custom power system solutions in addition to its main business in innovative retail power conditioning products. The new strategy would engage APC's design and manufacturing capabilities to serve new kinds of specialized customers, such as large data centers, businesses, hospitals, and other organizations.

Sounds straightforward and almost commonplace, doesn't it? So many companies choose a similar shift from products to solutions. But how many understand at the outset the immense array of decisions and activities such a move entails?

Creating this new power conditioning market would require myriad project investments at APC: projects that would drastically embellish all or parts of its manufacturing process to accommodate much more customization, upgrade the skills of its sales force to sell on a consulting basis, and realign its culture from one of tight manufacturing specifications and cost control to a more collaborative, solutions-oriented approach. The new strategy required investments that would leverage APC's reputation for "Legendary Reliability" to add legendary speed and flexibility, all without compromising its existing operations.

Factories that were measured on inventory control, throughput, and efficiency would now be asked to do custom work in the middle of a mass production facility while simultaneously reducing cycle time. As the company developed a market for power conditioning equipment solutions tailored specifically for customers' unique needs and facilities, its goals would change from market share to share of the customer's wallet. This would call on employees to work with clients' facilities managers, general contractors, and builders—a far different set of channel partners than those involved in producing and distributing a power supply in a box with a SKU bar code on the outside to be sold at a local electronics superstore.

APC's strategic shift was actually a full-scale revolution. This same strategic leap from a "make to offer" world to a world of "offer to make" confronted Louis Gerstner at IBM in the 1990s and John Chambers at Cisco in the early 2000s. Like these technology powerhouses before it, APC had achieved its early success through excellence in product design and manufacturing process development, as opposed to excellence in system integration and project management. Large portions of the organization were compensated very well for their performance in the old way of doing business, creating retail products for the shelf. But the new strategy required a whole new set of proficiencies to deliver custom solutions on a variable timetable to a global market.

When a company like APC contemplates shifting from being a products producer to a solutions provider, its leaders and managers must first work together to clarify the strategic intent, then define the rules for decision making, and align goals, metrics, rewards, decisions, and actions across the organization. They must begin to convert the abstract concepts of strategy, structure, culture, goals, and metrics to the actionable packets of work we call projects.

APC needed to make significant investments in projects to create new capabilities, establish new relationships, set new goals, and learn to measure success in new ways. These critical endeavors—all projects to transform the business—were crucial tasks in realigning the organization around its new strategy. Choosing the right transformative projects, and accomplishing them right, was the only way to travel from APC's existing organization to the new blend of ideas, interactions, and activities that would be essential to its new strategy.

Sometimes the most crucial transformative projects are the hardest to identify. Many execution failures stem from neglecting to identify and invest the resources to accomplish these *hidden projects of realignment*. APC's leaders needed to take a systemic look at the project investments necessary to drive the transformation, and disregard any project proposals that would not contribute to that goal.

Moreover, since APC intended to continue operating its successful retail product business, it faced an inherent conflict in allocating resources between projects working *in* and *on* the business and those that would *transform* the business, as described in "Three Types of Strategic Project Investments: Working *in* the Business, Working *on* the Business, and Working *to Transform* the Business."

Which projects and programs were essential to the new strategy? Which should be included in the portfolio, and which should be rejected or deferred? Which should receive the scarce resources that may have to be diverted from ongoing operations? APC needed a road map—a conceptual framework—to help sort through the array of possible project investments.

Earlier we emphasized the importance of aligning the portfolio of project investments with the corporate strategy in what we called the *engagement*

Three Types of Strategic Project Investments

Working in *the Business, Working* on *the Business, and Working* to Transform *the Business*

The bigger the shift in strategy, the greater the need for investments in projects and programs to accomplish it. Together, the leaders and managers must engage in conversations that identify and allocate resources to projects that accomplish three types of work:

- Working in the business
- Working on the business
- Working to transform the business

Working *in* the business means delivering products and services based on existing processes. Most of the ongoing work in a pure professional services firm or a custom solutions provider of hardware and/or software is project based. Such firms must engage continually in portfolio management to discern between those sales opportunities to engage in and those to decline. However, even a "make to offer" manufacturer must regularly initiate projects *in the business* to develop new products on a make to offer basis.

Working *on* the business is about improving current business processes to create better levels of performance. Working on the business requires prioritizing projects aimed at improving the current way of designing and delivering products or services. Working *to transform* the business is almost totally project oriented because transformation involves one-time strategic initiatives to move the enterprise to entirely new ground.[a]

a. Cathleen Benko and F. Warren McFarlan, *Connecting the Dots: Aligning Projects with Objectives in Unpredictable Times* (Boston: Harvard Business School Press, 2003).

domain. It turns out that *engagement* is only one of six domains that must align with each other and with the external environment for successful execution. Taken together, the six domains form the strategic execution framework, which we sometimes abbreviate as SEF. The SEF served as an essential tool for diagnosing potential misfits, choosing the right projects, and doing the projects right as APC traveled the path toward its desired future.

Aligning the Six Domains of the Strategic Execution Framework

Strategic execution can only happen when the six essential domains of the SEF are in alignment and when all six align with the external environment.

The first three domains constitute *strategy making*. Strategic project management investments must align with the company's overall idea of purpose, identity, and long-range intention (which we call *ideation*); with its *vision*, as articulated by its goals and the metrics it uses to evaluate progress toward them; and with its very *nature*, or the culture and structure that define its internal environment, as shown in figure I-2.[13] We call these three domains the *strategy-making* domains because their alignment forms the basis for a coherent strategy that the organization can execute. When a company's strategy aligns with these domains and with the external environment, the strategy makers have chosen to do the right things.

Doing things right requires strategic alignment of the project portfolio in the *project leadership domains*, which we call *synthesis* and *transition*, as shown in figure I-3. Synthesis is the art of putting it all together, the job of managing the strategic projects and programs in the project portfolio effectively. Transition is the essential final step of strategic execution. It transfers the skills, approaches, and technology from the realm of projects to the ongoing operations. It realizes the benefits and embeds them in the organization.

Engagement, as we have already noted, creates the crucial dynamic translation between strategy and action, by integrating action with intent. The

FIGURE I-2

Strategy making requires aligning the *ideation*, *vision*, and *nature* domains with one another and with the external environment

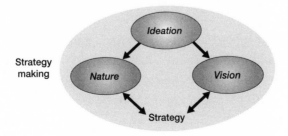

FIGURE I-3

Execution leadership requires aligning the *synthesis* and *transition* domains with one another and with the project portfolio

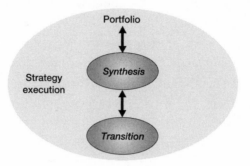

engagement domain aligns the ongoing portfolio of projects and programs dynamically with the organization's strategy as the latter evolves to meet the ever-changing demands of the external environment, as shown in figure I-4.

We have found that all six of the domains are critical. None can be ignored. An organization that focuses on achieving excellence in one or a few domains and falls down in others will not perform as well as a firm that is average across all the domains. And it is no accident that the six essential domains—ideation, nature, vision, engagement, synthesis, and transition—combine to form the acronym INVEST.[14]

Understanding and aligning the six domains is a continuous, dynamic, iterative process. As in any complex system, a change in the environment or in a single domain will trigger or require changes in all the others. So to understand and influence the whole, we must understand the parts. And to optimize each domain, we must understand all the others.

The Six Imperatives of Strategic Execution

The task of aligning the critical domains can be stated in the form of six simple imperatives, as shown in table I-1. The six imperatives are tightly related, and they must operate together although not necessarily in sequence.

Navigating the SEF does *not* require a step-by-step, sequential journey through the six domains. That is why we intentionally drew the framework as a set of interconnected domains rather than a linear, left-to-right

FIGURE I-4

The strategic execution framework (SEF)

Strategic execution requires aligning the six strategic execution domains among themselves and with the external environment. Note the pivotal role of the engagement *domain. It links the strategy developed in the strategy-making domains of* ideation, vision, *and* nature *with the portfolio of projects to be executed in the* synthesis *and* transition *domains of executing strategy.*

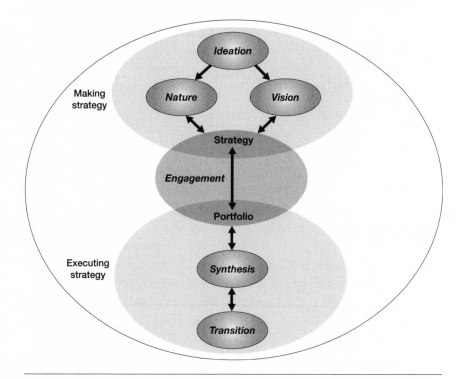

TABLE I-1

INVEST: Six imperatives of strategic execution

Domain	Imperative
Ideation	Clarify and communicate identity, purpose, and long-range intention
Nature	Align the organization's strategy, culture, and structure
Vision	Translate long-range intention into clear goals, metrics, and strategy
Engagement	Engage the strategy via the project investment stream
Synthesis	Monitor and continuously align the project work with strategy
Transition	Transfer projects crisply to operations to reap the benefits

progression. Your organization may be perfectly well aligned in and among one or more of the SEF domains. It may need only minor tweaking in a few domains. Or you may need major realignments, as APC did. But by using the SEF as a guide, you will be able to address the important issues systematically (see "The Antidote to Whack-a-Mole Execution").

We will provide rating instruments for each domain to help you decide where the misalignments are and thus where best to direct your project

---

The Antidote to Whack-a-Mole Execution

Without a systematic framework, strategic execution deteriorates to a game of "whack-a-mole." Anyone who has been to an amusement park or a pinball arcade can relate to the game of whack-a-mole. It features six "moles" that pop up through holes in the game board directly in front of the player. Each player is given a club—a "mole whacker." As the game starts, moles pop up through the holes at random. The object of the game is to whack the mole on the head before he drops back in his hole. The person who hits the most moles wins a fabulous prize. Perhaps a stuffed mole.

Whack-a-mole presents a direct analogy to corporate life. Performance problems rear their ugly head: time for Six Sigma! Whack! Oh, wait a second, metrics seem to be out of alignment! Time for Balanced Scorecard! Whack! Whack! Not so fast . . . people are resisting! Time for a cultural initiative! Whack! Whack! Whack! Funny as the game is, it only lasts two minutes at most. The "initiative of the month" syndrome that plagues many organizations lasts much longer and is much more exhausting.

Interestingly, the results can be strikingly similar between the arcade game and the organizational version. There are winners and losers and lots of energy spent on a nebulous outcome. Some people are rewarded, while others go away empty handed and frustrated. However, there are some important differences. The arcade game stops, and everyone moves on. The organizational game keeps on going, day after day of whacking moles, without even a stuffed animal prize to show for the effort.

Fortunately, the six imperatives—if addressed systematically together—offer an antidote to the whack-a-mole pattern. At the end of chapters 2 through 6, we offer rating instruments specific to each domain. Your organization's results will help you understand where your misalignments lie, and therefore where to start addressing the six imperatives.

investment dollars. The power of the SEF is that it will push you to rethink your stated strategy if the investments necessary to realign one or more of the SEF domains are too costly or too risky to undertake.

Some successful organizations fulfill all six imperatives instinctively, without the explicit aid of a strategic execution framework. For example, Toyota's long march toward dominance in the market for fuel-efficient hybrid automobiles addressed every key element in the six domains, as we will discuss in subsequent chapters. The company's sustained commitment to doing the right things and doing things right has propelled it to a market position rivaling GM as the world's largest auto manufacturer. In fact, many observers (including customers, employees, investment analysts, and shareholders) consider Toyota to be light-years ahead of GM in overall performance.[15]

Using the SEF Intentionally: Wipro

Like APC, the $2.4 billion Bangalore, India–based company Wipro has consciously adopted the strategic execution framework to guide a major corporate transformation. In the midst of changing from a skilled low-cost supplier of computer programming expertise to an integrated provider of technical solutions, Wipro embarked on a series of transformational projects to align the organization around its new strategy.

Incorporated in 1945 as Western India Vegetable Products Limited, the company changed its name to Wipro Limited in 1984 to mark the widening of its product line, which soon expanded from cooking oil and laundry soap to include technology services and hardware, toilet soaps, lighting, finance, biodiagnostics, and later software programming.[16] In the 1980s Wipro hired a team of computer professionals to create a strong info-tech presence for the company throughout India and beyond. By the turn of the millennium, chairman Azim Premji committed to a new corporate identity as a global IT services powerhouse.

Premji and his strategy-making team recognized the need for comprehensive change that would create new alignments across the organization. They consciously addressed the new ideation to be sure that it would be supported by the necessary structural and cultural changes, the right goals and metrics, the right array of project investments managed and coordinated in the right way, and the timely transfer of customer-driven program outcomes back to ongoing operations.

A 2005 study (one of many projects Wipro undertook to drive its transformation) revealed that Wipro's ability to grow in the burgeoning IT solutions market would be directly proportional to its ability to create a world-class cadre of strategy-savvy senior program managers.[17] These key individuals would need to understand in depth their customers' strategic needs and the organizational alignments necessary to attain them, so that they could become trusted advisers working to help design enterprise-wide IT solutions for major corporations. At the same time, they would need to understand, align, and mobilize the resources within Wipro to be able to deliver on the company's intended brand promise. These new skill sets were a far cry beyond Wipro's recognized excellence in providing speedy, low-cost programming skills for its IT outsourcing customers.

The study surveyed internal skill profiles and determined that in addition to the existing personnel, a significant number of customer-facing program managers would be required to meet the potential demand in the future. By 2008–2009 the need for such program managers would grow dramatically.

Using the strategic execution framework helped Wipro adopt a comprehensive, systematic approach to its strategic transformation. First, the company designed a simple way to communicate the new direction throughout the organization, summarized by the slogan "From 'Get it done!' to 'Get the right results!'" The human resource development project team then made a careful assessment of the differences between Wipro's existing project management capabilities and the desired new profile for senior program managers. It identified significant differences between the existing and the desired skill base in terms of business focus, delegating and coaching capabilities, change management and risk management, role identification, and primary plus supplementary abilities.

The strategy makers and the project leaders embarked on a series of transformational projects to create the program management cadre. All agreed that their work would involve sustained focus and investment in multiple dimensions of organizational development, including comprehensive recruiting, training, compensation, empowerment, and career path programs.

The SEF helped guide this significant commitment to investments in what could have remained a hidden project portfolio, which, if unaddressed, would certainly hamper execution. And in recognizing the value of using such a conceptual framework themselves, the strategy makers chose to pass that knowledge on to members of the program management cadre. Through extensive training investments, all members of the new cadre would eventually become proficient at using the SEF to identify and create critical organizational alignments for their customers and within Wipro. Thus at Wipro, the SEF became not only a tool for understanding key alignments but also a shared language for the executives and an empowered group of customer-facing senior program managers. And as we mentioned earlier, shared language and collaboration are essential elements of effective execution (see "Strategic Execution: Think Beyond 'Whose Job Is It?'").

Navigating the Six Imperatives

Our goal in this book is to explore the central role of engaging in strategic project portfolio management for successful execution. To achieve it, we devote a full chapter to each of the six imperatives. As we have noted, addressing the imperatives and aligning the domains to the ever-changing external environment is the *only* effective way to convert strategy into action. When organizations use the framework to select, align, and manage their strategic project portfolios, everyone at every level knows how to invest every available resource every day.

We begin with the *strategy-making* domains, where individuals and organizations decide which are the *right things to do*. Chapter 1 discusses the elements of ideation: the collective who, what, and why that guide all the organization's decisions, help recruit talented workers who share the organization's vision, and give its people a reason to participate energetically and passionately every day. Thus the *ideation imperative* asks us to *clarify and communicate identity, purpose, and long-range intention*. It gives us the starting point and the seeds of the future strategy and shapes the strategic choices that must be made throughout the organization.

Chapter 2 delves into the interconnections among goals, metrics, and strategy. Taken collectively, these three elements form the *vision imperative*: *clarify the strategy in goals and metrics*. We look at some conventional and unconventional wisdom regarding how these elements bear on the choice of the right strategic projects for the organization to undertake.

Chapter 3 covers the very *nature* of the organization: the links between its culture, its strategy, and its structure. This is the domain where the hidden transformative projects of realignment for strategic execution are most

Strategic Execution

Think Beyond "Whose Job Is It?"

We've emphasized that strategy makers must work *together* with strategy implementers to achieve strategic execution. Both groups must recognize project portfolio leadership as a core competency, with different responsibilities at different levels of the organization. When the system works well, everybody in the organization has a role to play.

Senior executives must take responsibility for deciding and communicating the company's purpose, identity, and long-range intentions, and creating the organizational structure and culture that will further those strategic directives. They must translate strategic intent into specific goals and metrics, and work with project leaders to determine which investments are required to attain them. They must take pains to identify the hidden work of realigning the SEF domains as needed, and undertake the projects necessary to accomplish it—in short, to do the right projects. They must establish a sponsorship system to ensure that the project leaders have the resources to do the projects right. And they must revisit these decisions regularly, with the help of project leaders, in a continuous mutual commitment to doing the right things right.

The project leaders, for their part, must go beyond a narrow focus on doing their projects right. They must pay attention to the broader strategic picture and understand the organization well enough to identify the barriers to execution. They must develop the communication skills to help influence the choice of projects, to question strategy when appropriate (as in the Iridium project), to identify and secure required resources, and to seek help with the project work when necessary.

We've observed that when strategic project portfolio management works well, project managers are empowered to *lead from the middle with support from the top*. Fortunately, this creates valuable learning opportunities for project leaders and begins to sketch out a career path that could prepare them for executive positions.

On a personal level, each individual has the ultimate responsibility for deciding how to invest the time, energy, and other resources available on any given workday. At this level, too, the strategic execution framework offers a guide to investment choices both big and small.

likely to reside. The chapter begins by exploring the power of culture and the perils of attempting to change it when the chosen strategy is severely out of sync with existing values and practices. It offers simple tools for testing the alignment between strategy and culture, and describes the types of structure best suited for each of the generic strategic value disciplines we outline in chapter 1. The *nature imperative* requires us to make choices and invest in projects to *align culture, strategy,* and *structure.*

In chapters 4 through 6 we switch the focus to the project leadership domains and shift the discussion from *doing the right things* to *doing things right.*

Chapter 4 explores the specifics of engaging in strategic project portfolio management. It begins with the critical work of clarifying strategic intent and communicating it throughout the organization in both words and deeds. It explores the importance of sponsorship and discusses how to establish the right sponsorship environment. It then turns to the delicate but crucial task of balancing the choice of strategic projects with the availability of resources to achieve them. Chapter 4 revisits in detail the *engagement imperative* we introduced at the beginning of the book: *engage the strategy via the investment stream.*

Engagement is the *central* imperative because it connects the difficult work of strategy making with the equally hard work of leading projects. It identifies and continuously realigns the specific *project outputs* that will deliver the right *strategic outcomes.*

Chapter 5 explores the principles and processes of the portfolio management system that launches, coordinates, monitors, and completes the project work. This embodies the *synthesis imperative: monitor and align the project work.* Chapter 5 describes how project portfolio management actually converts strategy into action and provides continuous feedback to strategy makers about the status of strategic initiatives and the availability of key resources.

Chapter 6 concentrates on how projects and programs become part of ongoing operations. Here, we explore the challenges of managing timely handoffs and realizing the strategic benefits the projects were designed to achieve. We call this the *transition imperative: transfer the projects to the mainstream to reap the benefits.*

In our concluding chapter, "Executing Strategy by Doing the Right Things Right," we begin by exploring the question we hear most often: Where should we start? At first glance, this may seem almost as enigmatic as asking, Where should I grasp a hula hoop? There are, however, concrete and actionable answers to fit every organization, and tools for understanding where the most important tensions lie. We offer a number of such tools throughout this book.

To illustrate all the imperatives in action, we have chosen an example on a grand scale: the Singapore National Library Board's (SNLB's) six-year, multimillion-dollar transformation of the national library system. This massive project represented no less than the strategic execution of an entire nation's desire to support a literate, cultured, intellectually and technologically advanced population.

Like Toyota's move to hybrid cars, the SNLB effort (in which we were privileged to participate and which was one of many experiences that propelled us to develop the SEF) instinctively addressed all of the six imperatives. By distilling the key principles *behind* these two success stories, the strategic execution framework and the six imperatives can guide other organizations, as they did APC and Wipro, toward similarly spectacular accomplishments.

We use these examples in part to illustrate the universal applicability of the framework and the six imperatives: nations can use the framework to direct their future economic and geopolitical strategies; corporations both large and small can apply it to attain their goals; schools, hospitals, arts organizations, and NGOs can adopt it to fulfill their purposes—just as we employ it to be the best teachers, researchers, and consultants we can be. We argue in the conclusion that the six imperatives offer a systematic path toward creating a better, more aligned workplace. Such a workplace can unleash stunning amounts of positive energy in its employees.

Individuals can adopt the six imperatives too, as we will discuss via the sterling example of Lance Armstrong. There is no better way to achieve individual purpose and goals than to align all the domains and to invest every precious minute, and every other personal resource, accordingly. So let us invest some of our time and yours in a journey through the six imperatives of strategic execution.

Part I

Strategy-Making Imperatives

One

Ideation Imperative

Clarify and Communicate Identity, Purpose, and Long-Range Intention

Clarity of purpose, clarity of understanding.

—Zen proverb

O N A TRAIN bound for West Berlin through East Germany in the early 1960s, a family huddled together in their berth. As one of the children sat quietly looking out the window upon arrival at Checkpoint Charlie, all he could see were some faint, distant lights in the late-night gloom. Suddenly the door burst open and through it strode a tall, stern-looking East German officer. The officer demanded to see passports and travel documents for all the family members. The young boy was frightened nearly to incontinence. The officer looked over the papers and asked three questions:

- Who are you?

- Why are you here?

- Where are you going?

Years later, that boy—now grown—can still recall in vivid detail every thread on the officer's coat, every button, and every wrinkle on his face. He can also appreciate the fundamental nature of the three questions. In retrospect, those three questions were all the officer needed to ask in order to test the validity of the family's travel plans. If who you are, why you are here, and where you are going don't make sense when considered together, then there is something wrong with your story, and it requires further interrogation. But if who, why, and where are congruent and clearly aligned, there is very little reason to suspect a problem. So it is with organizations. The questions of who, why, and where form the basis of ideation. The answers to these fundamental questions are the source of organizational energy and form what we call the ideation domain of strategic execution.

The *ideation imperative* requires identifying and aligning the organization's identity, its purpose, and its intentions—the collective who, why, and where that guide all its decisions, drive all its investments, and give all its people a reason to participate every day. In short, the ideation imperative asks us to *clarify and communicate identity, purpose, and long-range intention*—the current situation and the desired future of the strategy equation. Figure 1-1 shows the ideation domain in the strategic execution framework.

The Power of Ideation

The most effective individuals and organizations are those that take pains to understand and cultivate a sense of identity, purpose, and long-range intention. When an organization invests time, money, and energy to develop, align, and articulate these three components of its rationale for existing, it helps all potential stakeholders—including customers, employees, partners, suppliers, and shareholders—make their own decisions about whether to join up or not.

Strong, clear ideation helps differentiate an organization in ways that are far more powerful than slogans or numbers. It helps attract the best employees, who will be increasingly discriminating in their career choices as shifting demographics require organizations to replace the skills of retiring baby boomers. It helps equally discriminating customers make choices about where to make their purchases, where to spend their time, and where to seek help in accomplishing their own purposes and intentions. It helps potential investors decide where to place their faith and their funds.

The elements of ideation are anything but "soft" or trivial, as some corporate leaders seem to think. They represent the foundation of an individual's ability to find meaning or an organization's ability to create and sus-

FIGURE 1-1

The ideation imperative: Clarify and communicate identity, purpose, and intention

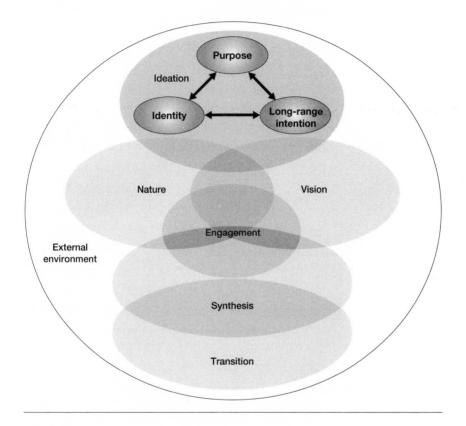

tain value. They are the first place to invest scarce resources for strategic execution, and they guide the choice of the appropriate strategy and the portfolio of strategic projects throughout the organization.

One of the most pressing issues of our time is society's attitude toward, and enslavement to, the ever-diminishing supply of fossil fuels. At least two major companies, BP (formerly British Petroleum and BP Amoco) and Toyota, have chosen to align their identities, purpose, and intentions around the future uses of petroleum and its derivatives. Unlike Iridium, which we profiled in the introduction, these two companies have recognized the need to realign their choice of strategic projects around an increasingly obvious and significant change in the external environment. Both BP and Toyota initiated the realignment by focusing on ideation. Without ever having been introduced to the strategic execution framework or the six imperatives, these companies understood that clarifying identity, purpose, and intention is the critical first step toward *doing the right things*.

BP began by investing in a major portfolio of projects designed to introduce a new, more forward-thinking sense of ideation for a formerly traditional oil company. As early as 1997, then-CEO John Browne took the first steps by withdrawing from the Global Climate Coalition, a group of large corporations that sought to debunk the risks of global warming, and making a series of speeches urging companies to start taking steps to prevent global warming rather than debating whether it would occur.[1]

In 2000 the company adopted the slogan "bp: beyond petroleum" to convey a strong commitment to a future of more responsible energy usage. But a slogan, however catchy and well crafted, has little positive effect on its own. Unless it holds meaning both internally and externally about the organization's true identity, purpose, and intentions, it can be as hollow as a weasel-word mission statement. BP reinforces "beyond petroleum" with investments in solar and wind power and other renewable energy sources. These projects and programs were consolidated in 2005 in a new subsidiary, BP Alternative Energy. Even the company's redesigned logo, a green, white, and yellow sunburst, deliberately connotes commitment to the environment and solar power and promotes BP as "the supermajor [oil company] of choice for the environmentally-aware motorist."[2] Its alternative energy Web site offers information and advice for customers interested in conserving energy and using renewable resources.

Nevertheless, many critics have doubted the sincerity of BP's approach. To counter commentary in articles with titles such as "BP: Beyond Prosperous," "Beyond Probity," and "Beyond the Pale," the company must make continuous investments to communicate its purpose, identity, and intentions and to *align all its actual activities* to that ideation.[3]

A serious corrosion problem in BP's Alaska pipeline in 2006 highlighted the perils of misalignment: all the best intentions and all the green rhetoric in the world could not prevent a potential disaster if the project portfolio did not allocate adequate resources for pipeline maintenance. In fact, key individuals had long been rewarded for *minimizing* maintenance expense—a clear failure to translate ideation into the ongoing investment stream.[4] Fortunately, BP operators found the corrosion in time to prevent a major leak from damaging the fragile arctic environment, but the ensuing long maintenance shutdown disrupted oil supplies around the world at a large remedial cost for the company.

In contrast, Toyota has done a better job of aligning its activities with its ideation. Much of the company's success with hybrid cars flows from the company's relentless attention to ideation and its ability to create the necessary alignments throughout the organization.[5] Again, without referring explicitly to the strategic execution framework, Toyota did, in fact, accomplish all six imperatives in aligning all six domains internally and with the external environment, beginning with ideation.

In *The Toyota Way Fieldbook*, authors Jeffrey K. Liker and David Meier describe the company's unique approach to management and the principles that underlie it. Principle one is "Philosophy as the foundation." The following illustrates the importance of ideation as the basis for Toyota's performance:

Cost reduction is not what drives Toyota. There is a philosophical sense of purpose that supercedes [sic] any short-term decision making. Toyota executives understand their place in the history of the company and are working to bring the company to the next level. The sense of purpose is like that of an organism working to grow and developing itself and its offspring. In this day of cynicism about the morals and ethics of corporate officers and the place of large capitalistic corporations in civilized society, Toyota gives us a glimpse of an alternative, provides a model of what happens when tens of thousands of people are aligned toward a purpose that is bigger than making money.[6]

As tangible outcomes of the Toyota Way, the best-selling Corollas, Camrys, and other vehicles have long enjoyed a reputation for reliability and fuel efficiency. Despite this success, the company embarked on a new campaign in the 1990s to realign around the external realities of dwindling petroleum resources and increasing environmental concerns.

In September 1993, while U.S. automakers focused on satisfying the demand for ever-bigger cars, trucks, and gas-guzzling SUVs, Toyota organized what would become a team of one hundred engineers for a project code-named G21. Their purpose was to develop the global car of the twenty-first century. At the behest of then-chairman Eiji Toyoda, energy efficiency was to be a chief concern—an admirably forward-looking idea when oil was selling for less than $15 per barrel.[7] The project team also adopted the long-range intention of environmental friendliness from Toyota's Earth Charter of 1992.[8]

With a strong sense of identity, purpose, and long-range intention—and a carefully targeted investment fund that eventually surpassed $1 billion—the G21 team stunned the global auto industry by unveiling the production version of the Prius gasoline-electric hybrid in October 1997 and announcing that the car would be available for purchase in Japan within three months. U.S. competitors had yet to design a prototype, and Toyota had beaten its original five-year timeline for moving from the G21 idea to a radically new and fully viable mass-produced hybrid automobile by an entire year. Three years later, Hollywood stars would begin showing up at the Oscars in their new Prius automobiles, and enthusiastic American "pioneer purchasers" would place orders over the Internet, enduring long waiting lists in their cultlike pursuit of a Prius.[9]

Only the two-door Honda Insight hybrid beat the Prius to the U.S. market, in December 1999. The Prius, however, introduced in August 2000, quickly surpassed the Insight in sales, profitability, and awards. In 2001, U.S. Prius sales totaled 15,556 units; Insight, 4,726.[10] Indeed, Toyota has so successfully dominated this market that Honda decided to stop production of the car altogether (it is developing a new, smaller hybrid expected to appear in 2009).[11]

Toyota is considered one of the most operationally efficient companies in the world. Yet the roots of its operational efficiency are not in the operations domain per se. Toyota's real success arises in the first instance from its deep-seated purpose, its commitment to taking the long-range view, its strong internal and external identity as a socially conscious global corporate citizen, and its willingness to make long-term investments to fulfill that ideation. By 2006 Toyota's market capitalization was more than double that of GM, Ford, and DaimlerChrysler combined.

Clarifying Identity: Who Are You?

Like strategic portfolio management, the choice of identity is *always on*, whether organizations and individuals opt to manage it actively or not. People and companies readily make choices that manifest their identity in externally recognizable ways. The outside world infers identity from these external clues, which can seem as trivial as an individual's choice of automobile, wristwatch, or mobile phone, or the dress code for a corporate event—or as serious as a publicly adopted code of ethics or a significant lapse of judgment. Even if the clues are inaccurate, they create a de facto identity and shape the way the world relates to people and organizations.

The more successful organizations and individuals make and communicate these choices consciously and carefully. They create, clarify, nurture, and consistently reinforce identity. Indeed, a strong identity is the first step to strategic differentiation, and it is central to a company's ability to compete. It goes beyond Who are you? to ask, What makes you different from anybody else?

Strategic Identity: What Kind of Company Are You?

One of the ways companies express their identity is through the type of strategy they choose. Michael Porter describes two fundamental kinds of strategies—or categories of strategic identity—that can yield above-average profits:

- Become a *cost leader* by charging the same prices as competitors (or less) but operating with lower costs.

- Become a *differentiated value provider* by operating with about the same costs as competitors but earning higher revenues by being able to charge higher prices than competitors for customers who value their particular form of differentiation.[12]

Geoffrey Moore, author of several books on how value and innovation are created, expands Porter's two categories into the four "value disciplines" that can characterize an organization's strategic identity.[13] *Operational excellence* corresponds closely to Porter's cost leadership strategy. The other three value disciplines define three kinds of differentiated value strategies: *customer intimacy*, *product leadership*, and *disruptive innovation*.

- *Customer intimacy* focuses on customer relationships and the customer experience as the central themes of decision making about the product and service offering.

- *Product leadership* strives to create best-in-class products, with an unbeatable combination of features, form, and function.

- *Disruptive innovation* creates a new category of business or attracts a new category of customer, thereby changing the game to a new playing field.

The choice of strategic identity has important implications for downstream projects, as the organization invests to align all six domains in the strategic execution framework. We will explore these implications in the chapters we devote to the relevant domains and imperatives.

Projects That Test Identity Strength

The simplest way to test the strength of identity is to ask people to fill in the blanks in this statement: "The _____ organization is a _____," where the first blank indicates the organization's name and the second asks for a descriptor that clearly delineates the company. A widely shared choice of descriptors represents the perceived identity and serves as the new de facto foundation for all decisions within the organization. In Toyota's case, a strong sense of identity pervades public perceptions of the company as well. Outside observers can easily complete the identity statement. For example, Professor Ryoichi Yamamoto, from the Institute of Industrial Science at the University of Tokyo, stated, "Toyota is a model company in the field of environmental management and resource productivity."[14]

Table 1-1 provides examples of descriptors that could identify the well-known companies it lists.

TABLE 1-1

Clarifying identity

Many companies can describe their identities in simple phrases such as the following:

Procter & Gamble	Brand management specialist
Wal-Mart	Retail seller
Accenture	Management and IT services provider
Cisco Systems	Component manufacturer and integrator
Intel	Component manufacturer
Flextronics	Low-cost manufacturer
Sony	Entertainment company
IBM	Comprehensive IT solution provider
Apple	Innovator in consumer electronics
Gateway	Low-cost computer company
Dell	Direct-to-consumer distribution channel

Ask any eight people to articulate your organization's identity. If you get eight different answers, you need to invest in projects to clarify and communicate identity.

This fill-in-the-blanks exercise is a simple but revealing project that any organization can implement immediately, with a relatively minor investment of employees' time, intellect, and perceptions. Have a meeting. Call in the team. Take a large sheet of paper and hang it on the wall. Write the fill-in-the-blank question on the chart and ask everyone to complete it by themselves. Then ask for a readout on the way people fill in the blanks. If a pattern emerges, it means that people are of a consistent mind, and identity is probably not an issue in your company's performance. A wide divergence indicates that clear company identity is not a strong asset of the organization and that project investments to clarify identity may be in order.

Sometimes the corporate identity can be too strong, too restrictive, or out of step with the external environment. For example, in *Seeing What's Next*, the authors document a fateful decision when Western Union contemplated investing in telephone technology.[15] Alexander Graham Bell offered the technology to Western Union in 1876 for what today would be a small investment even in inflation-adjusted dollars. But Western Union's leaders implicitly translated their view of the core business in long-distance communications to "We are a telegraph company." From that sense of identity, the option of investing in telephone technology (which, at the time, only had local area calling capability) received a straightforward decision. Western Union declined. Remember, strong ideation is a big help in deciding what *not* to do.

Was this a stupid decision? Maybe. Was it a consistent decision? Yes. It shows how the sense of identity affects the major strategic decisions as well as the smaller daily choices of what to work on today or which projects to suggest for the future. Identity may be strong or weak, but it runs continuously as a filter for all activities. Organizations can choose to manage it directly and actively or indirectly and passively.

The leaders at Western Union, for instance, might have made a different decision if they had chosen to manage the company's identity more actively, to make sure that "We are a telegraph company" continued to make sense in an evolving environment. Had they chosen "We are a long-distance communication company"—or even the more purposeful "We help people communicate"—they might have invested in the telephone technology and then invested further to develop long-distance telephone capabilities. The same argument has been made about Xerox. Having invented Ethernet, desktop computers with bitmapped screens, and a usable mouse, Xerox "fumbled the future" of personal computing, because its leaders viewed Xerox's identity as that of a "copier company."[16]

Projects That Reshape Identity

Lou Gerstner's celebrated turnaround at IBM in the 1990s offers a noteworthy example of how a consciously chosen shift in identity manifests itself as a set of important investment decisions. Most observers assumed that when Gerstner joined IBM in 1993 as the first outsider hired to be CEO in the company's history, the strategy was to break the company up into pieces that would compete in different product markets.

Gerstner struggled with the fundamental choice between IBM as a "products" company versus IBM as a "solutions" provider. He had been a customer of IBM in his former job at American Express, and he knew that his biggest problem at Amex was integration of systems. Breaking up the company made little strategic sense in light of such market demand for system solutions. Moreover, as Gerstner noted later in his book *Who Says Elephants Can't Dance?* he felt that dismantling IBM would be destroying a *national treasure*—as strong a source of identity as any we've ever encountered.[17]

Gerstner's decision to reinvent the national treasure as a "solution provider" versus a set of "product companies" had profound implications for the structure and culture of IBM as well as its vision, goals, and metrics. But the root of the project work that supported IBM's painstaking return to grace was this fundamental choice of strategic identity.

American Power Conversion (APC), the company we profiled in the introduction, has made a similar choice of strategic identity. Like IBM, APC will need to create a strong solutions organization while continuing to support its successful products organization. In effect, APC will need to create the right downstream organizations to support two types of strategic identity: cost or product leadership for the products business, and customer intimacy for the solutions side. To do so, it must make project investments to align all the key elements of the organization with this new, blended strategic identity. But unlike IBM, APC has access to the strategic execution framework and the six imperatives to aid in its choices.

In fact, navigating the framework helped break an execution logjam that had slowed APC's progress for nearly two years. The eight-point strategy, put together by a small group of senior executives, had effectively stalled in the organization. Realizing that they needed to take action, the management team decided to invest the time of twenty-five top leaders in the business, including project sponsors, and send them to an intense eight-day off-site workshop designed to identify and overcome the barriers to execution.

Projects That Clarify or Reinforce Identity

One of the first issues to surface at APC's off-site workshop was a widespread lack of clarity about the desired new corporate identity and its organizational implications. The company has a highly refined product development organization, but without a clear understanding of the new strategic identity, the product leaders could not know how to invest the resources at their disposal. Therefore, the very first step—the first successful strategic project investment—was to explore in detail what it means to be a provider of power systems solutions, and how that differs from the culture, processes, structures, and skills that have served APC so well in the past. Using the strategic execution framework to guide this exploration helped the APC teams identify and prioritize the hidden, transformative projects along with the more obvious projects working *in* the business and *on* the business.

Clarifying Purpose: Why Are You Here?

Fortunately, the strong sense of purpose at APC—*nonstop networking*—could encompass the new strategy as well as the old one. The most effective individual and corporate identities encapsulate such a sense of purpose. In fact, identity only becomes truly meaningful when linked and aligned to a purpose. A sense of purpose is critical to creating a sustainable organization or business. It gives people a compelling reason to come to work every day and to invest their personal resources in the collective endeavor.

Alignment around purpose helps combat ambivalence, apathy, and boredom. Stephen Covey cited a Harris Interactive poll that showed that only 37 percent of the people surveyed knew where their company was going and why.[18] That leaves almost two-thirds of people in the dark as to the purpose and long-range intentions of their organization.

When Joe Calloway, author of *Becoming a Category of One*, works with clients on brand development and competitive positioning, he starts by asking organizational leaders to clarify the collective *why*.[19] Calloway describes how a strong sense of purpose energizes employees, simplifies decision making at all levels, and delivers consistently high-quality results at companies such as BMW, Tractor Supply, and LensCrafters.[20]

For example, outsiders might describe LensCrafters as a successful retail eyeglass distributor. But LensCrafters employees have a much more meaningful way to think about their company and their jobs: they don't just sell eyeglasses. They help people see better, one hour at a time. They offer the gift of better sight "to those who have the least and need [LensCrafters] most."[21]

In 2006 this sense of purpose took another direction: in addition to helping customers see, LensCrafters employees also help them look their best. The expanded purpose recognizes and reinforces a shift in the external environment, as consumers increasingly value the chance to reflect personal taste and style in their choice of fashion eyewear. Like any other shift in purpose, LensCrafters' initiative required a series of project investments, including a new store concept and extra training for associates (and even a new employee dress code combining fashion with professionalism) as well as new marketing and ad campaigns.

In another telling example, while studying the motivation of construction workers, one of our colleagues asked electrical construction workers on two large power plants what they were doing. Electricians on the first project said, "We are terminating cables in the turbine-generator building." The answer to the same question on a second, virtually identical project was, "We are lighting up the southwestern U.S.!" Productivity, safety, absenteeism, and rework metrics on the second project were all significantly better than on the first.

Why Purpose Matters

Many executives place purpose high on the list of "fuzzy" words, along with mission, core values, and calling. For some, the idea of fulfillment of purpose seems so far out of the realm of business as to be irrelevant. But as the Austrian neurologist and psychotherapist Viktor Frankl observed in a concentration camp during WWII, purpose is actually a matter of life or death.[22]

Frankl's legacy, documented in *Man's Search for Meaning*, includes two major concepts that are critical to leading organizations.[23]

- People have an unassailable ability to choose their response to any given set of circumstances.

- When people lose their connection to purpose, they die.

Frankl wrote that "everything can be taken from a man but one thing: the last of the human freedoms—to choose one's attitude in any given set of circumstances, to choose one's own way."[24] He relates an experience of being ill and huddling in the corner of a hut, simply trying to survive. Sick and fatigued, Frankl made a choice to volunteer for a work detail on the basis of how much good he could do for his fellow prisoners even though the easiest thing to do would be to stay put: a choice of action driven by purpose.[25]

Even in more mundane circumstances and even in the most routine of existences, people need some connection to purpose. The decisions people and organizations make about where, how, and why to invest their energy all stem from this need.

Frankl identified purpose as a basic life force by observing the way his fellow detainees faced the dire circumstances and indeterminate duration of their incarceration. People used several mechanisms to cope in the prison camps: mental games, conversations, and serving in various capacities in the camp were all part of the daily coping rituals. Some prisoners' sense of purpose consisted of surviving to a specific date; some aimed to survive to reunite their families.

Frankl noted that those who lost their sense of purpose either died outright or committed suicide. One method for ending one's own life in prison camps was to "run into the wire." The barbed wire fences surrounding the camps were highly electrified. By running into them, people would essentially electrocute themselves.

Comparing a lack of corporate purpose with one of the greatest atrocities of the twentieth century may seem shocking to some. But when executives, managers, team leaders, and individuals diminish the importance of connection to purpose, they are making a fundamental error in human motivation and are encouraging people to "run into the wire." Working without purpose or checking all emotions at the door slowly sucks the life out of people and organizations. In contrast, executives who encourage a sense of meaning, articulate the higher purpose of the enterprise, and truly value the integrity of the human condition help channel the natural energies of people throughout the organization.

Purpose Trumps Circumstances

People can often withstand enormously negative situations if they have a strong enough sense of purpose. In the aftermath of Katrina, the 2005 hurricane that devastated wide swaths of the U.S. Gulf Coast, television images showed the New Orleans police chief, amid the chaos and destruction, emphatically declaring that his organization swore to protect the citizens of New Orleans, and they were going to continue to work toward that end no matter the circumstances. His sense of purpose was clearly in full force. His energy was in high gear. What he articulated as his motivation came from his sense of purpose, not his salary and benefits package. The police in New Orleans were facing spectacular challenges:

- No power

- No emergency response infrastructure (hospitals, ambulances, communications)

- Contaminated water supplies

- Insufficient assistance from federal emergency agencies

- Widespread reports of rape, looting, and assault (many of which were later discounted)

- Direct attacks from people they were trying to save

It may seem obscure, but these challenges constitute a project environment. There are things to deliver (provide medical help, break up fights, stop the looting), a very loose schedule, and a set of resources (the police officer, his team, and the equipment that survived the storm). The police had a limited number of ways of making or communicating decisions about what to do, where to go, what to accomplish, what not to do.

In this context, purpose became the driving force behind personal decisions, the most basic of which was whether to stay on the job or not. Dozens of police officers walked off the job. Two committed suicide: they "ran into the wire." Others, propelled, we believe, by their strong sense of purpose, stayed on to help restore order in a thousand barely visible ways each day. Despite the subsequent controversy about the larger disaster management effort, these purposeful officers made important individual contributions in the storm's immediate aftermath.

When circumstances become extreme in a business because of the difficulty of competing in a global marketplace, when overtime becomes mandatory for extended periods of time, when extraordinary effort is needed, a clear sense of purpose is what keeps people going. It gives people a reason to compete, a reason to volunteer their best efforts, or a reason to carry on despite seemingly impossible odds. The absence of purpose leads to burnout or worse.

Many people stay in organizations long after they have ceased to give the best they have to offer. They pour their passions and energies into outside activities, and work just to pay the bills. Some of this has to do with a disconnection to purpose, a lack of the most basic reason to perform. In a purposeless environment, people's efforts have no connection to the idea of a preferred future. Without a sense of purpose, there is little reason to expect high performance. In contrast, a strong sense of purpose can actually reduce the stress of the overworked, by helping people separate the unimportant tasks from the ones that propel the organization toward its intended future.

As we discussed in the introduction, the smallest building blocks of strategic execution are the individual, moment-by-moment choices of what to work on, what not to work on, and what level of effort and excellence to bring to the task. Without some collective sense of purpose, those individual investment decisions devolve to personal preference. Thus, creating a sense of shared purpose is far more important than the sharing of lofty thoughts in the executive suite. It is actually the microscopic fiber that connects individual choices to the real work of strategic execution.

The sense of purpose can vary from extremely strong to extremely weak, but it is always on. Even in organizations with no articulated purpose, people will find their own meanings and pursue their own individual agendas. Lack of clarity about purpose does not manifest itself as an immediate problem—rather, the organization can limp along or even appear to perform well for years. Sooner or later, though, companies with a weak or confused sense of purpose experience a breakdown or crisis, as happened in the spectacular meltdowns at WorldCom, Enron, and others.

Contrast those dispiriting examples with DNV (Det Norske Veritas), a global company with over 150 years of service in certifying the seaworthiness of oceangoing vessels and, more recently, of assessing and certifying the safety, quality, and environmental compliance of a wide variety of products and business processes. *Det Norske Veritas* means "the Norwegian truth." The name literally signifies that if DNV says the ship is seaworthy, that is "the Norwegian truth." DNV's purpose and its brand promise of assuring the safety, quality, and environmental compliance of products and processes are fully embedded in its name.

A DNV surveyor who detects a crack while inspecting the hull of a huge ocean liner does not have to think twice about applying the standard of "the Norwegian truth" to decide whether to report the ship's deficiency and require the defect to be corrected, potentially holding the ship in port for a week or more at a significant cost to its owners. Since the risk of adverse consequences from such a crack would only materialize if the ship hit a severe storm, ship and cargo owners may exert strong pressure for immediate approval to avoid expensive delays. In such cases, DNV reinforces its purpose and protects its internal and external brand promise by standing squarely behind the surveyor.

Even organizations with a strong sense of purpose and identity can suffer when their leaders fail to fully understand or respect what inspires their people. Pehr Gyllenhammar, former chairman of Volvo, learned this the hard way when he tried to engineer a merger with the French automaker Renault in the early 1990s. Under Gyllenhammar's guidance, Volvo had long enjoyed a distinct identity as the leader in automotive safety and as a pioneer in designing jobs for quality of work life.[26] What Gyllenhammar failed to understand was the company's importance as one of the flagships of the Swedish economy and an enormous source of national pride. Investors, employees, and even customers finally rejected the Renault connection when they perceived a threat to Volvo's very purpose within Sweden.[27]

Volvo's later, happier combination of its automobile division—but not its truck division—with Ford somehow avoided tarnishing that sense of national purpose and in fact created a much larger global platform from which to market the cars while maintaining their Swedish heritage.

Projects That Clarify Purpose

Some time ago, the manufacturing manager for the head and disk assembly area at IBM San Jose faced an interesting problem. The team had made several attempts to reduce defect rates in the manufacturing process for attaching data-recording head and arm assemblies to the device that moved them over the disk surface where they read and write data. Nothing had worked. Training, defect analysis, new tools, process reviews, design reviews, manufacturability studies, focus groups, and quality circles had all failed to generate any material effect. Similar problems occurred in other parts of the process, on different parts of the manufacturing line.

The manufacturing manager decided to try something unconventional. He held a short meeting (today it would be called a town meeting) with the manufacturing team. In the meeting, he asked whether people could describe how the eventual customer used the data storage devices they built. Silence. Not a person in the room had a clue as to the ultimate purpose of the product they worked on daily. The manager devoted the following hour to discussing how customers used the data storage device for banking, insurance, medical records, research, payroll, and so on. He then asked the group what it would mean to them if a data storage failure caused them to miss an important medical diagnosis or treatment, be denied a mortgage or a paycheck, or other equivalent results.

This was the first attempt to connect the dots between what the line workers did and the value it created for people at large—their version of "We are lighting up the southwestern U.S.!" Not surprisingly, quality performance improved. Not dramatically, but measurably. Where nothing else had worked at all, the effect of helping people connect to the ultimate purpose of their work changed performance for the better.

Connection to purpose will not happen by itself, and it is not merely a matter of a town meeting or two. What is needed is a set of project investments to accomplish some clear and specific connections to purpose. The right kinds of projects will clarify purpose and communicate it throughout the organization.

What Good Do You Do?

Purpose does not have to be on the scale of solving world hunger in order to be significant in creating motivation. It just has to be real. It has to be tangible.

For example, if a company disappeared, what would be the loss? How would the world be worse off? Conversely, what good does the company do? Why is the delivery of that "good" important? Why should anyone care? People who don't care are unlikely to deliver top performance.

Consider Southco Inc. Southco's purpose is associated with improving product touch points, by optimizing the experience people have in using things like a door handle, a glove compartment latch, or a center console lid in a car. Improving the ease, simplicity, comfort, and general feel of what it means to open a door, service a computer product, or close the hatch on a yacht may seem small, but touch is one of those things that create inherent value in a product—and Southco is dedicated to making that experience as much of a pleasure as possible. Doing the job well, and making customers' touch interface better, can serve as a unifying purpose for people in the company.

Determining what good an organization does and how the world is actually affected by its products and services may require a project investment. It might require investing in several projects or even several programs, some as simple as town meetings and others as elaborate as extended customer research programs.

Who Is the Beneficiary?

Understanding purpose means understanding the people or organizations that benefit from the good an organization does. In chapter 3 of *The Tipping Point*, Malcolm Gladwell describes how the producers of *Sesame Street* and *Blue's Clues* designed and refined their programming through understanding the factors that drive success in children's programming.[28] The creators of both these programs were motivated to offer programming that served children's developmental needs. That was their purpose. They conducted numerous exhaustive and innovative experiments to determine how the variations in program length, program makeup, character orientation, casting, and so on, affected young viewers.

Each of these experiments was a project in itself. Either knowingly or unknowingly, the creators of these shows engaged in focused project investments to determine the exact mixture of elements to serve the children who were the intended beneficiary of their purpose. The programming was designed to optimize the good the shows could do. By knowing everything possible about the good, and who benefits from it, the creative teams could produce enormously popular programs that were also highly profitable and received critical acclaim as *good* programs for children.

Another way to think about the beneficiaries of your work is to explore how you serve your customer's customers' needs. For people at the base of a supply chain, the purpose their product or service serves may be several steps away from them. Understanding how the customer's customers benefit from what a company does can help clarify its purpose in a way that is truly meaningful to its employees.

Clarifying Long-Range Intention: Where Are You Going?

Long-range intention is the seed of the desired future strategy. It provides both direction and a destination for the organization and is the first step in identifying strategic goals and the project investments that will be necessary to attain them. The only way to know about the validity of a short-term purchase or investment is to understand whether it will help or hinder the long-range intention.

Without a sense of long-range intention, individuals have no support for making good short-term decisions. In some cases, this means they will invest their energy in immediate goals that may hurt the organization in the long term (see "Ideation and Sustainability: Citigroup"). In more sinister examples, such as WorldCom, some individuals set their own intentions and grab for all they can get in the short run, even if it costs the organization everything in the long term.

Projects That Clarify Long-Range Intentions

Much has been written about the effect of short-term decisions to serve quarterly earnings at the expense of long-term organizational health. Yet

Ideation and Sustainability

Citigroup

Companies with strong long-range intention are in business for the long term. They invest in projects and programs to provide future value. More than a decade ago, in their extensively researched book *Built to Last*, Jim Collins and Jerry Porras documented the connection between long-range intention and investment. They described Citibank's intention of being "the most far-reaching financial institution there has ever been" and the investments it made to do so.[a]

For example, according to Collins and Porras, "Citibank consistently invested in important new methods earlier than Chase Manhattan, three decades earlier in some cases."[b] The list of such investments included divisional profitability statements, merit pay, management training programs, college recruiting, ATMs, credit cards, retail branches, and foreign branches.[c]

Years after Collins and Porras's observation, such long-range investments continue to lead to superior performance at Citigroup, the largest financial institution in the world. Yet the company occasionally runs into trouble when short-term performance goals get in the way of its espoused intentions—perhaps because it has not invested enough in projects that clarify the long-range intentions and align them with appropriate short-term goals and metrics.

In 2001, Citigroup's Japan Private Bank was audited for its operating practices. The auditors identified many irregularities that required correction, and Citigroup agreed to take action. In 2003, the auditors returned to find the same set of problems. The bank had reverted to using the old practices almost immediately after agreeing to stop them. As the 2003

here is the paradox: tomorrow's prosperity depends on today's investments. So buried somewhere in the list of things to invest in today are the projects that will drive the prosperity of tomorrow.

The problem is that any investment in creating and communicating these long-term intentions competes for resources in the short term. Executive attention and organizational engagement in satisfying short-term ob-

investigation continued, it became clear that Citigroup had engaged in prohibited activities, including selling securities without authorization, and at least thirty instances of inappropriate transactions, including deals that could help customers hide losses.

The investigators concluded that the irregularities stemmed from systemic problems that have created issues for Citigroup's private bank in other markets, such as Mexico in the mid-1990s. While the firm's intention became "world's largest financial institution," its purpose became "meet the numbers goals." In fact, some employees joked that DNA meant "do numbers always" at Citigroup. Thus their idea of long-range intention narrowed to meeting quarterly profit and growth targets. Under those circumstances, employees made highly risky and questionable decisions that eventually led to the cancellation of the operating license for Citigroup in Japan.

Oddly, Citigroup still appears to think this is a business controls problem. In reality, the corporation needs to invest in projects that clarify and communicate a unifying sense of identity, purpose, and long-range intention to guide decisions throughout the 275,000 employees. In the absence of such strong shared ideation, "do numbers always" does become the DNA of the organization. Chuck Prince and the other leaders at Citigroup will need to make further investments in clarifying identity, purpose, and intentions. Above all—and this is the most difficult part—they will need to eliminate conflicts between the ideation imperative and the goals and metrics used to interpret it, as we will discuss in chapter 2. The stain on Citigroup's reputation will subside over time, but it offers a painful and expensive lesson in how not to manage long-range intention.

a. James C. Collins and Jerry I. Porras, *Built to Last: Successful Habits of Visionary Companies* (New York: HarperBusiness, 1994), 108.

b. Ibid., 194.

c. Ibid.

jectives rob critical resources for developing the future. It is a balancing act between short- and long-term views. The key is finding the right balance between the two. The best diagnostic question is, What is the ratio of investment focus in your current portfolio between short-term survival and long-term prosperity? If the answer is 1:0, the strategy makers need to reshape and reinforce ideation.

Creating Sustainability Through the Ideation Imperative

Customers, employees, and investors will flock to an organization that meets their own needs for a healthy identity, purposeful work, and the chance to create a legacy. Thus, the elements of ideation are the elements of sustainability.

Without strong ideation, it is virtually impossible to achieve sustainability. The dot-com boom and bust created a long list of organizational casualties in companies that could not see beyond their initial gee-whiz enthusiasm about the uses of the Internet. They had ideas but lacked clear *ideation*, and they especially lacked the ability to choose and implement the right array of strategic project investments to bring life to their ideas.

One CEO we know lamented that the venture capitalists who funded his dot-com operation were constantly driving him to meet a spending target rate. The metric was built around dollars spent per day. It didn't matter how the money was spent. Just spend. No targeted investment and no sense of identity, purpose, or long-range intentions. Not surprisingly, that approach burned through millions of dollars and created very little sustainable value.

Contrast this with the strong ideation that characterizes the companies in Geoffrey Moore's research, as shown in figure 1-2. Returning to the categories of strategic identity we described earlier, Moore groups companies using a combination of strategic focus (operational excellence, customer intimacy, product leadership, or disruptive innovation) and type of market advantage (offer, customer, industry, category). What is significant here is that the intersection of the two reveals a combination of identity, purpose, and intention strong enough to distinguish the company and guide all its project investments. Economizers, for example, center their investments on cost control, delighters work on perfecting their offer to customers, reassurers focus on "guaranteeism," and flashers work on changing the way the offer is made. Each category invests in vastly different strategic projects and programs, driven by vastly different ideations.

Projects That Communicate Identity, Purpose, and Long-Range Intention

Visual mapping is one of the most effective ways we have seen for developing, refining, and communicating organizational purpose, identity, and long-range intention. It generates the overall picture in a readable and vi-

FIGURE 1-2

Strong ideation companies whose strategic identity helps drive all project investment decisions

	Offer advantage	Customer advantage	Industry advantage	Category advantage
Operational excellence	**Economizers** BIC, Motel 6, Costco	**Satisfiers** Kinko's, IKEA, Southwest Airlines	**Dominators** Wal-Mart, Dell, Visa, Exxon	**Reinventors** McDonald's, FedEx, Jiffy Lube, Charles Schwab, Centera Genomics
Customer intimacy	**Delighters** Nordstrom, Nike, Crystal Geyser, Hold Everything	**Includers** McKinsey, Martha Stewart, Saturn, Starbucks	**Market-makers** Merrill Lynch, NY Yankees, Disney	**Niche-carvers** AARP, MTV, Silicon Valley Bank, Pleasant Company
Product leadership	**Reassurers** Duracell, Sony, Tumi, Titleist, Agilent	**Excellers** REI, Adobe, Ferrari, Lawson, Retek	**Excluders** Cisco, Microsoft, Mercedes, Nokia	**Innovators** Palm, Apple, Sharper Image, Chrysler
Disruptive innovation	**Flashers** Priceline, E*TRADE, Netscape, Napster	**Enchanters** Home Shopping, TiVo Intuit, Pleasant Company	**Disrupters** Amazon, AOL Time Warner, Enron	**Sorcerers** eBay, Yahoo!, Nintendo, Polaroid

sually stimulating representation of how the organization chooses to operate in its environment. Visual mapping projects can be especially helpful in times of organizational transformation, organizational change, and environmental change. They use a process of interviews and iterative design steps to turn the spoken word and existing documentation into an effective visual representation—a map—that can be communicated throughout the organization.

Firms such as Paradigm Learning and The Grove Consultants International specialize in taking a team of people through a structured process to create visual maps. However, it is entirely possible for a company to design and implement its own visual mapping project. Even a depiction as simple as the training materials that illustrate Wipro's move from "Get it done!" to "Get the right results!" (as described in the introduction) can carry strong meaning throughout the organization.

The most effective visual mapping projects also include a series of group presentations and discussions to ensure that every individual understands and internalizes the map's consistent message about the organization's identity, purpose, and long-range intentions for competing in its external environment. Sometimes the presentations occur in training sessions that cascade from the top of the organization to the bottom or from the bottom up, where teams at each level discuss and absorb the map and its meanings and then "train" the next level.

One company we know encouraged a small group of interested employees to develop a series of visual maps that would clarify and communicate its identity, purpose, and intentions in an uncertain industry environment. The result was an elaborate but easily understood set of line-drawn images that featured the company as a dirigible held aloft by two distinctive hot air balloons (representing the two key businesses) as it crossed treacherous terrain toward its intended future, surrounded by other flying competitors and navigating industrywide challenges in pursuit of its strategy. After a companywide series of training sessions and a sustained communications program, employees at all levels frequently referred to the visual maps in explaining how they made personal decisions about their priorities at work every day.

Embedding the Elements of Ideation Throughout the Organization

With the level of turnover in most organizations, maintaining a clear sense of identity, purpose, and intentions as people come and go can be very difficult. If an organization has developed a keen sense of the collective who, why, and where, and has figured out how to communicate it through visual mapping, the remaining challenge is to sustain the right level of communication over time. Without a conscious effort to embed the map and its meanings in day-to-day activities and interactions—for example, in new worker orientation materials—the mapping project will quickly fade from view. By investing time and energy to make the transition between the original project and ongoing activities in the evolving environment, the visual map project leaders can complete the journey from ideation to transition.

To reap the maximum benefit from visual mapping and other ideation imperative projects, the organization must continually communicate and reinforce its message in every possible way:

- New worker orientation

- Company newsletters

- Company Web site

- Periodic communication meetings

- Management briefings

- Visual posting throughout the physical plant

- Advertisements in all kinds of media

Ideation and Brand

Identity, purpose, and long-range intention are important components of a company's *brand*. A strong brand is one of the most valuable assets a corporation can build. In addition to differentiating it from the competition, the brand helps customers and other stakeholders bond with the company and its product offerings. It creates loyalty. It contributes to the sustainability of any organization.[29]

A well-developed, consistent brand makes choices regarding investments of time, energy, and money easy to accept or reject. When people can discern which options are consistent with the organization's identity, purpose, and intention, they gain tremendous advantage in decision speed and quality.

Projects That Build Internal and External Brands

Many companies leave the work of branding to the marketing communications people, who create an outward-facing brand that offers meaning for target customers. But the organizations that best harness the power of ideation know how to link the external brand to the internal brand—the sense of what the company means to its own people as well as to its customers.

Figure 1-3 shows how Yahoo! accomplishes this linkage. It takes the strong external identity or brand statement "Yahoo! is a life engine" and translates it into specific internal meanings for employees, in terms of the core experiences, core competencies, and core values of the company's ideation.

Internal branding gives context and meaning to work and has a tangible benefit in attracting the right employees and guiding their daily decisions. It requires investments in projects that translate identity, purpose, and intentions to meanings for employees. Figure 1-4 diagrams how senior vice

FIGURE 1-3

Internal and external branding at Yahoo! provides a link between "Yahoo! is a life engine" and the company's core experiences, core competencies, and core values

© 2005 by Yahoo! Used with permission.

FIGURE 1-4

Translating the internal brand into specific projects and programs at Yahoo!

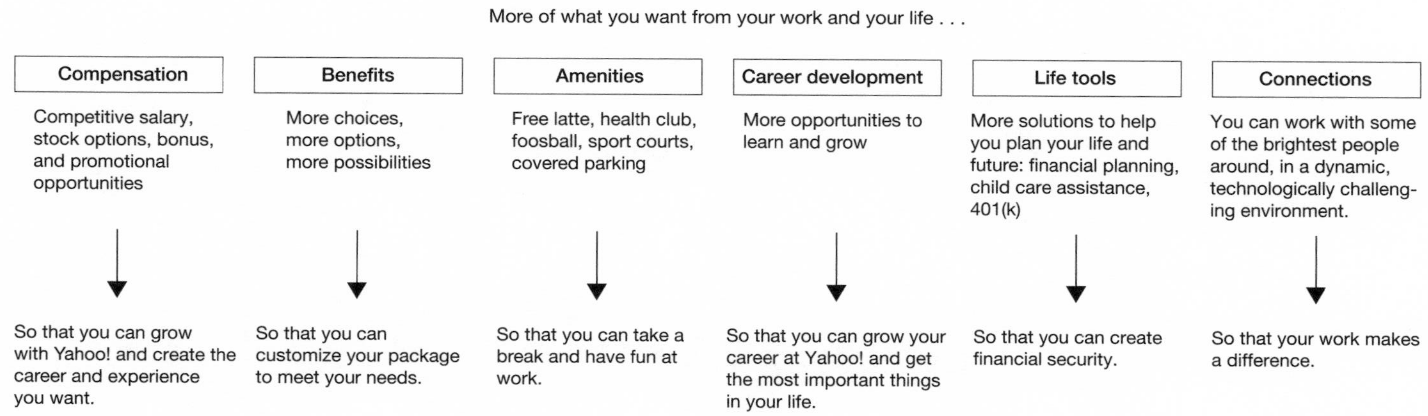

More of what you want from your work and your life . . . .

Compensation	Benefits	Amenities	Career development	Life tools	Connections
Competitive salary, stock options, bonus, and promotional opportunities	More choices, more options, more possibilities	Free latte, health club, foosball, sport courts, covered parking	More opportunities to learn and grow	More solutions to help you plan your life and future: financial planning, child care assistance, 401(k)	You can work with some of the brightest people around, in a dynamic, technologically challenging environment.
So that you can grow with Yahoo! and create the career and experience you want.	So that you can customize your package to meet your needs.	So that you can take a break and have fun at work.	So that you can grow your career at Yahoo! and get the most important things in your life.	So that you can create financial security.	So that your work makes a difference.

© 2005 by Yahoo! Used with permission.

president, human resources and Chief People Yahoo!, Libby Sartain and her project team translated the core ideation "Yahoo! is a life engine" into the internal brand "More of what you want from your work and your life"—and then clarified it in categories of employee life, outlined specific aspects of those categories, and described for employees the direct intended benefit from the offerings in the categories. Identifying each category and designing each benefit required targeted project and program investments. Notice also the downstream investment implications in each area for such things as health clubs, sport courts, and covered parking.

A great deal of evidence indicates that these projects and investments have generated significant returns for Yahoo! Jon R. Katzenbach, in *Peak Performance: Aligning the Hearts and Minds of Your Employees*, identifies Yahoo! as a peak performer and describes the internal environment of such companies as follows: "The most evident characteristic of any peak-performance workforce is the energy level it exudes. Walking into the workplace, you feel its energy, which is noticeably different from that of any average performing workplace. Activity levels are more intense, attitudes are more positive, interactions are less constrained, and formal positions are less evident. People work hard, but they have fun at work and take full advantage of a widespread sense of humor."[30]

This could be a significant factor in why Yahoo! has grown at double-digit rates and has a net profit margin of over 30 percent.[31] "Yahoo! is a life engine" condenses identity, purpose, and long-range intention into a strong, unifying internal and external brand.

Cultivate the Meaning of Your Brand

An organization that is fully aligned around strong, clear ideation can distill much of the purpose and meaning of its existence in a single symbol or logo. In fact, the word *logo* itself comes from the Greek *logos*, which means "cosmic reason . . . the source of world order and intelligibility," according to *Webster's Dictionary* (New Riverside University Edition).

As we described with the example of Western Union, strong ideation also tells a company what not to do. Sometimes this restricts brand and logo choices in unexpected ways. When brand identity is extremely ingrained, it has tremendous staying power—which can work to an organization's detriment if it tries to do something that the marketplace does not associate with its brand.

Coca-Cola learned that lesson painfully in one of the largest and most public branding disasters in history. Loyal consumers staged a near revolt when the company attempted to replace its iconic brand name and product formulation with an innovative "New Coke." The enormous emotional reaction to New Coke underscores the importance of the meaning customers ascribe to brands.

In taste tests compared with Pepsi, New Coke led by 6 to 8 percentage points, and participants preferred New Coke to the original formula as well. Yet when the company replaced Coca-Cola with New Coke, the market simply refused to accept the change. Plummeting sales eventually forced the reintroduction of the old formula under the brand Coca-Cola Classic, and New Coke virtually disappeared. The ill-conceived New Coke project was reduced to a very expensive lesson: strong brand identity trumps numerical research.

If clarifying, building, and reinforcing the brand requires significant investments, attempting to change a meaningful brand may require even greater investments—if it is possible at all. If the marketplace sees a company's brand in a particular way and that way conflicts with a new strategy, then the company must include rebranding investments in its project portfolio in order to make the strategy work. Market perceptions may in fact even eliminate some strategic options for some iconic brands.

Case in point? A large technology firm one of the authors worked with decided to explore the possibility of offering Web-based consulting services for Microsoft products. Such a service would provide a major cost benefit to some customers because much of the work could be done remotely, thus avoiding the travel and occupancy costs associated with on-site consultants.

In researching how the marketplace might view this offering, the company found that customers loved the idea but could not imagine the company's brand as a provider of Microsoft software services and support. Multiple focus groups set up by a third party unanimously and overwhelmingly thought that the market offering was a good one. But when the company offering the service was revealed, the focus groups unanimously rejected the idea, because they could not imagine themselves purchasing the service from that company. The company had all the product knowledge and services expertise to perform brilliantly and had proved it. But the market simply could not see the company in this way—or at least not without a massive investment to reposition the company's identity, purpose, and intentions.

The market analysis was so conclusive that the company canceled the project, saving millions of dollars in development costs. If the entire service offering had been built, the market resistance would have been overwhelming and that money would have been wasted. So investing in projects that check the brand recognition and brand identity implications of new product proposals is a critical part of strategic execution. "The Project List For Building Stronger Ideation" suggests a broad range of specific investments that can help create and reinforce the necessary alignments in this domain.

Ideation and Strategic Execution

As we will demonstrate in the next two chapters, the ideation domain links closely with the domains that determine a company's vision and its nature. The company's long-range intention sets the trajectory and determines the structure, goals, and metrics by which to fulfill it. Its identity and purpose create its culture. Together, these three domains—ideation, vision, and nature—illuminate the right portfolio of strategic project and program investments that are necessary for execution.

We noted in the introduction that the domains must operate in alignment with each other and with the external environment. It is important to remember, however, that each domain and each imperative plays a critical role on its own. We therefore offer a few simple suggestions for testing your organization's performance on the ideation imperative, as we will for each of the other imperatives in turn.

Rate Your Organization on the Ideation Imperative

The power of ideation manifests itself in tangible ways. The following questionnaires, answered either informally or formally through-

The Project List for Building Stronger Ideation

The list of projects to strengthen ideation is limited only by the imagination. Many require little more than an investment of precious time and creativity. Others are more elaborate and may require outside assistance. But since ideation is the first imperative, the time to start clarifying identity, purpose, and long-range intention is now.

- Develop the ability to articulate company values.
- Invite employees to participate in company-sponsored community service projects.
- Reinforce external brand image.
- Translate external brand to internal brand.
- Develop and communicate the long-range intention of the company.
- Undertake a global trend analysis to refine the long-range intention.
- Create focus on strategic identity, approach to competition, and type of advantage.
- Find creative ways to communicate "who we are" both inside and outside the organization.
- Communicate the stories that encapsulate the organization's ideation.
- Redesign hiring processes to increase ideation "fit."
- Upgrade facilities to set the right tone.
- Establish standards of behavior and conduct.

out the organization, help measure its ideation strength. When the results show weak ideation or vary considerably from unit to unit or at various levels of the hierarchy, investing in projects to strengthen ideation can yield significant improvements in the organization's ability to execute.

Measuring Identity

On a scale of 1–10, 1 = seldom true, 5 = sometimes true, 10 = almost always true.

TABLE 1-2

Measure your organization's identity

	Rating (1–10)
We understand the basic reason for the organization to exist. We know the inherent value the business has.	
Our business processes are designed to deliver the inherent value of the business.	
Managers and leaders often talk to the organization about the underlying idea of the company and why it is important.	
Our information system contains relevant data about things that would affect the validity of our originating idea.	
Our brand image is recognized immediately by our customers and suppliers.	
We know what our intrinsic value-add means to our customers.	
We know what our extrinsic value-add means to our customers.	
Our sense of identity guides decisions on its own without meetings and escalation.	
People in the organization self-govern and hold each other accountable for decisions that fall outside the identity of the company.	
What constitutes a good company investment is instantly recognizable to people in the organization.	
	Average score:

Interpretation of average score:

➤ Below 3: Individual identities drive the organization.

➤ Between 3 and 6: There is no internal or external brand advantage.

➤ Above 6: Brand is an asset internally and externally.

Measuring Purpose

On a scale of 1–10, 1 = seldom true, 5 = sometimes true, 10 = almost always true.

TABLE 1-3

Measure your organization's purpose

	Rating (1–10)
The organization has a clear purpose for why it is in business and the value it brings to the world.	
The core purpose of the organization is used to design and evaluate business processes.	
The management and leadership behave in ways that are demonstrative and supportive of a clear purpose for the organization.	
Systems in the organization constantly provide information on where we stand in supporting our purpose.	
	Average score:

Interpretation of average score:

➤ Below 3: The organization is strictly utilitarian.

➤ Between 3 and 6: There is inconsistent messaging.

➤ Above 6: People have a reason to believe.

Measuring Long-Range Intention

On a scale of 1–10, 1 = seldom true, 5 = sometimes true, 10 = almost always true.

TABLE 1-4

Measure your organization's long-range intention

	Rating (1–10)
We clearly understand what we will create in our organization 5, 10, 20, or more years into the future.	
We review our long-term goals several times per year and adjust our plans to be in alignment with the long-term view.	
The leaders of the business clearly demonstrate their support and dedication to the long-term goals of the organization.	
Our long-term goals are integrated into the communication systems; we know where we stand relative to reaching our long-term goals.	
	Average score:

Interpretation of average score:

➤ Below 3: The organization is living hand to mouth.

➤ Between 3 and 6: Low consistency leads to low motivation.

➤ Above 6: Long-range intention is an asset.

Two

Vision Imperative

Translate Intention into Strategy, Goals, and Metrics

Vision without action is merely a dream. Action without vision merely passes the time. Vision with action can change the world.

—Joel Barker

O
N AN ICY MORNING early in 2004, twenty executives from the Shared Services Team (SST) gathered at a beautiful conference center with hopes of creating the next level of effectiveness for their organization. Nestled in the woods and picture postcard perfect as the snow drifted down among the trees, it seemed the ideal place to gain perspective. The group's task seemed simple: create a plan to communicate the new strategy so that people at least four levels down in the organization would know what action to take.

The group included the SST's manager, a senior vice president, all the vice presidents who reported to her, plus selected subject matter experts—all bright, talented, and motivated executives with extensive experience in the company. They felt no ambiguity about the strategy because it had been created with their input over the course of many months. From all appearances, the group seemed poised to create tremendous traction for the organization during a time of extreme anxiety over a significant strategy shift. Yet before they got through a quarter of the agenda, the meeting started to fall apart.

The participants split into four subgroups, each focusing on one business unit area. They were asked to take some blank chart paper and create a simple list of three or four strategic outcomes for their unit. But when they returned to the meeting room, their charts were blank or filled with unintelligible content.

How could a set of goals be so difficult to create? How could such an experienced team crash into a wall when the strategy was so well documented? Their strategy document had all the presentation prerequisites: words, text, and graphics. Lots of color, diagrams, and arrows. Logical flows and connections. Not too much on a page. By all indications, communicating the strategy deep into the organization should be straightforward. The team was not on unfamiliar ground. This was not rocket science. What gives?

It turns out that although their strategy was well past the buy-in stage, the SST actually had no concept of where they were going or what it would look like when they arrived. They had no idea how to translate the starting point and the desired future long-range intention into the specific goals and metrics leading to a clear strategy, or the desired *strategic outcomes* to the relevant *project outputs*. This seems unbelievable in a team that manages multibillion-dollar information technology investments, but as we have come to see, it is not unusual. Many organizations fail to execute because people simply cannot connect the dots between what the strategy says, what specific goals it is directed toward, and what metrics can be used to navigate forward progress. Many lack line of sight to their goals.

The SST executives had a general understanding of the words and diagrams of the strategy but were unable to take action because the strategy lacked end points: there was no clear description of the desired end state, and little situational awareness of the starting point. Without a clear understanding of where they were and where they were going, they were unable to define the path to strategic execution. The SST needed to review the elements of ideation and link them to the vision domain, as shown in figure 2-1. They needed to address the *vision imperative: translate intention into strategy, goals, and metrics.* In so doing, they would discover that the very process of defining goals and metrics both clarifies and refines the strategy, making it far easier to communicate throughout the organization.

Addressing the vision imperative creates goal clarity and ensures the integrity of investment choices to serve the chosen goal. This means that organizations must set clear, well-communicated goals and then choose

FIGURE 2-1

The vision imperative: Translate intention into strategy, goals, and metrics

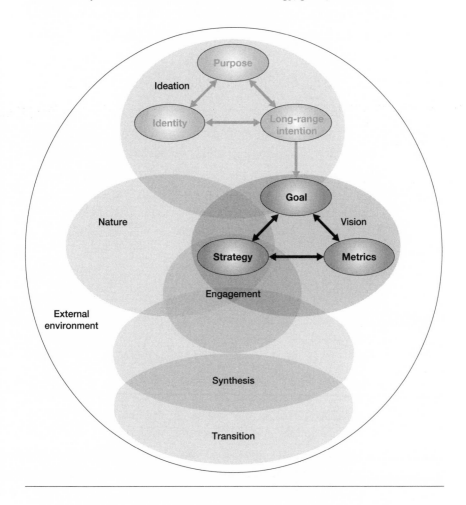

the best way to apply available resources to reaching those goals. Setting goals, setting standards for meeting them (metrics), and devising ways to get to the goals (strategy) are all part of the creative process. Approaching these decisions effectively requires forward-looking, positive, active choice.

Oddly, the lack of goal clarity can be exacerbated by early success. In one company we studied, for example, when a technological innovation gained market acceptance and sales began to accelerate, the goal of the organization shifted from inventing new products to meeting quarterly shipment and revenue numbers. Before long, anything beyond one to two quarters in the future was seen as long-range planning, relegated to a single person who generated a rolling five- to seven-year product development road map. For everyone else in the organization, the goal of continuous innovation disappeared from view. Such goal confusion or lack of goals pervades today's fast-paced, short-term performance–based thinking.

Translating Long-Range Intention into Specific Goals

Most corporate leaders endorse the need for goals, but few organizations actually articulate goals in ways that are generally understood, widely communicated, and clearly linked to the elements of ideation we discussed in chapter 1. Goals translate identity, purpose, and long-range intention into clear and tangible outcomes for the organization to accomplish.

One widely used approach to goal setting is to define "SMART" goals, which are:[1]

- Specific

- Measurable

- Achievable

- Resourced

- Time bound

SMART goals target outcomes that are *specific* enough to be recognizable. They include *measurable* indicators—either tangible or intangible—to evaluate relative success. They are seen by the organization as *achievable*, and they are endowed with the necessary *resources* to be accomplished in a defined *time* frame.

The vision imperative requires defining specific, measurable, and achievable strategic goals and metrics at all levels of the organization—exactly the challenge that stymied the SST executives. Once they define the goals and metrics, the strategy makers and project leaders must translate them into time-bound projects to be endowed with resources and managed as part of the strategic portfolio in the *engagement* domain, as we will discuss in chapter 4.

Use Creative Choice to Combat Backward Thinking and Self-Limiting Attitudes

The first and simplest step in defining goals and metrics is simply to choose to do so—an act that is far less obvious than it may seem. Active, creative choice overcomes ambivalence, self-limiting beliefs, and the fear of accountability, all of which conspire against establishing and embracing clear and measurable goals for both individuals and organizations (see "Overcoming Ambivalence: Balancing Belief and Desire").

Defining the right goals and metrics requires creative and integrative thinking, which differs from problem solving: it is forward-looking and positive rather than backward-looking and negative. For example, in a small consulting firm we know very well, employees asked the CEO in an all-company meeting, "What are our goals for next year?" The CEO replied, "All I know is that I don't want to have another year like last year." This statement indicates a problem-solving mentality in the world of lagging indicators, which focus on past performance rather than on a desired future.

Focusing on the past is a critical failure in leading strategic execution. Furthermore, avoidance is not a goal. There is no way to gear a set of metrics, or create a strategy, around what the goals are not. What is not wanted is infinite. What is desired—the goal or the preferred strategic outcome—is finite and focused. Choosing a preferred future also means recognizing mutually exclusive trade-offs and drawing the line that separates the specifically chosen goals from all the other infinite possibilities.

Even in the presence of a clear and compelling desire, without the discipline of choosing SMART goals, little sustainable progress can take place. Unfortunately, in our experience, too many organizations tend to make choices by default. By failing to choose and articulate clear goals, the organization's leaders fail to lead. As Robert Fritz put it, "The deadline is missed. The contract is unsigned. The go ahead is not given. The vote is not cast in the election. Because of the inability or unwillingness to choose, the person in this mode assigns the power to the situation and abdicates his or her own power. Such refusal to choose cripples any effective action in its earliest stages. All that is left is reaction."[2] When this happens in a company, *reaction* not only characterizes the management process, it *becomes* the management process.

Another human foible in organizational life is the tendency to adopt a process but not choose a desired result. As individuals, we may choose a diet and exercise without choosing health, we may choose a school without choosing an education, we may choose a job without choosing a career.[3] It should come as no surprise that organizations, too, enact the rough equivalent of choosing processes over results.

Overcoming Ambivalence

Balancing Belief and Desire

In *The Path of Least Resistance*, Robert Fritz describes how the conflict between beliefs and desires affects people's ability to set clear goals.[a] There
is an enormous difference between believing something is either achievable or desirable and actually declaring it a goal. People, and therefore organizations, tend to declare something a goal while simultaneously not believing that it can be achieved. This creates tensions in two directions: one
tension is toward the desired goal; the other is to justify self-limiting beliefs. When we move toward our goal, beliefs pull us back. When we move
to make our self-limiting beliefs come true, our desires pull at us as if we
were stretching a rubber band. As soon as a goal is stated, the individual
engages, and therefore organizational belief systems engage. When a
company or an individual states a desirable target outcome, there are
barely audible voices that begin to whisper, "This is never going to happen."

There are two approaches to deal with these opposing tensions. First,
we can try to manipulate belief and put a happy face on the situation
through the power of positive thinking. The unfortunate reality of positive
thinking is that it may lack truth. The lack of truth gets in the way because
it pollutes our understanding of the current reality or the starting point
of strategic execution. This is dangerous because, as one of our customers found in a study of scores of its projects, the single biggest factor in

Many big-name processes have blurred the focus on results over the
past twenty-five years:

- Six Sigma process versus predictable and repeatable results

- Total Quality Management versus product excellence

- ISO 900X versus stable, repeatable processes

- Capability Maturity Model versus performance

- Enterprise resource planning versus efficient use of resources

- Customer relationship management versus customer loyalty

project failure was the lack of situational awareness. Teams of people simply did not know where they were and therefore could not find their way to where they needed to be.

The second way to resolve the opposing tensions is to become vague or disconnected from the clear statement of desired outcome. If we believe a desired outcome is unattainable, we are less likely to be clear and conscious about adopting it as a goal. In a sense, our true desires go underground.

People often do things on the basis of subconscious thought patterns.[b] Thus, it is possible that some goals remain subliminal: they drive our behavior subconsciously. But if the goals of the organization lie in the subconscious of a select few, how will they be actualized through a coherent strategy and a coherent investment portfolio?

The solution is neither to give up on goals nor to try to eliminate beliefs. If we extrapolate a bit on Fritz's work, the most powerful lesson about understanding the tension between desire and belief is that *choice trumps belief.* A person or an organization may have a belief about what is possible and what is not possible, but that does not preclude the ability to invest in critical activities to serve the goal.

a. Robert Fritz, *The Path of Least Resistance: Creating What You Want to Create* (Salem, MA: DMA, 1984), 82–88.

b. Among the many sources that illuminate this phenomenon, we particularly appreciate Malcolm Gladwell's books *The Tipping Point: How Little Things Can Make a Big Difference* (Boston: Little, Brown, 2000) and *Blink: The Power of Thinking Without Thinking* (Boston: Little, Brown, 2005).

The list of process initiative casualties bears the brunt of office humor. Employees use terms like *program of the month* and *initiative du jour* to deride the process initiative life cycle. "This too in time shall pass" is a cubicle mantra. That is because processes without goals cannot yield measurable results.

Defining Metrics: What Success Means

There's a time-honored expression in management lore: *you accomplish what you measure.* But what you measure—your performance metrics—must align with your strategic goals. Some businesses measure things because they can, not because they are the right things to measure. Measuring the right things encourages the behaviors that lead to success. And the appropriate metrics will be different at different levels of the organization.

For example, almost every company has some form of customer metric. Sometimes this is abbreviated as *customer sat*. But what does customer sat really mean? It can take a dozen forms:

- Service level

- Product quality

- Initial product quality

- Features

- Form

- Function

- Product performance

- Reliability

- Value

- Price

Consider the differences among the following customer measures:

- *Customer satisfaction:* Customers say they got what they wanted.

- *Customer insistence:* Customers insist on buying only from one source.

- *Customer loyalty:* Customers repeatedly buy from a business.

- *Customer reference:* Customers regularly refer a business to their friends.

- *Customer emotional response:* Customers experience a positive visceral reaction.

Each of these *strategic outcome* measures can translate into an effective *project output* metric if it serves a chosen goal. But each will encourage slightly different behavior patterns. Choosing the right metric requires understanding which behaviors to reinforce to drive progress toward the goal.

Projects to Clarify Goals and Metrics

Victor R. Basili, Gianluigi Caldiera, and H. Dieter Rombach offer a creative thought process for designing metrics by asking fundamental questions about the goals.[4] Motorola, NASA, and Hewlett-Packard have all used this structured approach as a systematic way of developing goal/metric clarity. The first step is to split the goal into the component parts of purpose, issue, object, and viewpoint. For example:

- *Purpose:* Increase

- *Issue:* The rate of

- *Object:* Customer referrals

- *Viewpoint:* From the sales force perspective

Next, identify the underlying questions relative to the goal. In this instance, the question might be, How many sales result from existing customers recommending our company to others? Answering the question points to the appropriate metric, such as *percentage of sales transactions from referrals.*

What Basili et al. did not point out is that in selecting the goal, question, and metric, the strategy becomes more clearly defined in order to meet the metric, answer the question, and achieve the goal. In the process, it becomes obvious which project investments will be necessary to execute the strategy. To illustrate:

- *Emergent goal:* Create incentives for referral volume

- *Investment:* Projects to build incentive programs

  - Referral processes and systems

  - Tracking systems

  - Compensation systems

If the goal remains the same and the question changes, the metric changes and the project investment changes. Some examples:

Question: Does referral business contribute to our business?

Metric: Business volume generated through referred business

Strategy: Generate greater dollars per sale

Investment: Seek referrals to large-volume buyers

Question: Is referral business profitable?

Metric: Profit contribution from referrals

Strategy: Prioritize referral leads on profit potential

Investment: Opportunity analysis systems based on profit

Question: What is the advantage of a referral?

Metrics: Sales cycle time, conversion rate, total value of referral sale

Strategy: Act on referrals that create the most value to the business

Investment: Data mining system to analyze booked revenue

The question that underlies the goal significantly affects the way metrics are constructed, how strategy is formulated, and the investments that result. There is a saying attributed to Oliver Wendell Holmes Jr: "A moment's insight is sometimes worth a lifetime's experience." The generation of better and better–quality questions is a way of generating insight.

The significance for an organization could be as dramatic as the difference between seeking greater numbers of referrals, greater dollar volume, more profit or sales pipeline efficiency. All of these could be associated with increased rate of referral but drive very different investments. So the goal-question-metric approach requires great care in choosing the right questions to ask.

Ask the Right Questions: Problem Solving Versus Appreciative Inquiry

Problem solving is a critical skill that focuses on eliminating undesirable results. Appreciative inquiry is a critical skill that capitalizes on what works to create a better set of results.[5] Of the two kinds of thinking, appreciative inquiry offers more leverage in designing positive metrics.

In analyzing information about performance, we tend to concentrate on what is not happening. If people get a test score of 85 percent, they tend to focus on the 15 percent missed. If organizations are at 85 percent of a target, the 15 percent deficit gets the focus. Many management processes begin with a gap analysis. Focusing on closing gaps is a full-time business for consulting firms. The theory goes that if a consultant cannot identify a gap and demonstrate the negative consequences of not filling it, then the consultant is unlikely to generate business.

But gap analysis leads to a problem-solving mentality, not the creative thinking that the vision imperative requires. Problem solving is an avoidance mechanism, focused on avoiding the negative results that a problem generates. Unfortunately, the tendency toward problem solving and risk aversion has a major influence on the type and quality of questions asked in goal-question-metric processes.

Of course, in dire or rapidly deteriorating circumstances, solving problems is critical—but by itself, it is insufficient. An earthquake or a hurricane, for example, presents enormous, seemingly insurmountable problems to solve: stop the flooding, stop the looting, stop the suffering, stop the death, stop the illness. But after addressing those issues, problem solving will not *create* anything to replace the devastation. What must take over at that point is the leverage of what works.

The roads, power grids, water systems, and other infrastructure elements *that are still working* will be the starting point of creating a better set of results for people in the affected regions. Recovery will be built on things that work, not on things that are broken. The roads that work will be used to carry supplies so that recovery can take place. The focus will be on building from what is accessible and expanding from the base of what works.

In their work on appreciative inquiry, David Cooperrider, Diana Whitney, and Jacqueline Stavros outline an approach to organizational change and achievement based entirely on processes other than problem solving.[6] Consider their example of British Airways, an organization that constantly looks for ways to improve service in order to enhance customer satisfaction and retention. Baggage loss is a problem for all airlines and is a major satisfaction issue for travelers. Any traveler who has lost a bag knows the situation all too well. The feeling of knowing that the luggage has been misplaced lasts a long time in the mind of the customer.

One of the British Airways approaches to this problem was to study and attempt to minimize the amount of time it took to recover a lost bag. After all, one of the cornerstones of customer service is responsiveness to problems. A problem-solving mentality could set a goal for responsiveness using the following thought process:

- *Purpose:* Increase

- *Issue:* The speed of

- *Object:* Recovering lost baggage

- *Viewpoint:* From the customer's viewpoint

- *Emerging obvious question:* How fast can we get the bag back to the person?

- *Obvious metric:* Baggage recovery speed

- *Obvious strategy:* Find delay causes and improve recovery systems

- *Obvious investment:* Baggage tracking and recovery processes, tools, and so on

This is perfectly sensible, logical, and straightforward. But the whole construct of improving lost baggage systems is a bit like trying to reduce heart attacks by speeding up the ambulance service. The recovery system does not get at the root of the customer outcome that would make a difference in satisfaction and retention. If customer service and retention are the overall intent, then baggage handling is tied to "exceptional arrival experience." If we use appreciative inquiry, the key question would be, What do we do well that, if we did more of it, would improve the overall travel experience for our customers? Or, in order to increase the odds of an exceptional arrival experience, What do we do right that gets most bags where they're supposed to be?

Cooperrider et al. demonstrate with case after case that the right metrics focus people's attention on doing the right things. If we focus on deficit, we get more deficit. If we focus on what is working, we get more of what is working. British Airways is one of many that benefited greatly from shifting from a study of deficits to a creation mentality based on appreciation of what is working.

Contrasting the goal-question-metric exercise under appreciative inquiry versus problem solving offers telling insights:

PROBLEM SOLVING

Goal: Reduce baggage recovery time

Question: How long does it take to recover a lost bag?

Metric: Time to close a lost-bag incident

Strategy: Create a best-in-class baggage recovery system

Investment: Lost-baggage tracking systems and reporting dashboard

APPRECIATIVE INQUIRY

Goal: Exceptional arrival experience

Question: What do we do well that, if we did more of it, would most affect the customer's perception of an exceptional arrival experience?

Metric: Customer compliments, customer retention

Strategy: Improve the customer touch points from end to end

Investments: End-to-end processes based on demographic and psychographic research of customer delight factors, including the timely arrival of luggage

The positive orientation of appreciative inquiry creates a whole new set of possibilities in terms of better goal clarity and better choice of questions, leading to better metric design, clearer strategies, and more appropriate project investments.

Use Leading Rather Than Lagging Metrics

Aristotle once noted, "A vivid image compels the whole body to follow."[7] But a vivid image of what? What lies ahead, what lies behind, what we want to lie ahead, what we wish did not lie behind? Most companies manage by tracking quarterly performance indicators such as:

- Profit
- Margin
- Inventory
- Production volume
- Revenue versus last quarter
- Revenue versus same quarter last year
- Quick ratio
- Acid test ratio

- Debt/equity ratio

- Price/earnings ratio

This data offers a vivid image of the past but does little to guide future actions and investments. All the items in this list are lagging indicators derived from past activity. In many ways the give and take between publicly traded companies and market analysts is a game of making a future prediction of what the past will turn out to be. A company is then rewarded or punished in terms of stock price based on the conformance to expectations of the analysts. But as analysts always note, past performance is not predictive of future profitability.

What has happened in the past is very seldom useful to lead an organization. Looking at the past actually reinforces old attitudes about what is possible and not possible, which, as we discussed earlier in this chapter, can limit the organization's ability to make positive choices that create a better future.

If an airplane pilot used only lagging indicators, the plane would take off, and the navigation metrics would be:

- Miles flown

- Average speed

- Fuel consumed

- Average altitude

- Route flown

But using only these indicators wouldn't help the pilot fly the plane predictably to a specific destination. Instead, the pilot needs to work with forward-looking information:

- Destination

- Current course compared with flight plan

- Current ground speed

- Distance from destination

- Fuel level

- Fuel required according to projected conditions

- Weather conditions between present position and destination

- Weather conditions at destination

Using this information, pilots can navigate. Concentrating on the turns they did or did not make and how they handled turbulence in the air behind them is irrelevant. An executive running an organization by looking only at accounting figures is the rough equivalent of a pilot using a rearview mirror.

To improve the safety performance of their companies, top managers will naturally reward those managers whose business units have achieved below-average accident rates in the previous period. Tracking near misses and doing causal analysis of the factors that created the near misses—which are much more frequent than accidents and help identify potential future accidents—is one step better than tracking past accidents. But companies that want to achieve safety records that approach zero accidents must take a more proactive approach in using leading indicators—they must analyze all their current and planned work methods in order to identify and proactively eliminate potential hazards from the workplace.[8]

Some organizations are extremely adept at using leading indicators to their benefit and can translate leading indicators into quarterly results. Others stick slavishly to the backward-looking measures that Wall Street prefers. In the process, they miss the opportunity to define leading metrics to focus behavior on the desired *future* results.

Align Meta, Mega, Macro, Midlevel, and Micro Metrics

Many levels of metrics guide and align the individual activities of strategic execution. We define these as:

- *Meta:* Metrics that measure achievement of purpose

- *Mega:* Metrics used to make strategic choices that serve goals and purpose

- *Macro:* Metrics to gauge top-level goal attainment

- *Midlevel:* Metrics to optimize the business to serve goals

- *Micro:* Metrics for individual contributors to the other metrics

Building multilevel goals and metrics to serve customer outcomes is a critical competence in strategic execution. When these metrics align with each other and with strategic goals, people at all levels know exactly how their own successes contribute to the organization's success. Southwest Airlines offers a powerful example of translating its heralded low-cost strategy into goals and metrics that align across multiple levels of the organization (see "Aligning Goals and Metrics at Southwest Airlines: Aircraft Turn Time").

Aligning Goals and Metrics at Southwest Airlines

Aircraft Turn Time

Aircraft turnaround time is not the whole story of Southwest's success, but it gives us an example of goals and leading metrics that are aligned at each level:

Meta goal: Freedom to travel

Offer air travel as a preferable alternative to other forms of transportation and do so in a way that is fun, safe, and affordable.

Mega goal: Coverage of primary and secondary airport market

Provide low-cost service to primary and secondary airports where sufficient demand exists.

Macro metric: Aircraft utilization, cost per available seat mile

A low-fare airline must have high utilization. Utilization is based on the ability to serve the right market efficiently and fly full.

Midlevel metric: Aircraft turn time

Utilization and cost per available seat mile are served by keeping aircraft in the air. Planes make no money while sitting still.

Micro metric: Refueling time

One highly critical element of the Southwest business model is the performance of all the small tasks that contribute to the centerpiece of turn time. Refueling time is one of many leading measures that contribute to a team performance metric.

Starting with the goal of offering affordable air travel at frequent inter-vals, the metric of *cost per available seat mile* gives Southwest a measure of efficiency. But this metric cannot be used to directly guide or measure a ground crew, or a pilot, or a flight attendant, or the CEO. Therefore, South-west needs other measures to drive activities at all levels of the business.

Cost per available seat mile is related to airplane utilization. When fleet size can be cut because of higher utilization rates per plane, cost per avail-able seat mile goes down at constant miles of flight. Fleet utilization can-not be directly controlled by most individual employees, so it would not make a good micro-level metric. It does, however, point to the midlevel metric called *flight turnaround time*. The faster the turnaround time, the fewer airplanes required and the higher the utilization. At this level, indi-viduals can embrace and influence performance as defined by the metric.

Flight attendants can affect turnaround time by working to clean and prepare the plane and helping passengers load and unload more quickly. Ground crews can look at times required to fuel, clean, and service the plane. Gate agents can prepare the next group of people to be ready to load when the plane is ready. All the hundreds of tasks in a landing and a take-off can now be optimized to lower the delay of a plane on the ground. So the people who handle the fuel hose know exactly what they do that con-tributes to the business model that drives overall goal achievement. All these micro-level metrics align with the larger goals. Managing the busi-ness becomes a matter of executing to the metrics daily.

Unfortunately, most business models are not as simple as Southwest's. Many airlines (United, Continental, and Delta) have tried a similar market offering and failed. Southwest has inspired JetBlue, easyJet, and others that are successful in using a similar model but with their own carefully de-signed goals and metrics. The fact remains that without clear goals linked to appropriate multilevel metrics and supported by coherent investments, strategic execution is almost impossible—or at the very least, it is a ran-dom chance event.

Spotting Misaligned Goals and Metrics

Organizations often have conflicting metrics at various levels of the busi-ness. For example, most professional services firms struggle with the con-flict between customer service delivery metrics and employee time utilization metrics. On the top line of a professional services firm, there are metrics of profitability, customer loyalty, differentiated offerings, and so on. To remain profitable, the professionals in the company must maintain a level of billable hours. Here is where the conflict arises. Remaining billable means forgoing anything that would jeopardize utilization, including:

- Finishing projects ahead of time

- Implementing cost-saving steps

Misaligned Metrics

The Call Center Fiasco

Organizations with customer contact hotlines that are managed as call centers provide a common example of misaligned metrics. Most organizations that sell consumer electronics—and especially makers of personal computers and peripheral products—have telephone help lines for customers.

In the early days of the personal computer, the call centers were tiny in comparison to the challenge of serving millions of neophyte customers with thousands of configurations of equipment, software, applications, and uses. As personal computer margins got squeezed over time, the pressure to reduce cost of service became inevitable. Call automation and cost reduction through menu sorting, online help, fax-back help lines, and the like became the rule of the day as companies struggled to reduce costs. Many decided to establish call centers in far-flung locations with technically astute workforces and favorable cost structures.

If a company has an efficiency motivation, the focus on cost reduction is perfectly rational. It is also, however, the source of unintended outcomes. Most personal computer products have a relatively short life span. The time from purchase to obsolescence is often a year or slightly more. Getting a customer to come back for the next purchase is relatively crucial because of the cost of acquiring a new customer versus maintaining an existing customer. Thus, for some companies, customer satisfaction may become as important a goal as efficiency.

Various means of call recording, surveys, interviews, and direct customer contact provide appropriate metrics for customer satisfaction. Yet in virtually all call centers we have encountered, companies at one time or other

- Exploring alternatives

- Exiting low-value services as they emerge

In these cases, the time utilization metric for the people at the customer interface apparently is tied to the top-level metric of profitability, which may make intellectual sense—but unfortunately contains a set of motivations that are counter to the top-level metrics of customer satisfaction and loyalty. The example in "Misaligned Metrics: The Call Center Fiasco" illustrates

measured the customer service representatives primarily on *call time*, or, more specifically, on the time it takes to complete each call. The implicit assumption was that the faster the customer problem is solved—the shorter the call time—the more satisfied the customer. And the shorter the call time, the greater the cost savings in use of employees' time. Thus, call time became a metric for both customer satisfaction and cost reduction.

This is flawed thinking. The motivation of individuals measured primarily on call duration is to manage the duration even if it sacrifices customer satisfaction. Call duration is directly in the hands of the person at the customer interface, but customer satisfaction is too high-level a goal for any one individual to take on. So call center employees do exactly what they are measured on. They strive to shorten call time using strategies such as these:

- Transfer the call

- Give a solution (any solution) and ask for a callback

- Escalate the call to a supervisor

- Hang up

The rough interpretation of the above from a customer point of view:

- The runaround

- Incompetence

- More incompetence

- #@**%%!!!%%^^&&***!!!

Clearly, call time is a poor micro-level metric for achieving customer satisfaction. When translated to the operational level, it creates a misalignment between high-level intentions and personal goals.

how such misaligned metrics can end up destroying customer relationships rather than strengthening them as intended.

Championing Clarity and Accountability

Goal clarity is the ability to identify the result being sought. Metric clarity is the ability to measure the path toward the goal and the level of goal achievement. For some people and organizations, this clarity has a downside.

- Goal and metric clarity leave less wiggle room to claim the actual result meets the stated goal. Staff meetings, board meetings, and performance review meetings become much less ambiguous when goals are clear.

- When goals and metrics are clear, smart talk, double-talk, stories, and excuses won't work. No amount of talk can get people out of the results they behaved themselves into.

- Plausible deniability is taken away. Changing the story, twisting the data, telling half-truths, all become useless as tools to explain away poor performance.

- Accountability becomes inevitable, and many people shrink from situations where accountability is clear.

In its simplest form, accountability is the opposite of stories and excuses. For example, in a seminar setting, people were asked to commit to be back from breaks on time. *On time* had a specific definition that all could understand clearly. On time meant that they had to be seated by the time the music of a specific song stopped. If people were not on time, a staff member would take them aside and point out respectfully that they had broken their agreement. The response from people in this situation often took the form of stories and excuses right out of early school years. Dog ate the homework, my watch isn't working, lost track of time, got a phone call, had to go to the bathroom, and on and on.

Accountability is different from blame and assumes no right or wrong. Accountability is the ability to:

- Acknowledge the truth about the results that have been created

- Accept ownership of the choices that drove the results

- Declare a path forward consisting of the choices that will be made in the future

Accountability is not complex and it is not difficult. Yet stories and excuses abound. Clear goals and clear metrics render such stories and excuses useless. Even when people recognize the need for goals and metrics, there is a clear tendency to resist them until goals, metrics, and strategy are woven into the fabric of the organization at every level. The *San Jose Business Journal* summed up accountability in a small sign we noticed in its offices: "At the end of the day, we either have reasons or results. Reasons don't count."

Corporate Social Responsibility: Choosing Goals and Metrics for the Triple Bottom Line

Sustainability has become a global watchword—or, in our terms, a meta goal—in assessing the actions of governments and increasingly also of large corporations, especially those with global brands. There is ongoing debate about what sustainability means, but a broad consensus has developed that it involves rigorous assessment of an enterprise's investments and business practices against three Es: economy, ecology, and equity.

This framework for assessing investments and business practices has come to be called "triple bottom line" accounting. It is enshrined in the metrics used to evaluate investments at multilateral lending institutions like the International Finance Corporation (IFC) of The World Bank, and in the "Equator Principles" that have now been voluntarily adopted by private lenders, including Citigroup and Deutsche Bank, which are collectively responsible for more than 75 percent of global project financing.[9]

These investment criteria use conventional accounting measures to assess economic sustainability but generally extend the assessment window over a longer, "life cycle" time frame than traditional financial assessments. Ecological sustainability is assessed in terms of minimum acceptable criteria for a set of environmental services such as protecting or even enhancing air quality, water quality, species biodiversity, and so on. Equity sustainability is assessed in terms of minimum standards for managing and compensating displaced populations, requiring "free prior informed consent" (FPIC) from indigenous groups for development to proceed on their ancestral lands, and so on.[10]

Companies that adopt triple-bottom-line goals and metrics are usually high on the scale of corporate social responsibility (CSR). Many companies recognize that their young, media-savvy customers and prospective employees are increasingly concerned about the environmental and social justice aspects of CSR. These global consumers increasingly vote with their pocketbooks and résumés to reward good corporate citizenship. And they avoid buying from or working for companies whose business practices around the world may be legal in terms of local laws, but that the prospective customers or employees have come to believe are harmful to the environment (such as wasting energy or causing air and water pollution) or create social injustices (such as employing child labor or displacing settled populations).

Witness the growing popularity of hybrid automobiles, running shoes assembled in factories that are certified to employ no child labor, "LEED certified" green buildings, and many other "green" products and services.[11] For companies that sell to or seek to recruit high-CSR customers and employees, earning the reputation of being a high-CSR enterprise may involve some extra costs. However, the high-CSR brand that they develop provides a hefty payback to shareholders: it increases sales to socially conscious consumers, attracts investment from socially conscious investors, and helps recruit and retain scarce, socially conscious employees in specialties like information technology.

For these kinds of reasons, many companies have decided that it is in their long-term interest to practice the same kind of triple-bottom-line accounting used by IFC and large investment banks.[12] Ben & Jerry's (ice cream) of Vermont was an early example of a "green" company that started small and developed an "ultrahigh" CSR brand; it grew to become a large enterprise that was acquired by Unilever PLC in 2000.

It is not easy for managers to set measurable triple-bottom-line goals. As the *Economist's* review points out, "One problem with the triple bottom line is quickly apparent. Measuring profits is fairly straightforward; measuring environmental protection and social justice is not. The difficulty is partly that there is no single yardstick for measuring progress in those areas. How is any given success for environmental action to be weighed against any given advance in social justice—or, for that matter, against any given change in profits? And how are the three to be traded off against each other?"[13]

It is true that a single bottom line may be less ambiguous than a triple bottom line. However, some progress is being made in quantifying both the ecology and equity dimensions, as described in "Measuring Corporate Responsibility: Ecology and Sustainability" and "Measuring Corporate Responsibility: Equity and Fairness." And the contribution to the firm's long-term single-bottom-line financial returns by setting the ecology and equity bars high can be significant.

Measuring Corporate Responsibility

Ecology and Sustainability

To better assess the ecology bottom line, new kinds of metrics are beginning to be developed for quantifying the costs and benefits of diminishing or enhancing a set of "ecosystem services" currently provided by the natural environment.[a] Walt Disney Imagineering, the internal group that designs Disney's theme parks around the globe, is developing techniques to assess the value of the ecosystem services provided by portions of the natural environment that could be affected by its projects. For example, the ecosystems of existing wetlands provide flood attenuation, water filtration, "biotreatment," and wildlife habitat. Whenever and wherever Disney builds a park, Walt Disney Imagineering needs to mitigate any loss of such wetlands and also reinforce, replace, and enhance those ecosystem services.

Elements of the built environment can potentially provide similar ecosystem services. Flood control barriers, water treatment plants, and even new wetlands, created by flooding adjacent locations, can be developed to compensate for—or exceed—the losses in ecosystem services caused by buildings, roads, monorails, and other facilities related to theme parks that impinge on existing wetlands. A great deal of ongoing research in this area promises to help assess the ecology dimension of sustainability in a more rational manner in the future.

a. Robert Costanza, Ralph d'Arge, Rudolf de Groot, Stephen Farber, Monica Grasso, Bruce Hannon, Karin Limburg, Shahid Naeem, Robert V. O'Neill, Jose Paruelo, and Robert G. Raskin, "The Value of the World's Ecosystem Services and Natural Capital," *Nature* 387 (997): 253–260.

Measuring Corporate Responsibility

Equity and Fairness

The equity dimension of the triple bottom line is undeniably the most difficult area to quantify unambiguously. And because the social costs and benefits of any intervention are usually unequally distributed across multiple stakeholders, equity assessment metrics and processes will ultimately always be political, even if their social costs and benefits could be quantified. The approach of the most progressive organizations in assessing equity goals has been to set minimum standards for meaningful involvement of affected stakeholders in early-stage feasibility review and planning processes. This allows all stakeholders to be heard, and social equity issues to be broadly assessed and globally optimized, before early decisions—especially those that are difficult to reverse later—become cast in concrete. As we will discuss in chapter 4, following a "fair process" has been shown to increase participant acceptance of and compliance with ultimate outcomes, even if participants do not agree with the outcomes.[a]

A fair process will not necessarily result in an outcome that meets all the goals of all stakeholders. However, it ensures that their goals will be considered in choosing alternatives through early participation, when they can potentially have the most influence over outcomes. The keys to setting up a fair process are to engage all affected stakeholders from the outset in meaningful dialogue to present and rebut anticipated costs and benefits of each alternative, provide clear explanations of the rationale for all decisions that were made, and set clear expectations for the timing and nature of future decisions and actions.[b]

Thus, setting fair process standards is a readily available means to begin setting and enforcing meaningful equity goals and metrics for an organization's business investments and practices.

a. W. Chan Kim and Renée Mauborgne, "Fair Process: Managing in the Knowledge Economy," *Harvard Business Review*, January 2003, 127.

b. Joel Brockner, "Making Sense of Procedural Fairness," *Academy of Management Review* 27, no. 1 (2002): 58–76.

Achieving the Vision Imperative: Start Simple

As we saw in this chapter's opening example of the SST, the most difficult part of the vision imperative for many organizations is determining where to start. The last thing a team of people engaged in creating alignment in an organization needs is a 300-pound, twelve-swim-lane, Six Sigma, ISO 900X, Baldrige-based document that no one can understand and few can even lift. Starting simple is the best way to create the right alignments between long-range intention and the strategic goals and metrics that will drive the progress toward it. Table 2-1 offers a simple way of beginning to lay out the connections.

We use the table as a starting point to help teams of leaders get a handle on alignment within the vision imperative. In the area of outcomes, we could start off with a goal-question-metric approach, or we could use the triple-bottom-line approach, or we could use any of a myriad of established processes for identifying SMART goals. The reality of working with executive teams is that when asked for outcomes, executives seem to have a very difficult time articulating clear end results. If the problem is the inability to articulate outcomes, then there is little point in developing an elegant strategy without a clear understanding of where the organization wants to be in the future. The simple tool shown in table 2-1 gives an approach to help the executive team define:

- The strategic outcome they are looking for

- The links to the overall organizational strategy

- How the outcomes are to be measured

- How to articulate a simple high-level description of the strategy for getting to the outcome

- Which indicators can be used to measure progress toward the outcome

- The tangible work product in terms of project outputs that must be created to reach the outcome

This may seem elementary, and in some ways it is. But the question remains as to why so many organizations and groups of people struggle to

TABLE 2-1

Linking strategic outcomes to project outputs: Connecting goal to metric, to strategy, to deliverable

Goal or strategic outcome	Linkage to overall strategy or question	Measurement and target value for measure	Strategy path	Leading indicators	Deliverables or project outputs
This is the future outcome, stated as if it has already occurred.	Which aspect of overall company strategy will this outcome help us reach?	How will we know we have reached the outcome? You don't measure the strategy—you measure the outcome.	Broad and *simple*—the "path"; *how* will we reach the outcome?	What things will tell us whether we are making progress toward reaching the outcomes?	Hard, tangible things we deliver along the way, plus the final outcome.
Customer validation	What does the customer think? Does he or she agree with what we think our outcome and measurements are?				

answer such a simple set of questions. After all, what is so complicated about answering the questions of where you are, where you are going, and how you are going to get there?

Rate Your Organization on the Vision Imperative

After the organization gets done with the ropes course and the hymn sung in the forest while holding hands, executives need to get down to setting goals, providing metrics, and linking them to strategy. As in the other imperatives chapters, we offer here a rating instrument, to be administered either informally or formally throughout the organization to help you determine whether your organization needs investments to align the vision domain. When the results vary considerably from unit to unit or at various levels of the hierarchy, investing in projects such as those described in "The Project List for Translating Intention into Strategy, Goals, and Metrics" can yield significant improvements in your organization's ability to execute.

The Project List for Translating Intention into Strategy, Goals, and Metrics

- Top-down and bottom-up goal formulation processes
- Facilitated sessions for structured goal setting
- Strategic execution office creation
- Strategy mapping
- System risk assessments
- End-to-end metric design
- Incentive system redesign
- Executive compensation realignment
- Metric-based strategy creation
- Expansion of definition and scope of scorecards
- Scorecard alignment from top to bottom

Measuring Goals

On a scale of 1–10, 1 = seldom true, 5 = sometimes true, 10 = almost always true.

TABLE 2-2

Measure your organization's goal-setting ability

	Rating (1–10)
Our organization sets clear goals for the near term (1–5 years) that are supported by our strategy and the way we measure performance.	
There is an organized and defined process for setting goals.	
Management exhibits discipline and resolve in achieving goals.	
Our systems provide information on goals, including who is accountable for meeting them.	
Goals in the organization provide clarity about both outputs and outcomes for the organization.	
Goals are created in a way that makes it clear whether they are reached or not.	
Goals are selected on the basis of affirmative topics that emphasize what the organization wants more of.	
	Average score:

Interpretation of average score:

> Below 3: The organization is lost in space, and individuals are making choices for the organization on whatever basis they choose.

> Between 3 and 6: There is a mixture of individual and organizational goal clarity advantage.

> Above 6: The organization is reaching goal clarity.

Measuring Measurements

On a scale of 1–10, 1 = seldom true, 5 = sometimes true, 10 = almost always true.

TABLE 2-3

Measure your organization's ability to measure

	Rating (1–10)
Our measurements of the business are consistent with the way people are measured and are clearly connected to our strategy.	
Measurements are created in a well-developed process that makes who, what, how, how much, and when easy to understand.	
Managers and leaders clearly articulate the measures of the business and how individual and business measurements relate.	
We know how to measure the right things to predict success and avoid pitfalls; we understand the key performance factors for the organization.	
The organization's scorecard is built on lead indicators and uses lag indicators for historical purposes.	
Metrics of the organization measure the leading-indicator aspects that are central to the business model.	
	Average score:

Interpretation of average score:

➤ Below 3: Measurements are too vague to help deliver strategy.

➤ Between 3 and 6: Measurements are present but ineffective.

➤ Above 6: The organization can navigate well.

Measuring Strategy Connected to Vision

On a scale of 1–10, 1 = seldom true, 5 = sometimes true, 10 = almost always true.

TABLE 2-4

Measure how well your organization connects strategy with vision

	Rating (1–10)
Our strategy lays out a clear path for us to reach from where we are to where we want to be according to our goals.	
Strategy is developed for the organization through a clear and defined process.	
Management is clear on the strategy, and when strategy changes, we have a repeatable process for making necessary adjustments to goals and metrics.	
We have the systems, data, and ability to design strategy based on solid information.	
	Average score

Interpretation of average score:

➤ Below 3: The strategy is disconnected.

➤ Between 3 and 6: There is a high risk of missteps and missed targets.

➤ Above 6: The strategy is reaching coherence.

Three

Nature Imperative

Align Strategy, Culture, and Structure

I came to see, in my time at IBM, that culture isn't just one aspect of the game—it is the game. In the end, an organization is nothing more than the collective capacity of its people to create value. Vision, strategy, marketing, financial management—any management system, in fact—can set you on the right path and can carry you for a while. But no enterprise—whether in business, government, education, health care or any area of human endeavor—will succeed over the long haul if those elements aren't part of its DNA.

—Louis Gerstner[1]

THE STORY of Louis Gerstner's efforts to change the strategy of IBM in the 1990s shows how critical it is to align an organization's culture and structure with its strategy. Gerstner understood the importance of consciously initiating a series of projects to realign IBM's structure and culture and transform the company from a maker of branded products to a provider of custom integrated IT solutions for global clients. The new strategy, structure, and culture—the very *nature* of the company, or the nature domain—needed to align with its new ideation, supported by new goals and metrics in the vision domain.

A more recent case shows what can happen when there are misalignments of strategy, structure, and culture in the nature domain and with the ideation and vision domains. In July 1999, Carleton (Carly) Fiorina took over as president and CEO of the legendary company founded by Stanford engineering alumni William Hewlett and David Packard. Fiorina came from a sales-oriented, nonengineering background, with years of experience as a telecommunications executive at AT&T and Lucent Technologies. With the support of HP's board, she launched a series of dramatic strategic initiatives, including a hotly debated merger with computer manufacturer Compaq Computer Corporation in an attempt to create a large, low-cost supplier of commodity personal computers and servers.

She managed to eke out some initial cost savings by eliminating redundant staff, but otherwise her execution of the merger and the new commodity strategy stalled far short of success. On February 9, 2005—less than six years later, with HP's market capitalization drastically reduced—Fiorina was unceremoniously fired by HP's board. What went so badly wrong for Carly Fiorina at HP?[2]

HP's directors, individually and collectively, insisted that the new strategy was appropriate but that Fiorina had failed to execute it effectively. Industry pundits disagreed. Several opined that by attempting to be a large commodity supplier of personal computers, servers, and peripherals while simultaneously expanding HP's corporate IT services—the second thrust being similar to what Gerstner had done at IBM—Fiorina's strategy lacked sufficient focus and was therefore inherently flawed.

We find a more nuanced explanation more plausible: the Compaq merger was a reasonable strategic move if HP wanted to become profitable in the rapidly commoditizing PC and server markets, but the strategy represented a gaping disconnect between HP's ideation—created by its founders and epitomized in its service mark, "HP Invent"—and its culture of product leadership and employee cultivation, a disconnect that Fiorina failed to address. Two months after Fiorina left, HP's board brought in Mark Hurd, the "cash-register guy" from NCR, to repair the damage. Hurd had a much lower profile than Fiorina and was personally similar to HP founders Hewlett and Packard in many ways.

Hurd did not fundamentally change HP's strategy. Rather, after taking the helm in April 2005, he initiated a set of internal projects, some of which we will discuss in this chapter, to begin retooling HP's ideation and to work on realigning its culture and structure to fit the new strategy.

To begin with, Hurd portrayed himself as just another one of the employees who was not looking for self-enhancement but to help the company return to continued success. As it turned out, he was a great fit for HP's culture. He was very honest about the challenges HP faced post-merger, but focused more on everyone's role in achieving success together—another hallmark of founders Hewlett and Packard—rather than spending too much time selling the merits of the strategy and the merger.

Just two years out, the results of Hurd's efforts toward internal realignment were already showing. By August 2006, HP had far surpassed Dell in PC sales growth and had matched its profitability. And HP continued to lead Dell in PC shipments in the fourth quarter of 2006. All the company's divisions were profitable and outperforming analysts' high-end expectations, and the stock price was up by 50 percent.

Many strategists focus on designing strategies that fit the external environment. They underestimate, as Fiorina and the HP board appear to have done, the equally important issue of strategic fit with the *internal environment*. As Hurd's early results revealed, the idea of combining with Compaq was not inherently flawed but misaligned with the *nature* of HP—its DNA, as Gerstner might put it.

Thus Fiorina's failure stemmed, at least in part, from neglecting the *nature imperative: align the organization's strategy, culture, and structure* among themselves and with its ideation and vision, as shown in figure 3-1.

The nature domain links strategy, structure, and culture, all of which are essential aspects of an organization's internal environment. Of the three, culture is the most difficult to manipulate, so it is crucial to consider both the existing and the desired culture when defining strategy and structure. The most astute corporate leaders know they must either choose a strategy in line with the existing culture or be prepared to make significant investments to modify or create new cultures.

Structure and culture can both be viewed as sets of formal (articulated and written) and informal (unarticulated and unwritten) rules, respectively, about how people should behave in an organization.[3] One powerful lever for culture change is to change the organization's structure, which defines rules about groupings and reporting relationships to determine how information, authority, and resources flow between individuals and business units.

FIGURE 3-1

The nature imperative: Invest in projects to align culture, structure, and strategy

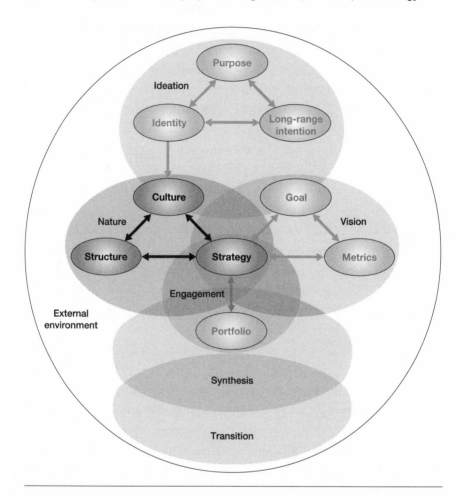

Culture is tightly linked with identity in the ideation domain, described in chapter 1. And like strong ideation, strong culture is hard to change. Nevertheless, by realigning structure and strategy in the nature domain with the right goals and metrics in the vision domain, it is still possible to move organizational culture in a new direction.

In chapter 1, we described how the ideation imperative—clarifying and communicating identity, purpose, and intention—defines the beginning and the desired end points in the strategy equation. In this chapter, we explore how to understand the size of the gap between the two, or the length and difficulty of the path to strategic execution. We first consider cultural issues and then turn to organizational structure. In each section, we discuss ways to identify and invest in the right kinds of projects to address the nature imperative. Much of the alignment work in this domain consists of transformative projects that can easily remain hidden. Strategy makers who overlook these critical projects inevitably create execution traps.

The Nature Domain at Hewlett-Packard

At their core, the founders and leaders of HP were engineers who knew how to extend and package electronic technologies into innovative and useful devices for millions of customers. Guided by Fred Terman, dean of engineering and provost of Stanford University (who came to be known as the founder of Silicon Valley), Bill Hewlett and Dave Packard deliberately created and nurtured two key elements of identity, which became reflected in the cultural rules that developed at HP. First, as Terman's protégés, they valued *engineering innovation* as the basis for competitive advantage. Second, they believed that innovation could not be directed from above, so they consciously developed a caring and consensus-oriented environment that cultivated long-term employees and allowed for bottom-up influence on strategic direction. This Hewlett-Packard identity was reflected in the unique combination of culture and structure that the founders shaped during the first few decades at HP—"the HP Way"—and it attracted many talented engineers to spend their entire careers at the company.

HP's initial product was a compact and user-friendly—for that time— audio-oscilloscope that Hewlett and Packard designed and prototyped in their Palo Alto, California, garage, and produced for Walt Disney's Imagineers to use in fine-tuning the sound track for the movie *Fantasia*. In the early 1970s, HP developed world-beating handheld calculators with sufficient power and ease of use to transform engineering practice. Almost overnight, these HP hand calculators obsoleted slide rules for engineers and mechanical hand calculators for accountants. Continuing in this tradition, the inkjet personal printers and replacement cartridges that HP Labs invented in the late 1980s and continuously reinvented during the 1990s provided about 50 percent of the company's revenue—and 75 percent of its profit—at the time that Fiorina left the company in 2005.

In each case, competitors copied HP products and arguably produced superior and less expensive imitations, often within just a few years. Earlier than many other companies, HP recognized that product life cycles were shrinking, and it embraced the strategy that truly innovative products should account for the bulk of the company's revenue. So HP aimed to be the initial leader in each of these product areas, relying on its engineering inventiveness to produce new breakthrough products. In terms of the strategic identities we introduced in chapter 2, HP was a disruptive innovator: as companies like Texas Instruments and Casio subsequently began to commoditize hand calculators, HP deemphasized them and began to focus on laser and inkjet personal printers and the even more profitable toner and ink cartridges for them. Along the way, HP kept innovating and patenting the innovations to its printer cartridges, inks, driver software, multifunction home office copiers–printers–fax machines–scanners, and so on, at a rate that competitors could not match for the fifty years before Carly Fiorina joined the company.

As we noted in chapter 1, Michael Porter argues that the only way to earn above-average profits in low-margin, commoditizing businesses (like personal computers and servers by the late 1990s) is to become a low-cost provider, which typically requires large-scale operations and an aggressive focus on cost cutting.[4] So the Compaq merger strategy was a good one if HP wanted to emphasize building and selling personal computers and low-end servers.

Dell has been a low-cost, consumer-friendly computer assembler and distributor from the outset, so this strategy is entirely consistent with Dell's history, capabilities, and culture. Trying to replicate this strategy at HP flew in the face of a deep-seated identity and culture that continued to be incorporated in HP's service mark, HP Invent, through the six years that Fiorina attempted to lead HP in the opposite direction and beyond. The example that best illustrates this disconnect—one that deeply rankled many long-term HP employees—involved pasting HP's brand onto Apple's iPod digital music players and reselling them as "HP Apple iPods."

For these long-term employees and many outside observers, a strategy better attuned to the company culture would have eschewed the merger with Compaq and instead invested scarce managerial and engineering resources on inventing the next generation of breakthrough products—as HP had done so many times in the past—rather than attempting to become a completely different kind of company with an expertise in low-cost manufacturing and distribution of commodity products.

No matter how well a strategy is designed to address the dynamics of a given marketplace, if it flies in the face of the organization's culture and is not supported and enabled by its structure, it will require conscious and concerted project investments to realign the nature domain. When corporate leaders fail to address these critical alignments, as we argue Fiorina did, the essential transformative projects remain hidden—or at best unfinished—and the strategy inevitably fails.

So why was Mark Hurd able to succeed where Fiorina failed? For one thing, he acknowledged and paid attention to the cultural and structural adjustments that the new strategy implied. As one business writer said, "In the end, they [HP] got the best of both worlds—a charismatic CEO who brought about a hotly contested but transformational merger, and a no-nonsense, operations-oriented CEO determined to make the combined company work."[5] Hurd paid attention to the company's rich history and culture, while not dwelling on them, and acknowledged its core values, manifested in the ideation and vision domains, which underpinned everyone's activities.

The Power of Culture

Since culture is the most difficult to change of the three elements in the nature domain, and the most powerful help or hindrance for strategy, it is in many ways the anchor of strategic alignment. Corporate leaders should think long and hard about whether they can identify attractive strategies for their industries and markets that align relatively well with the existing culture, before attempting to move mountains in changing the nature of an established organization.

Organizational culture provides a set of guidelines in the form of multiple unwritten rules about what is appropriate behavior. This set of cognitive frames and schemata helps people make sense of the world around them, including the behavior of other people in the workplace. A strong culture helps employees understand what kinds of behaviors to value, and which ones to emphasize when a particular decision or action appears to enhance one or more valued outcomes at the expense of others. The HP Way culture placed the greatest emphasis on technological inventiveness and respect for all employees. In contrast, the sales-oriented culture of a company like Compaq placed primary emphasis on increased market share and lower unit prices.

In most new enterprises, the cultural values of the founding team become deeply embedded after just a few years.[6] Founders hire an initial set of managers whose values match their own. These managers then screen and hire the initial cadre of employees in part on the basis of whether the new employees appear to share the cultural values of the organization. And so on: managers at every level teach and model culturally correct behavior to their subordinates and tend to reward those who conform to the organization's culture (see "Sources of Organizational Culture"). Employees who do not share the organization's values or who violate its cultural norms start to feel increasingly ostracized. If the cultural gap is large enough, they will generally choose to leave the organization or will be forced to exit after a time.

Sources of Organizational Culture

We often think of cultural values and conventions as being determined primarily by national origin, class, profession, or ethnicity. Employees raised in different countries working in the same profession—even within a single company—can have quite different values about things as simple as timeliness or as complex as the importance of individualism versus collectivism, the appropriate level of deference to authority, the need for rules and regulations to guide behavior, the importance of achieving given outcomes versus maintaining group harmony, and the relative importance assigned to short-term versus long-term outcomes of decisions and actions.[a]

However, even within a single country, there are significant differences in the cultures that founders define by their words, deeds, and initial hiring decisions. Moreover, different variations of the corporate culture may exist in different parts of the organization, depending on the kinds of work each unit has to accomplish. Many companies require and value inputs from diverse individuals and far-flung groups with complementary skills. The most successful of these invest regularly in training programs, internal brands (as discussed in chapter 1), and other projects and programs to create and nurture a coherent overall culture.

a. Geert Hofstede, *Organizations and Culture: Software of the Mind*, 2nd ed. (New York: McGraw-Hill, 2005).

A Typology of Culture

There is a world of significant research and literature on the concepts and content of organizational culture. The contribution we find most useful identifies four generic types of culture, based on the relative emphasis that members of the organization place on four different kinds of values. Following William Schneider, we call these the *four Cs of culture*: competence, collaboration, cultivation, and control.[7]

- A *competence* culture believes in the "Field of Dreams" principle: make great products and people will flock to buy them. It values technical excellence above all else. Companies with a strong competence culture are typically headed by engineers or scientists. Many start-up technology companies embody the competence culture. HP's culture glorified technical excellence and stressed modesty and self-effacement. Cofounder Bill Hewlett was the archetype of an HP engineer—brilliant, but humble, and always happiest when talking to researchers or engineers about the innards of their latest project. In contrast to this cultural ideal, Fiorina was viewed by many at HP as "flashy" and "imperial" and lacking in appreciation for the technical merits of HP's great products. In contrast, Hurd reflects self-effacement and considers every team member an important contributor with a valuable role to play.

- A *collaboration* culture is the polar opposite of a competence culture. It places great value on understanding the unique needs of each customer. Companies with a strong collaboration culture prefer their product offerings and features to be pulled by customer requirements, rather than pushed by the unique technical competence of their hardware or software engineers. Service-oriented businesses and businesses that develop and deliver custom hardware and software solutions must generally develop collaboration cultures to be successful. Notably, the custom solution services business that depends on a strong collaboration culture is the area in which HP has been least successful. Its performance in this sector has consistently lagged behind that of IBM, even after two years under Mark Hurd's leadership.

- A *cultivation* culture places a high value on recruiting, retaining, and nurturing highly creative employees to produce unique products.

Media companies, advertising agencies, and boutique consultants are archetypes of cultivation cultures. The HP Way of bottom-up, consensus-driven decision making is an excellent example of a cultivation culture at work—and it helped foster a series of technological breakthroughs that resulted in disruptive innovations throughout the company's first fifty years of operation.

- A *control* culture is important for companies in mature commodity businesses, mature service industries such as accounting or utilities, where profit margins are small and reliably producing standard outputs with consistently low costs is the key to success. Compaq had developed a strong control culture as a commodity PC and server supplier. But the control culture was totally foreign to HP at the time that Fiorina engineered the merger with Compaq—and she did not do enough to change this dimension of the HP culture in the years after the merger. In fact, despite her strong intention to reshape the postmerger culture into an entirely new one—the combined HPQ—she didn't invest in the right projects to achieve such a transformation. This was what Mark Hurd, the "cash-register guy," was brought in to accomplish, and he appears to have succeeded at doing so.

According to Geoffrey Moore, an organization's culture can be defined by the kinds of values it cherishes and the kinds of people, activities, and achievements it celebrates. Culture determines how an organization sets its priorities, the kinds of questions it asks, and the style of leadership it adopts. It encompasses the prevailing way of organizing work, and the type of people the organization attracts.[8] Table 3-1 uses these dimensions to describe the four cultural archetypes.

In chapter 1 we discussed Moore's four value disciplines, or generic categories of strategic identity, which can be mapped to Porter's cost leadership and differentiation strategies. Moore elaborated on these categories to describe the appropriate culture alignment for each one. Thus, an *operational excellence* (cost leadership) strategy fits best with a culture that emphasizes *control* (especially of costs) and *competence* (with respect to streamlining and standardizing processes). In contrast, a *differentiation* strategy requires a culture that emphasizes *collaboration* with customers to

TABLE 3-1

The four archetypes of organizational culture

Which cultural values align with your chosen strategy, and what kinds of project investments do you need to cultivate them?

	Competence	Control	Collaboration	Cultivation
Cherishes	Achievement	Order and security	Affiliation	Self-actualization
Celebrates	Top performers	Making the plan	Teamwork	Creativity
Prioritizes	The work	The system	The people	The idea
Asks	How?	What?	Who?	Why?
Leads by	Expertise	Authority	Process	Charisma
Organizes as	Work projects	Hierarchy	Persistent teams	Little as possible
Recruits for	Competitiveness	Loyalty	Trustworthiness	Brilliance

© 2002 HarperCollins. Reprinted from Geoffrey A. Moore, *Living on the Fault Line: Managing for Shareholder Value in Any Economy*, rev. ed. (New York: HarperBusiness, 2002), 235.

understand their needs and *cultivation* of employees who possess the unique skills required to develop and deliver differentiated value for the organization's products and services. To show this graphically, we can superimpose a strategy arrow for each of Moore's four value disciplines on the Schneider culture typology, as shown in figure 3-2.

FIGURE 3-2

Align strategy with culture: Charting your culture egg

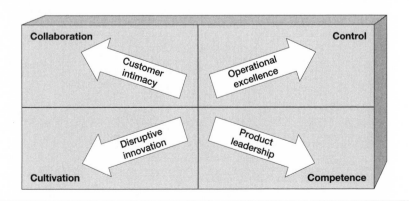

A Quick Project to Assess Your Organization's Culture

No company fits perfectly into any of Schneider's cultural archetypes. But a company can diagram its particular cultural profile as a "culture egg" showing where its primary values lie.

First, score your organization's degree of emphasis on each of the four cultural archetypes on a scale from 0, in the center (corresponding to "no emphasis"), through 5, in the outside corner ("strong, primary emphasis"). Next, plot these points on each of the diagonal axes. Then sketch the culture egg by drawing an oval through the scores on each dimension. The culture egg depicts the specific blend of values, priorities, leadership style, and attitudes toward work that is peculiar to your organization.

Figure 3-3 shows the culture egg for a custom hardware manufacturer, whose primary cultural emphasis is on collaboration to understand the unique needs of each customer, with a secondary emphasis on competence to differentiate the kinds of custom solutions that it can provide from those of its competitors.

To test how well your organization's strategy aligns with its culture, draw your culture egg in figure 3-4. Then superimpose the appropriate strategy arrow in the quadrant corresponding to the primary strategic

FIGURE 3-3

The culture egg for a custom manufacturer

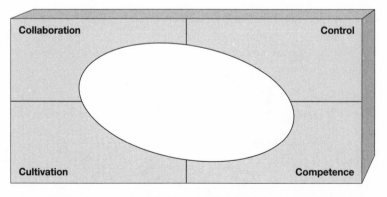

FIGURE 3-4

Template for testing the alignment of strategy and culture

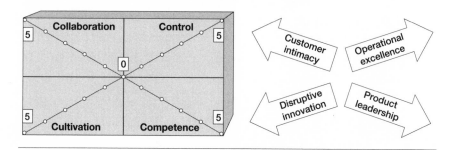

identity that you identified as your company's long-range intention in chapter 1.

If your strategy arrow overlays the largest part of the egg, your strategy and your culture are well aligned. If not, prepare to make significant investments in culture change or to watch your strategy fail.

To drive home the point, figure 3-5 maps HP's traditional and proposed new strategies to its pre-Fiorina culture in 2000. It is evident from this alignment map that HP's attempt to impose an *operational excellence* (cost leadership) strategy was severely misaligned with HP's longstanding culture,

FIGURE 3-5

HP's strategy-culture alignment map

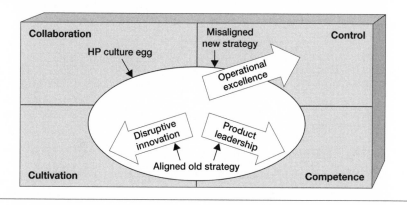

which emphasized *competence* in leading-edge electronic product development and *cultivation* of its employees. HP's culture was perfectly aligned with its traditional strategy of combining product leadership and disruptive innovation—and severely out of sync with its new *operational excellence* strategy for delivering low-cost PCs and servers. So at least one reason for Fiorina's downfall was her failure to identify and invest in the right projects to support such a major culture shift.

Tackle, If You Must, the Challenge of Culture Change

As we have stressed repeatedly, culture is difficult—but not impossible—to change. The corporate landscape of the last few decades offers precious few examples where a new leader has been able to drive a significant change in the culture of a large, established organization. Three conditions hold in virtually all these cases:

- First, the leader is an articulate individual whose core values mirror the values of the culture he or she is attempting to create. Personal authenticity is critical to employees' acceptance of a change in cultural direction from a manager.[9] Workers are acutely able to spot any inkling of hypocrisy in corporate leadership. A manager who espouses one set of values while behaving otherwise cannot be effective in generating cultural change.

- Second, the employees must be convinced that their current culture is so badly misaligned with the changing industry environment that persisting with the existing cultural values will cause the organization to fail.

- Third, the organization's leaders must invest in projects and programs that will reshape and realign the internal environment. These projects may include changing the business units' structure and leadership and bringing in managers who are archetypes of the desired new set of cultural values.

All these conditions were in place when Lou Gerstner succeeded in shifting IBM's culture to emphasize customer solutions over brands, which meant deemphasizing its product leadership strategy in favor of customer intimacy.

Gerstner clearly understood the nature imperative. He chose to sharpen and reinforce the best aspects of IBM's culture while introducing new cultural values and business unit leaders to support the new strategic direction. Significantly, his first step along that path was to design a structure to foster the new layers of culture appropriate to a global systems provider.

He began by creating IBM Global Services as a customer intimacy organization and giving it some unusual capabilities. For example, people in the Global Services unit could include non-IBM products in an IBM customer solution for the first time ever. Before this, IBM culturally could not and would not support such a "radical" idea. Thus the new structure offered an opportunity to begin changing the long-ingrained corporate culture.

At the same time that Global Services was created, the remainder of IBM was organized into business units that collectively became known as "brands." At that point, the overall identity of the company became one of system solution provider, split structurally into a global services segment and a brands segment.

Both parts of the organization benefited from Gerstner's determination to return IBM to the status of the national treasure it once was. But both required significant investments in projects to support a return to excellence under the company's new strategic identity. "Realigning the Nature Domain at HP" recounts Mark Hurd's efforts to accomplish a similarly profound transformation at HP.

For every success story like Gerstner's at IBM and Hurd's at HP, we can identify a litany of failures—including one at IBM—that occurred when managers tried to implement strategies that required culture changes they either failed to recognize or did recognize but failed to implement.

In the 1980s, IBM attempted to take over Rolm, a successful telecommunications start-up company, to acquire its technology and expertise, but proved unable to realign Rolm's culture with its own. Key managers of the vibrant young acquiree departed the merged company, and the expected benefits failed to materialize. IBM eventually divested Rolm and achieved little or no value from this acquisition. This is a very common— and horrendously value-destroying—result when corporate leaders embark on culturally misaligned mergers and acquisitions and then fail to invest in projects and programs to realign the internal environment. Another success story (see "Investing in Projects to Align Corporate Culture: SAS Institute") illustrates the range of investments that may be necessary.

Realigning the Nature Domain at HP

When HP's board brought in Mark Hurd, the *Economist* described him as "an understated operations geek."[a] In contrast with the flamboyant Carly Fiorina, Hurd fit HP's strong competence cultural archetype of self-effacing and modest engineers. He was the type of leader HP had known throughout its history (even though his background, like Fiorina's, was mostly in sales).

And Hurd really cared about operations. Eschewing media contact, he refused to comment on the wisdom of HP's strategy and set about retooling the structure and incentives to make it work. He knew he had to introduce strong fiscal accountability to make HP more competitive in the volume operations model. He thought the highly profitable printer business had been masking the weakness of the PC business, so he broke up the two units (which Fiorina had combined) to make them more accountable. In the same way that Gerstner had modeled the *collaboration culture* at IBM, Hurd modeled the *control culture* from his first day on the job. He initiated aggressive cost-cutting measures that eliminated most outside consultants and eventually cut the workforce by 10 percent.

Simply put, he focused on operations and alignment, continuing the role Packard had performed so well for years, which had lapsed through

What Executives Do Affects Culture More Than What They Say

Citigroup is one of the most decentralized financial institutions in the world. It has experienced a number of ethical lapses in the business practices of its various business units, including the one we described in chapter 1. Following several such widely reported incidents, the company invested substantial resources in creating a set of executive education programs to develop a strong culture of commitment to ethical and legal work practices. At the same time, Citigroup managers, like their counterparts in other financial services companies, continue to be evaluated heavily in terms of short-term financial metrics. So a tension remains between the espoused culture of ethical behavior and the formal structure (which defines the rules about performance metrics for employees and the rewards tied to them) in the nature domain, and between structure in the nature

the 1990s during Fiorina's tenure. To emphasize his focus on control culture values, he took the unprecedented step of bringing in outsider R. Todd Bradley, an operations-oriented executive from palmOne, to head the new and refocused PC business unit.

Within days of taking office, Hurd made a highly symbolic decision, in recognition of the HP Invent tradition that had been so badly bruised by Fiorina, to terminate sales of the HP-branded Apple iPod. From informal conversations with many HP employees, we have learned that this inconsequential (in terms of revenue) but important action earned Hurd huge reservoirs of support in the ranks of HP's engineers.

At the same time, Hurd made several key changes to the sales and product divisions to reinforce the desired cultural change. The result was a slow but steady reorientation of the culture to promote the control orientation that enables low-cost volume operations. Hurd's persistent investments of his personal time and the company's resources gradually began to boost employee morale and improve the company's performance, just as Gerstner's efforts to change the cultural emphasis from competence to collaboration had done at IBM.

a. "Mark Hurd, Hewlett-Packard's Cash-Register Guy," *Economist*, March 16, 2006.

domain and organizational performance metrics (what organizational outputs are measured to assess progress toward long-range goals) in the vision domain.

This tension between espoused corporate values and executive actions led to yet another scandal for Citigroup in 2004, code-named the "Dr. Evil" trade. Citigroup CEO Chuck Prince had given multiple speeches to his employees about how important it was for Citigroup traders to follow scrupulously ethical business practices, and he had made significant investments in ethics training for all employees. Yet the perpetrators of the Dr. Evil trade were not disciplined. Understandably, this caused many Citigroup employees—like the anonymous employee cited in "Executive Actions Versus Corporate Values: Citigroup's 'Dr. Evil' Trade"—to be confused about the firm's core values.

Investing in Projects to Align Corporate Culture

SAS Institute

Even in the absence of dramatic strategy shifts, there is always a dynamic tension between an organization's culture and its environment. And even when the environment is stable, building a strong culture requires investing in projects to grow and nurture it, especially when the company is widely decentralized or growing fast.

The founder of the SAS Institute, a fast-growing software company based in the Research Triangle of North Carolina, decided to develop a culture of cultivation for its creative software developers. Because SAS grew so rapidly, the culture could not be transmitted organically by relying on longer-term employees to socialize new employees. Instead, the company made deliberate and costly investments in several areas to refine, grow, and nurture its unique culture, including such projects as:

- Setting up and maintaining elaborate screening and recruiting procedures for new hires, to ensure their cultural compatibility with the company's values at the outset

- Offering free child care for employees' children on-site, long before other U.S. companies adopted this costly benefit program

- Chasing workers out of the building at 6:00 p.m. each day and locking the doors to ensure a balanced work-home life

Aligning Structure to Strategy

If culture encompasses the implicit and explicit informal norms about appropriate behavior in an organization, structure constitutes the more formal definitions of authority, reporting relationships, individual jobs, patterns of interaction, information flows, and employee performance evaluation and incentive systems. An aligned structure links and allocates scarce resources to the strategy and supports the appropriate culture. It

The concern for workers' families and home life was an important dimension of the cultivation culture that CEO James Goodnight both preached and modeled by his own behavior. All these actions reinforce SAS's cultivation culture by aligning what managers do with what they say. Besides helping recruit skilled and creative employees, this strong cultivation culture at SAS Institute contributes to an extraordinarily low turnover rate. This not only reduces HR costs but offers other, more subtle benefits to SAS as well.

Richard Florida, in *The Rise of the Creative Class*, points out the importance of retaining employees in creative companies:

Companies should limit turnover not just because replacing workers costs a ridiculously high amount of money, but also because it breaks up those long-term relationships. The SAS Institute and other incredibly creative companies constantly monitor and learn from their environment. They see users and customers not only as the source of money, but as the source of key relationships, and SAS has a 98% customer retention rate. So if a customer works with the same salesperson, and the salesperson works with the same sales engineer, and the sales engineer can call someone on the development team that he's known for years, they build up an accumulated stock of knowledge and interaction. This is real creative capital, but it's stored in the relationships that exist among the employees and customers of organizations—and it's invaluable to both inventing new products and solving problems.[a]

a. Richard Florida, "Managing Those Creative Types," interview by Jennifer Robison, CreativeClass.org, August 11, 2005, http://www.creativeclass.org/_flight_article_managingcreatives081105.shtml.

places decision-making authority and accountability at the level where fast-changing information about customers, competitors, and markets lies. And it measures and rewards behaviors that contribute to strategic objectives. All these elements of structure, if properly aligned, direct the organization's energy toward its goals. Naturally, different strategies and different corporate life stages require different structures to support daily investment decisions.[10]

Executive Actions Versus Corporate Values

Citigroup's "Dr. Evil" Trade

A *Financial Times* special report on corporate ethics described the Dr. Evil trade at Citigroup:[a]

> In July 2004 the [Citigroup] European government bond desk was under pressure to increase profits. So the traders planned a move that came to be known as the Dr. Evil trade. It aimed to exploit a weakness in the structure of the Italian-based MTS electronic bond market, in which marketmakers had to commit themselves to quote prices for bonds for at least five hours a day for minimum amounts.
>
> On a quiet day in August the trading desk placed sell orders worth €11.3bn in 18 seconds, which was equivalent to a full average day's trading volume on MTS. Together with further sales of €1.5bn on other domestic bond markets the total sale of no fewer than 200 different bonds was worth nearly €12.9bn. It then bought back bonds the same morning at a lower price, earning a profit on the deal of €18.2m. Competitors were stung for losses of €1m–€2m apiece . . .
>
> From a business perspective the trade was a disaster. Angry European governments withdrew business from Citigroup. Britain's Financial Services Authority imposed a fine of £14m ($26.4m) for a failure to exercise due skill, care and diligence, together with

Most companies start out as simple structures, in which many or most employees are generalists capable of performing a wide variety of functional tasks, and all command and control is centered in a single charismatic individual. As companies grow in size and complexity, they typically move to a functional or divisional organization to emphasize either specialized functional inputs or product/customer outcomes, depending on the company's strategy and the demands of its industry.

As Lawrence and Lorsch pointed out in the 1970s, functional hierarchies risk slipping into a silo mentality, where employees have trouble understanding how their departments and others fit into the overall strat-

failures of internal control and risk management—its highest ever fine. An investigation by MTS's own independent appeals board found that Citigroup had prejudiced the smooth operation of the market in the long run; shown a lack of professionalism in its disregard of how the trade would affect MTS; and been incompetent in the execution of the trade because of a failure to test software properly.

In a leaked e-mail, Tom Maheras, Citigroup's head of global capital markets, admitted that "we did not meet our standards in this instance and . . . we failed to fully consider [the transaction's] impact on our clients, other market participants and our regulators." Chuck Prince called the trade "knuckleheaded." *Yet in due course the traders, briefly suspended, returned to work. There was no news of anyone being fired* [emphasis added].

The morale of those who did believe in the values was thus undermined. As one (understandably anonymous) employee put it to us: "Not to fire these bond traders or their management is to internally celebrate their doings and it has led to an uncomfortable vacuum about what values the organisation stands by and what the strategy is."

This, then, was a classic example of how a huge effort to instill values could be subverted by top executives' failure to enforce them.

a. John Plender and Avinash Persaud, "The Day Dr Evil Wounded a Financial Giant," *Financial Times*, August 22, 2006.

egy.[11] They offer fewer opportunities for nurturing general management skills and are sometimes slower to focus on market developments. In fast-moving environments or as companies grow and diversify, they typically switch to a divisional organization focused on different products or customer segments, and then often add functional overlays to support some level of creative tension between the objectives of functional excellence and product/customer focus.

A functional organization that is attempting to produce multiple different products may appoint project managers to help direct functional resources toward specific clients or entire markets, in order to make it more responsive. In contrast, a product line organization that continues to grow will feel pressure over time to overlay functional groups, such as mechanical engineering, that cut across product lines, creating scale efficiencies and helping functional employees within each product or service line develop, formalize, and standardize companywide best practices. In some cases this takes place in loosely organized "communities of practice" that also provide guidance and mentoring for employees about technical issues.

Communities of practice are often more attractive than formal functional groupings, particularly in fast-changing technologies like biotechnology or computer science, where senior functional employees do not necessarily possess high levels of knowledge about the current state of the technology. Imagine a young molecular biologist seeking technical guidance from her functional supervisor, trained in cell biology, or her supervisor's supervisor, who was trained in plant or animal biology. Young biologists need a broader functional community—either colocated or virtual—through which they can tap the expertise of knowledgeable peers who are likely to be recent graduates or current researchers, including peers outside the company.

Virtual communities of practice spring up in many companies as an on-line substitute for physical colocation of functional or technical experts. The rapid growth of knowledge management initiatives within large organizations is a direct response to the breakup of previously colocated functional groups in many organizations, in which colocated specialists could share ideas around their cubicles, coffee machines, and water coolers.

Formalizing the Matrix

The classic matrix structure illustrated in figure 3-6 formalizes the need to combine functional excellence with a focus on products or other outputs. If it operates correctly, it encourages every employee to weigh both of these considerations in every investment decision and every action taken. By the end of the twentieth century, many large and complex organizations had evolved to become multidimensional matrix structures, often with as many as four or five dimensions of formal control and influence.

In multidimensional matrix organizations, many people end up reporting to two or more managers, each with their own set of functional, product line, regional, customer, platform, or other objectives, and who employ different metrics to assess performance against their specific objectives.

FIGURE 3-6

Formal matrix combines functional excellence with product/program focus

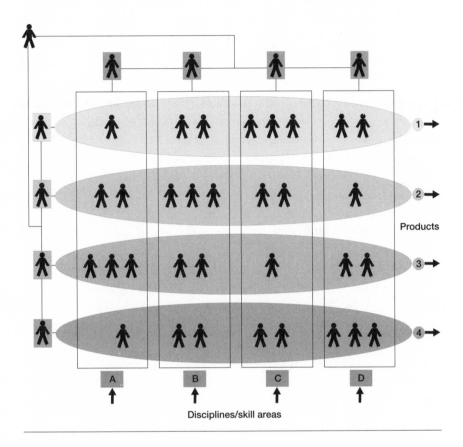

Products

Disciplines/skill areas

Such organizations require regular project investments to keep them healthy and relevant, as described in "Taming the Matrix: Invest in Projects to Fend Off Chaos and Adjust Matrix Strength."

Adjusting Matrix Strength

Even the most basic function/product line matrix structures may not place equal influence on those two dimensions. The relative influence of product/service line managers versus functional managers translates into what organizational experts call the *matrix strength*:

- A *strong matrix* structure exists when the product or service line managers—the customer-facing managers in the matrix—have a

Taming the Matrix

Invest in Projects to Fend Off Chaos
and Adjust Matrix Strength

There's an old joke from the early days of the complex matrix organiza-tion: "If my boss calls while I'm out, get his name." Sadly, the risk of chaos is very real in a poorly designed matrix, and several authors have de-scribed ways to make multiple command structures work more effec-tively.[a] All of them require routine investments in projects and programs designed to maintain an effective structure, nurture an overall culture, and keep both aligned with the strategy.

One such investment might involve setting up a project/program man-agement office (PMO) community of practice with centralized tool sup-port, training, and mentoring for project managers dispersed throughout multiple functional departments, business lines, or other dimensions of the matrix. Another potentially "hidden" project might redefine the work location, reporting and performance evaluation structure, and processes, metrics, and incentives for the employees in a particular business unit.

These are projects that adjust the "matrix strength" to fit the strategy and culture. Adjusting matrix strength in a well-designed organization can be far more effective than the major restructurings that some compa-nies undertake far too frequently.

a. For an excellent guide to designing effective matrix organizations, read Jay Galbraith, *Designing Orga-nizations: An Executive Guide to Strategy, Structure, and Process* (New York: Wiley, 2002).

strong, primary influence on decisions and actions of workers, and the functional managers' control is weaker.

- A *weak matrix* structure exists when an organization groups workers primarily by function but also has product/project managers.

- A *balanced matrix* structure accords relatively equal influence to each dimension and requires employees to negotiate continuous trade-offs in daily decision making.

The terms *strong* and *weak* do not imply a value judgment here: there is no uniformly right or wrong way to set up a matrix structure. The relative emphasis given to the customer-facing dimension versus the functional

FIGURE 3-7

Identify the appropriate alignment of strategy, structure, and culture

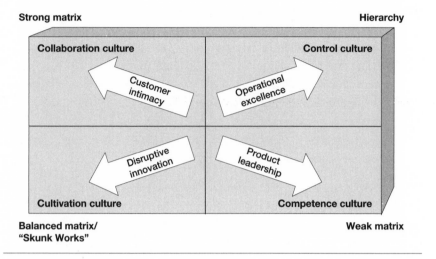

dimension must align with the organization's strategy and culture, as shown in figure 3-7.

The chief goal of alignment is to design an organization and a set of decision-making systems that automatically guide everyone toward the right investments in the right projects all the time. So the choice of structure depends on the strategic value discipline and the types of daily decisions an organization requires, as summarized in "Aligning Structure with Strategy and Culture."

Choose Traditional Hierarchy for Operational Excellence Strategies

United Parcel Service (UPS) has traditionally competed with both the U.S. Postal Service and privately owned FedEx. Against these two competitors, cost and reliable on-time delivery are the primary performance metrics, respectively. UPS must therefore pursue a strategy of cost leadership to maintain low-cost operations, and standardize and refine its business practices to achieve high reliability, in order to survive and grow.

For UPS and other companies with cost leadership strategies, a matrix organization with its additional layer of management is too costly, and the dual focus on technical excellence and customer responsiveness may not be necessary. UPS needs to execute standard sales, logistics, invoicing, and other processes reliably and efficiently. Even in its traditional package

Aligning Structure with Strategy and Culture

- An organization driven by *operational excellence* and *control* might avoid the matrix altogether: the additional managerial overhead of coordinating multiple dimensions exceeds the benefits of either a weak or a strong matrix structure, especially for relatively standardized operations somewhat sheltered from rapid change. Organizations in this category include electric utilities, package delivery companies, insurance firms, and the like.

- For organizations with a *product leadership* strategy and a *competence culture*, a *weak matrix* structure that prioritizes creating and enhancing deep technical expertise is often most appropriate. Examples include some pharmaceutical firms and makers of sophisticated but standardized manufacturing or testing equipment based on complex technology.

- Companies targeting *customer intimacy* and *collaboration* generally prefer a *strong matrix*. A strong matrix promotes agility and responsiveness over the weak matrix's advantages of enhancing technical depth and excellence. This strategy-structure-culture combination typically works well for high-end professional service firms, custom homebuilders, and other organizations whose technologies are beginning to mature, and when responsive delivery of customized products and services is the key to success. The strong matrix is the form that most closely ties *project outputs* to *strategic outcomes*.

- A *disruptive innovation* strategy depends heavily on a *cultivation* culture that supports the unique creative skills of key employees but also adapts rapidly to market changes. This often requires isolating the key employees involved in designing and producing the disruptive technology from the rest of the organization under a charismatic team leader in a small, flat, and informal "tiger team" or "Skunk Works" structure that strikes a balance between the weak and strong matrix structures but is less formal in its structure and work processes than any of the other three structures.

and letter delivery businesses, UPS must continually innovate its business processes in order to remain cost competitive, but the rate of technological innovation in the package delivery business is far slower than that faced by companies in fields like biotechnology. So UPS is primarily organized as a traditional hierarchy, relying on standardized work practices and clear chains of command to drive efficiency and reliability.

Choose Weak Matrix for Product Leadership Strategies

Maintaining state-of-the-art technical excellence is the key to success for companies with product leadership strategies. For such organizations, the breakup of functional groups is too high a price to pay for the market responsiveness of a strong matrix. Moreover, in many organizations, product lines or projects are too small to require significant numbers of dedicated employees. As a result, functional specialists must split their time across multiple products or projects to minimize idle time, so the organization may choose to colocate functional workers with other members of the same function rather than with product line or project team members.

Workers in a weak matrix structure are generally assigned to multiple product lines or projects. They receive their primary direction from their functional manager, who helps them mediate among competing demands for their time. Because functional managers are in the best position to monitor the performance of workers located in their departments, they play a correspondingly larger role in performance appraisals, often integrating inputs from the product or project managers.

Functional managers in weak matrix structures typically "own" resources such as budgets for employee salaries. Product or project managers may "pay" functional managers for the use of their staff via internal transfer pricing mechanisms, thus increasing their bargaining power over the allocation of employee time and expertise. Absent transfer pricing mechanisms, product and project managers typically submit requests to each of the functional managers for allocation of specialists via some kind of work order or requisition process. In the latter case, functional managers accrue even more influence in setting priorities and allocating their employees' time.

Functional colocation and budgetary authority, together with day-to-day direction and performance appraisal by functional managers, increase the influence of functional managers over workers' decisions and actions.

This makes the weak matrix structure less responsive to customers and markets than is the strong matrix. But it is more responsive to developing best practices and standards to create, maintain, and enhance technical expertise within each of the key disciplines of the organization's core competence. And it is more efficient at avoiding standby, idle time for workers with narrow specialties.

Weak Matrix: Pharma Inc.

A firm we'll call Pharma Inc. offers a good example of a weak matrix structure. Pharma is a 50-year-old global pharmaceutical company with more than 20,000 employees and over 150 new diagnostic and therapeutic products at various stages of development. Pharma needs scale economies and efficiencies in using scarce equipment and people, so its functional specialists (biostatisticians, chemists, pharmacologists, etc.) are located in specialized lab buildings with functional peers and split their time working for two or more product managers. All functional specialists are evaluated by their functional supervisors, according to input from each of the product managers for whom they provide services during the year. Product managers must reserve functional resources in a work order queue, so they find it extremely challenging to coordinate the diverse specialists from multiple functional groups who are assigned to their product, especially when there are changes in requirements or technologies that require rapid and simultaneous response from multiple functional groups. Pharma has developed an unsurpassed reputation for quality and innovation. However, its competitors have beaten it to market with two important new products during the last eighteen months.

The Pharma example shows how a weak matrix structure can reduce the organization's agility or responsiveness in the customer-facing or market-facing direction, making it less nimble in its marketplace. However, a weak matrix structure offers several important advantages:

- First, if the scope of work for most product lines or projects is relatively small, dedicating specialized workers to a product line or project can result in significant amounts of idle time for lightly used specialists and is therefore inefficient. Locating workers by function allows functional managers to spread workers' time across multiple projects, thus utilizing even workers with very narrow specialties more fully.

- Second, colocating specialists allows functional managers to pool the cost of specialized training, software, and equipment among a larger group of workers than any single product line or project could support. This provides significant cost advantages.

- Third, the weak matrix really excels in terms of technical knowledge management. Workers who are colocated with others of the same specialty can easily access the knowledge of more experienced or higher-skilled workers in their discipline. This allows for the efficient sharing and accumulation of technical expertise, lessons learned, and best practices within the firm.

- A fourth, little discussed benefit of grouping workers in functional departments is that it tends to provide more stable career paths for workers who must otherwise move from one project manager and location to another, often leading to anxiety about potential layoffs as projects or product lines wind down. For many highly skilled but risk-averse technical workers, being part of a stable, cohesive functional group is a significant benefit that a company can offer in attracting and retaining them as employees.

Choose Strong Matrix for Customer Intimacy Strategies

The strong matrix promotes the responsiveness and agility that are required for customer intimacy strategies and in fast-changing markets. In a strong matrix structure, workers receive primary day-to-day direction from their product line or project managers, with only occasional direction and supervision from functional specialists. Consequently, the product line manager has the primary responsibility for directing day-to-day work and for carrying out performance evaluations.

Product or project managers typically "own" the budgets for their deliverables, and they reimburse functional managers via internal transfer pricing mechanisms for the services of all of the specialized workers from each function assigned to their product line or project. Most functional employees are dedicated to specific products or projects, rather than splitting their time among multiple projects. This implies that typical product lines or projects are large enough efforts to require multiple dedicated employees from all or most of the functional areas in the organization, typically colocated with the project team. If colocation is not feasible, team members meet frequently, either face-to-face or virtually, to maintain tight coordination around the goals of the project.

Strong Matrix: Fluor Corporation

A good example of a strong matrix structure is Fluor Corporation. Fluor designs, procures, and builds large petrochemical, power, and process plants for industrial clients. Hundreds of engineers from about eight key disciplines (including chemical process designers, piping engineers, structural engineers, mechanical engineers, electrical engineers, civil engineers, and others) typically work together to design a large refinery or process plant.

In the 1980s, Fluor developed a unique facility in Irvine, California, to house multidisciplinary teams in its specially designed hexagonal office building. Each large project claimed a specific floor. The project manager was located in the center of the floor, and the workers from each function were grouped into a wedge running from the center of the building to the exterior windows. The most senior functional specialists sat at the point of the wedge near the middle of each floor, closest to the project manager. The most junior engineers and drafters were located around the periphery of the building at the windows. (Contrast this to a typical professional services firm in which window offices indicate high status!) Fluor designed modular furniture for this office so that when workers completed their role on a particular project, they could transport their desk, file cabinet, chair, and trash can on a specially designed moving dolly to the elevator to relocate to the floor of their next project assignment.

During the 1990s, pressures for outsourcing production engineering to lower-wage locations led Fluor, along with Bechtel of San Francisco and many other competitors, to find ways to perform the majority of its engineering work in less expensive locales. Fluor initially relocated engineers from Irvine to Greenville, South Carolina. Eventually, like other large engineering firms, Fluor began to outsource more and more detailed engineering production work to even less expensive locations overseas. But the same form of strong matrix structure continues to be used at Fluor and most other large engineering construction firms, albeit through virtual colocation of teams connected by high-bandwidth communication channels and application sharing software, rather than on physical colocation.

The design phase of a typical Fluor project can run from six months to two years or longer. Thus, project managers provide the primary guidance to, and performance evaluation of, the technical workers assigned to their projects over extended durations, whether they are colocated or not. Since Fluor's customers often need to make significant changes to their designs to respond to pricing, environmental, technological, and other market changes, this strong matrix, project-oriented governance structure with actual or virtual colocation of dedicated specialists to projects allows the project manager to coordinate all the specialists in real time, to adapt their designs rapidly to customers' evolving requirements. And Fluor has developed a state-of-the art knowledge management capability to share best practices through multiple virtual communities of practice that link practitioners across its global business units.

Strong Matrix: Biotech Inc.

A second example of a strong matrix organization is a company we'll call Biotech Inc. Biotech's two hundred employees work to exploit new and emerging scientific knowledge about the human genome. The state of knowledge in this field changes from week to week, so agile adjustment to changes in the emerging science base are critical for Biotech. Most Biotech specialists are fully dedicated to a single product development team. Only a few scarce senior scientists split their time across products. Product managers negotiate with one another in weekly meetings to allocate functional resources. They evaluate the specialists' work quarterly, with secondary input from the functional heads who do the recruiting, provide technical leadership, and arrange continuing education for workers in each of the functional specialties. Biotech has had to answer numerous FDA questions about the adequacy and consistency of its test procedures and reports. In spite of these concerns, by mid-2006 Biotech had begun distributing one product and had two products in the Phase III FDA approval process, placing it ahead of all its competitors.

Notice that both Fluor and Biotech make investments to support product or customer-specific inputs. Colocating workers by product line, together with day-to-day direction and performance appraisal of workers by product managers, strengthens the influence of product or project managers in guiding the decisions and actions of all workers, makes the strong matrix structure very responsive to rapidly changing customer or market requirements, and puts the technical objectives of each functional department into a supporting, rather than a leading, role.

At the same time, since they are denied the advantage of colocation by functional group, functional managers within a strong matrix organization must find alternative ways—such as virtual communities of practice—to accumulate and share technical expertise and best practices across products and project.

A strong matrix thus forgoes the advantages of scale efficiencies and deep technical competence that a weak matrix achieves. However, the strong matrix structure provides several compensating advantages:

- Most importantly, the strong matrix optimizes cross-discipline coordination, increasing agility and responsiveness to rapidly changing customer and market requirements.

- Second, a strong matrix makes it easy for a manager to tie workers' incentives to customers' values, or *project outputs* to *strategic outcomes*, as we've discussed in earlier chapters. Since most workers work on a single product line or project for extended periods, their performance incentives can be closely linked to the customer's objectives on the project. This aligns individual and team goals with customer requirements.

- Third, a strong matrix structure provides the organization with a training and proving ground for future general managers. It exposes specialists to a broader view of customer needs and technical solutions than they would get in a functionally oriented department. Product or project managers operate with dedicated technical staff, so they play a role that is equivalent to that of the manager of a small division of the company. This helps uncover and expose leadership potential both of product line and project managers, and of the technical specialists who work on their projects and would be far less visible to senior managers if they were located inside functional departments.

For all these reasons, many organizations that operate in fast-changing marketplaces opt for this form of structure. Customers at every stage of the supply chain have become empowered by Internet-enabled global competition among their vendors and suppliers striving to excel at serving their unique requirements. This has led to the commoditization of many kinds of products and services and has forced firms that formerly produced and sold "boxes"—standardized offerings of products or services—to adapt so they can provide highly customized solutions. To make this transition from "make to offer" to "offer to make," such firms must switch from a weak matrix structure that created product excellence in the past to a strong matrix structure that can responsively redirect organizational resources toward satisfying each customer's unique and constantly changing requirements. This is precisely the transition in structure that Louis Gerstner implemented at IBM to align with its custom solutions strategy and responsiveness culture. Both Wipro and APC (described in the introduction), as well as Cisco Systems and numerous other technology companies, have wrestled with this same challenge.

A strong matrix structure confers considerable authority on product line or project managers. Its success depends on the managers' understanding the value trade-offs embedded in the company's culture, so that they make "good" decisions in investing the resources under their control. Specifically, strong matrix organizations need to invest in nurturing technical communities of practice to maintain the excellence that got them to a product leadership position initially, while exploiting the strong matrix to make themselves more responsive to demanding customers wanting custom solutions (see "Moving Sales to a Strong Matrix Structure at HP: The Demise of the Five-Taurus Sales Call").

Choose Balanced Matrix or Skunk Works Structures for Disruptive Innovation Strategies

A disruptive innovation strategy often depends on a combination of cutting-edge technologies and extreme market/customer responsiveness, combined with a lack of formality. EBay has effectively emphasized all these dimensions to grow from a part-time start-up selling Pez candy dispensers to a megacorporation in record time. EBay's technology for managing millions of simultaneous auctions requires state-of-the-art integration of multiple information and communication technologies; at the same time, its responsiveness to its customers is legendary.

EBay achieves this balance by emphasizing technological excellence through functional groups and communities of practice for its infrastructure development and maintenance, while emphasizing project groups for new product and feature rollouts. The resulting balanced matrix combines efficiency and product leadership to drive eBay's extraordinarily impressive results.

Moving Sales to a Strong Matrix Structure at HP

The Demise of the Five-Taurus Sales Call

Mark Hurd introduced several key changes to align HP's structure with its evolving strategy and changing culture. Like Louis Gerstner at IBM, he used the structural changes to influence the culture.

Hurd believed that the high margins in the printer business were shielding the PC business from adequate scrutiny, so he reorganized HP's sprawling businesses into three overarching divisions: enterprise computing and services, general tech hardware (PCs, handheld devices, etc.), and imaging and printing. After he created these three product line divisions, Hurd's second major structural change initiative was to slim down the corporate sales force and decentralize authority for sales back to the operating divisions.

Sales had functioned in a weak matrix fashion, with the centralized sales force having most of the budgetary authority and providing primary leadership for sales of any size, working in parallel with more specialized salespeople from each of the business units. This weak matrix for sales resulted in what HP's customers called the "five-Taurus" HP sales call, when multiple HP salespeople, each in a corporate Ford Taurus, would show up at a customer site to close a sale.

Hurd transformed sales to a strong matrix orientation, placing budgetary resources and primary authority in each of the product line divisions, thereby sharpening their ability to compete with stand-alone printer companies like Lexmark or laptop manufacturers like Lenovo. Under the new organization, the corporate sales group provided coordination for sales to large global accounts. This type of "front-back" organization allows global customers to see HP as a single global entity through the corporate account managers, while the back office sales and engineering groups develop efficiencies of scale and specialization. IBM and Nokia also reorganized to work this way during the late 1990s and early 2000s.[a]

a. Jay R. Galbraith, "Organizing to Deliver Solutions," *Organizational Dynamics*, Special Issue, May 2002.

Amazon.com also uses a balanced matrix to achieve both cost efficiencies and extreme customer responsiveness. It relies on a traditional functional organization augmented by strong project managers to deploy advanced information technology that draws both its suppliers and customers deeply into its core business processes.

In both eBay and Amazon.com, the balanced matrix structure creates the needed combination of sophisticated project management for IT and functional management for logistics and other cost- and quality-sensitive business processes. However, eBay and Amazon.com are becoming mature businesses that no longer rely on their ability to produce disruptive innovations to remain competitive. For example, eBay acquired PayPal to get an electronic payment processing system and then acquired Skype for its highly disruptive, free Voice over IP telephony capabilities. And Amazon.com, having pioneered online sales of books, has now become a large online distribution channel, selling products for multiple vendors on its Web site. So these firms may have lost their ability to develop disruptive innovations internally, as they have grown larger and appear to be losing the struggle to avoid becoming more formalized, which besets most large organizations.

A small number of companies, including 3M and HP, have been able to continue generating disruptive innovations despite their size, by sustaining cultures that combine technical virtuosity with customer responsiveness and providing slack resources to individuals and groups to work on innovations.

However, to conceive, develop, and prototype the next disruptive innovation, most large and relatively mature companies must create Skunk Works, sometimes also called *tiger teams*—semiautonomous minidivisions or true corporate spin-offs that share the parents' high-level goals and can access all of their considerable resources but that have the freedom and flexibility of start-ups. This is done by creating formal or virtual groups that have a respected leader, a simple and highly informal structure, and the financial backing and marketing clout of the large parent organization.

Lockheed's World War II Skunk Works was so successful at doing this that the company has repeatedly used it to develop innovative products, and the name Skunk Works has become firmly embedded in the business lexicon. (See "The Skunk Works at Lockheed Martin.") Many excellent

The Skunk Works at Lockheed Martin

Lockheed Martin, the U.S. aerospace company, set up its Advanced Development Programs unit—nicknamed Skunk Works—during the Second World War. A small facility, it was given huge resources and top personnel to develop cutting-edge technology in secret.

Some of the world's most famous military aircraft—such as the SR-71 Blackbird, the high-speed and radar-resistant reconnaissance aircraft—emerged from its hangars. Still operating from an air force base in California, Skunk Works is now a registered trademark and a widely used term for any secret innovation-led project.

During the 1970s, similar units were set up inside many organizations to think "disruptively"—to look at products or markets outside their usual offering.

One of the most famous was Project Chess, the twelve-man team at IBM that developed the first personal computer in 1981. Similarly, the Macintosh computer was launched in 1984 by a dedicated Apple team that was deliberately relocated to its own separate building. One of the authors visited the Macintosh team building in 1985 and was ushered into a large central atrium filled with the sounds of employees vigorously playing on dozens of free pinball machines, together with another employee playing Chopin's "Minute Waltz" on a Bösendorfer concert grand piano in the center of the atrium. Steve Jobs described the Macintosh development program as an "intrapreneurial venture" within Apple—since it would compete with the Apple II, previously the company's core product.[a]

a. Paul Tyrrell, "Smart Companies Show 'Intrapreneurial' Spirit," *Financial Times*, July 24, 2005.

books and articles have been written on the subject of how to organize for disruptive innovations.[12]

Align IT with the Chosen Structure

Whichever structure an organization decides to use, project, functional, regional, product line, and other managers need timely and accurate information to support the allocation of authority and influence in that structure and to provide them with accurate and current information related to the metrics for which they are accountable. Thus, any attempt to change authority and responsibility relationships—for example, by switching from the hierarchy to a strong matrix structure—will require investment in projects to realign and upgrade information systems to support and motivate each of the managers in the new structure.

In a traditional hierarchy, information flows up and down within each functional discipline, appropriately summarized for each level of management. In contrast, a strong matrix structure requires project and product line managers to communicate horizontally across the hierarchy. This requires information systems that can break down the functional information at each level by project, program, or product and provide accurate and timely reports to the lateral managers. Organizations with bridges to external alliance partners also need information systems to support those partnerships.

Recently, UPS has begun to provide a broader set of customized logistics solutions for large customers like catalog vendors. This requires powerful and robust new information technologies and a "collaborative" systems integration capability to link its IT infrastructure seamlessly with its customers' IT systems. Even in the IT area, UPS—unlike other examples we've described in this chapter—has primarily worked with a traditional functional hierarchy, using a set of structural overlays such as steering committees and informal communities of practice to manage its IT workforce and vendors. The teams change over time according to strategic needs and are supported by extensive use of crosscutting processes and IT systems to maintain adequate levels of market and customer responsiveness. This allows UPS to innovate at a fast enough rate for its marketplace while keeping its organization structure simple and its management costs low.

Invest in Projects to Tune Matrix Strength

If an organization's structure is misaligned with its strategy and culture, it is relatively easy to tune its matrix strength anywhere along the scale from a one-dimensional functional hierarchy through a weak matrix, balanced matrix, and strong matrix to a product-line hierarchy. Several simple types of projects and programs are the levers of structural adjustment. These *structural levers* include changes in policy and practices that provide relatively more or less formal power and authority to product line or project managers versus functional managers.

For example, a high-end professional services organization with a customer intimacy strategy might appropriately have a collaboration culture but adopt a misaligned weak matrix structure where functional managers take precedence over project managers. As manager of this company, you can adjust the structural levers to calibrate the relative influence of the functional managers versus customer- or market-facing managers until the structure is perfectly aligned with the customer intimacy strategy and collaboration culture.

Build Cross-Functional Project Teams

The first lever of structure is the physical (or virtual) colocation of employees by function rather than by product line or project. In this case, if employees are currently grouped and located according to functions, they can be regrouped, and potentially also physically relocated, into cross-functional project teams to make them more responsive to customers and market. If the workers are geographically dispersed in ways that are difficult to change, then the colocation can be virtual rather than physical. Periodic face-to-face meetings help make distributed groups more cohesive, and frequent online interactions and structured events, such as design reviews, can help maintain group cohesiveness between meetings. If projects are too small to merit dedicated functional specialists, then the manager should leave the employees from those disciplines in their functional groups and increase the matrix strength of the organization using one or more of the other structural levers.

Adjust the Evaluation Process

The second structural lever is the relative weight given to the evaluations of project versus functional managers in the performance appraisal process. This is a very easy lever to reset: it can be infinitely fine-tuned to lie at any point between 100 percent weight for functional managers' evaluations through 100 percent weight for project managers' evaluations. To strengthen the matrix, it should be moved in the direction of project managers, thereby making workers more responsive to customer requirements.

Decide How to Allocate People to Projects

The third structural lever is defining the process by which functional experts are assigned to projects. At one extreme, functional managers establish work order queues according to requests from project managers; at the other extreme, project managers negotiate with one another over the assignment of functional resources. The former gives functional managers almost absolute power over this lever of structure, resulting in a very weak matrix. At the same time, however, it encourages project managers to plan ahead for the resources they need, which helps the organization optimize the use of its scarce human resources.

The latter approach increases the influence of project managers, strengthening the matrix. In our example, this lever should swing toward giving project managers more say in the functional resources that are assigned to their projects. A version of the work order queue that encourages forward planning but still gives the organization more responsiveness is one in which senior managers define a "hot list" of about five to ten projects during each period that are brought to the front of the work order queues of each functional group, in rank order. This retains the incentive for project managers to plan ahead, while subsequently providing them with the flexibility to escalate requests for priority to senior management, according to changing customer or market needs.

Assign Budget Ownership

The fourth lever of structure is the process used to budget and control funds. Having functional managers "own" the budgets for their employees' salaries and requiring product or project managers to request services from a functional pool dramatically weakens the matrix. Giving product line or project managers ownership of budgets, and having them "purchase" technical support from functional departments whose managers are evaluated in part by what fraction of their subordinates' time is billable to projects, dramatically strengthens the matrix. Allowing project managers to buy functional services from external groups when they are dissatisfied with the quality or timeliness of internal functional services gives ultimate power to project managers. As we noted earlier, this "unthinkable" culture-shifting move was one of Gerstner's first actions at IBM.

Companies that give project managers authority to purchase functional services on the outside need to keep an eye on both the efficiency implications of this—since the organization's functional resources may be underutilized if project managers exaggerate their need for specialists—and the long-term implications of losing critical competencies. In our example, the lever should be adjusted to give project managers budgetary authority to purchase services from functional managers, and possibly to outsource them subject to review.

Align Incentives with Strategy and Structure

The final element of structure that needs to be aligned internally is the set of incentives for workers and managers. The vision imperative aligned long-range goals and metrics with strategy, as described in chapter 2. In addition, the reward systems for each functional, project, product, and geographical business unit need to be carefully aligned so that managers who do the right things in the right way to achieve these metrics receive credit for doing so. This sounds like a platitude, but the complexity of accounting systems, especially with Sarbanes-Oxley and other regulatory constraints, can greatly distort individual behavior.

One forceful example comes from BP's record on worker safety. The company has had a series of fatal accidents on its refineries in the mid-2000s. Like many other companies, BP allocates many of the costs of preventing accidents—such as safety equipment, training, or time for safety meetings—to its plants and projects. However, the property damage, medical, and disability costs of accidents are not captured by BP's accounting system and therefore not charged to projects or plants.

Workers' compensation (WC) insurance for craft workers on plants or construction sites is the biggest single safety-related expense: it can range from 12 to 25 percent or more of labor cost and is experience rated. So at first glance, experience rating of WC insurance should create a powerful incentive for managers to invest in safety. However, on closer inspection, two factors undermine this incentive. First, experience rating is done not by project but for all of a company's operations in a single- or multistate region, so the effect of the incentive is diffused. Second, because insurance claims often take a year or more to settle, up to two years can pass before the costs of an accident show up in increased workers' compensation premiums for the company, so any incentive effect of WC insurance is also delayed by up to two years.

Thus, a project or plant manager pays the costs of preventing accidents but is almost completely insulated from the near- to medium-term cost of accidents. Given these incentives, rational plant or project managers who are evaluated and rewarded for minimizing plant or project costs in the current quarter—or even the current year—would spend nothing to prevent accidents! Nor, as became evident after the shutdown of BP's Alaska oil pipeline in 2006, would they spend money on critical maintenance projects.

Simply changing the incentive system to allocate an estimated cost for an accident to the project or plant on which an accident occurs immediately—even though this estimate is not a current period cost in the conventional accounting sense—has been shown to produce a dramatic decrease in accident rates.[13] Yet few companies have implemented such a system to date.

This is just one example of how misaligned incentives for individuals or groups can create behavior that works against strategic objectives. Product quality and customer relations are two other critical areas of corporate performance that often get distorted by incentive systems that focus on short-term "costs" or "profits."

In aligning an organization's structure and culture for strategic execution, managers must pay very careful attention to setting up performance appraisal systems that tie individual incentives tightly to strategic metrics at all levels of the organization and for each of the relevant performance dimensions in multidimensional matrix structures.

Getting It Right: DPR Construction

DPR Construction of Redwood City, California, went to great lengths to align its internal environment, and achieved spectacular success as a result. The company was founded in 1990. From the beginning, the founders strove to offer differentiated value and a delightful customer experience by developing an exceptionally high level of customer intimacy with semiconductor and pharmaceutical companies in need of turnkey construction projects to be accomplished rapidly and with uniformly high quality.

The founders engaged Jerry Porras and Jim Collins, authors of the book *Built to Last*, as consultants to help them develop, refine, and articulate their organization's culture to support this ideation. They developed a corporate vision statement that clarified the company's purpose, "DPR exists to build great things," and began recruiting employees who identified with this vision. New workers were extensively screened by multiple managers before being hired, to ensure a good cultural fit with DPR's values. Even after careful hiring, the founders did not leave development of a strong corporate culture to chance. Rather, they engaged in extensive training and orientation of new and continuing workers to promote a collaboration culture to support their extreme customer intimacy strategy.

With this well-aligned strategy and culture, the DPR founders set up a highly decentralized strong matrix structure. Relatively young project managers were placed in charge of each customer project and given an unusually high level of authority and responsibility. They were expected to take initiatives that were faithful to the company's values in dealings with customers. For instance, a relatively junior DPR project engineer decided, on his own initiative, to pave the excavated foundation for a building before the weekend at his company's expense so that construction on an urgently needed facility could continue on Monday, following forecasted rain over the weekend. This cost several tens of thousands of dollars but saved precious days of delay on a facility whose time-to-market value to the customer was measured in hundreds of thousands of dollars per day. Customercentric decisions and actions like this by empowered workers at all levels generated very loyal customers for DPR.

DPR attempted to relate strongly to its customers in other ways. The company's headquarters building was laid out with open floor plans and *Dilbert*-style cubicles to match the typical office layouts of its customers. And its young, tech-savvy workforce communicated easily with their high-tech counterparts in customer organizations.

While giving its young project managers unusually high levels of authority and responsibility, DPR adopted the kinds of tough internal rankings that Jack Welch used so successfully at General Electric. Managers ranked in the lowest 10th percentile of performance were put on notice that their continued employment was dependent on improving their rankings.

With initial financing from second mortgages on their homes, the founders grew DPR from zero to almost $2 billion per year of turnover in a period of about ten years—an unprecedented growth rate for labor-intensive, service-oriented construction companies. Much of their growth in volume was based on repeat business from satisfied clients.

As might be expected, such a rapid rate of growth put severe strains on DPR's working capital reserves, and the need to hire new employees at a rapid clip resulted in some hires whose values did not match the company's or who lacked the ability to work intimately with customers in an industry with a long tradition of lump-sum contracts and adversarial relationships. As a result, not all of DPR's projects were totally successful, and it did lose some customers over the first decade.

Nevertheless, the overall record of accomplishments accumulated by this company in such a short time is exceptional, in comparison to its peer organizations. Clearly, the careful attention that the three founders paid to aligning strategy, structure, and culture has paid off handsomely. Having successfully weathered the technology downturn following the collapse of the dot-com economy in the San Francisco Bay area after 1999, the company is once again growing rapidly.

The strategy-structure-culture alignment diagram for DPR's first decade in figure 3-8 shows how well the elements of this company's internal environment were aligned. "The Project Investment List for the Nature Imperative" will help you achieve similarly strong alignments in your own organization.

FIGURE 3-8

Achieving the nature imperative at DPR: Aligning strategy, structure, and culture required careful ongoing investments

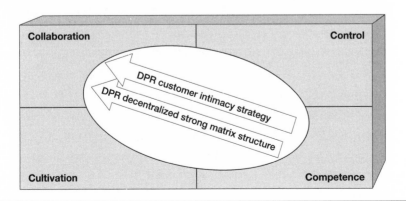

The Project Investment List for the Nature Imperative

- Ensure that strategy has been clearly articulated with crisp goals and metrics from the vision domain.

- Assess your culture to determine strategic fit.

- If you have a culture-strategy misfit, carefully consider whether you can change the culture fast enough to succeed in implementing the misaligned strategy. If not, revise the strategy to fit the culture more closely.

- If you decide to change the culture:

  - Drive an internal branding campaign to reinforce purpose in the culture.

  - Model the desired new culture by all your actions and decisions—what you do means much more than what you say!

  - Teach culture constantly: when asked for guidance by peers or subordinates, don't tell them what to do—teach them how to decide!

- Assess the structure-strategy-culture fit.

- If you have a structural misfit:

  - Use levers and dials to adjust the matrix between weak and strong to fit your strategy and culture.

  - Design project- and program-level metrics and rewards to align incentives at all levels.

- Make sure your enterprise and project information systems provide program and project mangers with the information they need, sliced according to their areas of authority and responsibility.

  - In strong matrix structures, project managers need P&L statements by project; functional managers need forecasts of resource demand and availability across projects.

  - In weak matrix structures, functional managers need work order systems to track and manage project requests for resources; project managers need visibility into the functional work order system so they can escalate requests for priority when needed.

Rate Your Organization on the Nature Imperative

Getting culture, structure, and strategy into alignment is no small task. After nearly a decade, there are some indications that Lou Gerstner himself wondered whether he had actually changed the culture of IBM. Situational awareness is a first step in understanding what you have to work with and where you need to focus additional investment to create a better-aligned natural environment. The following rating instruments should shed light on the leverage points for your organization.

Measuring Culture

On a scale of 1–10, 1 = seldom true, 5 = sometimes true, 10 = almost always true.

TABLE 3-2

Measure your organization's culture

	Rating (1–10)
Our company culture as it is today is well suited to carry out our strategy and works well with our structure.	
Our business practices are designed in such a way that they support our culture and make our jobs easier.	
Managers and leaders are active in shaping the culture of the organization in effective ways.	
The type of information that flows in the organization keeps our culture alive and strong.	
The artifacts of our culture (processes, language, rituals, stories, physical environment) are consistent with and supportive of our strategy.	
Our culture is a competitive advantage for us because of the way it attracts and motivates people with the skills we need.	
The subcultures within structural areas of the organization are complementary to the overall culture of the organization.	
	Average score:

Interpretation of average score:

➤ Below 3: Culture is a competitive disadvantage and is a blocker to getting strategy executed.

> Between 3 and 6: Culture is not likely to be in the way but is not a competitive advantage.

> Above 6: Culture is becoming a competitive advantage.

Measuring Structure

On a scale of 1–10, 1 = seldom true, 5 = sometimes true, 10 = almost always true.

TABLE 3-3

Measure your organization's structure

	Rating (1–10)
Managers and leaders of the organization design the organization to optimize business performance.	
The way we organize ourselves makes doing our jobs and executing our strategy easier.	
Our structure is created through a well-defined business process that takes into account strategy and culture.	
Our information systems break down organizational barriers by openly sharing information across business boundaries.	
Because of our structure, people know how they relate organizationally to the strategy.	
There is cooperation between organizational units that supports the execution of our strategy.	
We resolve disputes across organizational boundaries quickly and in a fashion that creates sustainable agreements.	
The measurements in organizational units are consistent with the way the overall organizational metrics are set.	
	Average score:

Interpretation of average score:

> Below 3: Structural misalignment is slowing things down and is an impediment to execution.

> Between 3 and 6: Structure is creating some problems that could be one of the fastest ways to improve strategic execution.

> Above 6: Structure is one of the things that sets you apart and makes you effective.

Measuring Strategy Within the Nature Domain

On a scale of 1–10, 1 = seldom true, 5 = sometimes true, 10 = almost always true.

TABLE 3-4

Measure your organization's strategy within the nature domain

	Rating (1–10)
The strategy of the organization is clear and well understood by people throughout the organization.	
Our strategy is created in a systematic way, and changes to it are made clear to the organization.	
Managers and leaders support and act in alignment with the strategy.	
Our strategy is developed on a very strong fact- and information-based foundation.	
People in the organization get a clear sense of what they can do to support the strategy.	
Our strategy drives coherent action.	
Our strategy can be executed, given our culture, with a reasonable level of organizational change.	
We know how to best organize to execute our strategy, and the necessary reorganization can be done without cultural conflict.	
Average score:	

Interpretation of average score:

➤ Below 3: The strategy is at great risk of failure.

➤ Between 3 and 6: There are significant issues to be addressed in the nature of the organization, and if not addressed, they will slow down execution.

➤ Above 6: The nature of the organization is an advantage to execution.

Part II

Project Leadership Imperatives

Four

Engagement Imperative

Engage Strategy Through the Project Investment Stream

*You can have anything you want—
you just can't have everything you want.*
—Anonymous

W
E HAVE WORKED with many organizations whose strategies
seem to ask them to do it all: produce leading-edge technology and be operationally excellent while developing the total customer experience and maintaining a focus on radically different customer solutions. This type of multifront strategy is almost always a nonstarter. It produces a broad set of investments in projects that lack enough focus in any one area to be successful. By trying to be all things to all people, the company ends up being mediocre to some at best. What differentiates one organization from another in terms of strategic execution is the discipline of engaging the strategy with the tailored portfolio of projects and programs that will bring it to life. In a world of limited resources, it is as much about choosing what *not* to do as about deciding which strategic projects and programs to invest in.

We call this *engagement* because the company can only commit to its espoused strategy by engaging in the appropriate project portfolio, as shown in figure 4-1. Engagement directs the scarce resources of time, money, equipment, and attention to the right mix of projects and programs. It calls

FIGURE 4-1

The engagement imperative: Engage strategy through the project investment stream

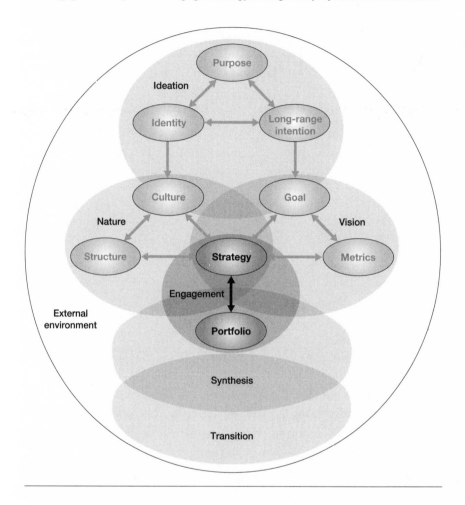

on strategy makers and project portfolio managers to engage in a bilingual conversation that uncovers the right strategic priorities and translates them to the right array of projects and programs.

The engagement imperative compels the strategists and project sponsors to engage with the managers, understand their specific, concrete needs, and react accordingly. It requires project managers to engage with the executives, understand the bigger issues of strategic intent and decision quality, and react accordingly. And like the meshing of gears when a race car driver engages the clutch, it propels the organization from strategy to action.

Engagement, then, is the central imperative of strategic execution. To state the imperative another way: get your investment governance right, choose the right projects, and endow the projects with the resources they need to be done right. Or more succinctly, as illustrated in figure 4-1: engage strategy through the project investment stream.

The engagement imperative is what Louis Gerstner of IBM referred to as the hard part.[1] It is where strategic execution fails or succeeds. It is where the work required to achieve goals based on metrics, and to transform structure and culture, meets the demands of ongoing operations.

Designing an organization to achieve the engagement imperative requires significant project investments in itself. These potentially hidden transformative projects must become part of the explicit strategic execution agenda. Moreover, organizations that do not already have strong portfolio and project management capabilities may need help in learning how to approach the task.

The challenge is fivefold:

1. Deciding how to decide

2. Identifying the projects and programs that will convert strategy into action

3. Developing criteria for prioritizing project investment decisions

4. Dealing with an overload of qualified projects

5. Reshaping the project portfolio as circumstances change

Project priority decisions often require trade-offs between improving or enhancing an existing process and building a new one to support the transformation of the company. Designing strategy around available resources is probably not the best way to drive innovation and change. But strategies that collectively require resources far in excess of the capacity of the organization are doomed from the outset. Figure 4-2 outlines the steps to accomplishing the engagement imperative. It begins with establishing the portfolio sponsorship environment and proceeds through the other essential tasks we will describe later.

FIGURE 4-2

Accomplishing the engagement imperative: establish the governance/sponsorship environment, match projects with resources, monitor and reshape the portfolio as circumstances evolve

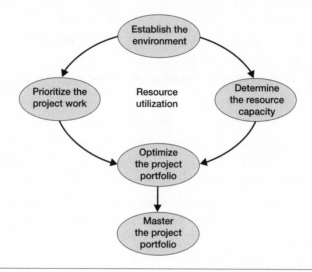

Establishing the Portfolio Governance Environment

In large measure, the success or failure of strategic execution rests on how an organization governs its project portfolio. The governance system creates the portfolio management environment. It establishes who will sponsor the projects, who will (and how to) decide which projects to undertake, who will identify and assign resources to the projects, and who will manage each project and program in the portfolio. This may be accomplished in several ways, from assigning senior executive sponsorship for the portfolio to creating a portfolio management team (PMT) or a portfolio or program management office (PMO).

Sponsorship is one of the most critical governance processes of strategic execution, and one of the most difficult to create. In fact, establishing the best way to sponsor and manage the portfolio may be the first and most important strategic project to undertake. Sponsorship is the element of portfolio supervision that keeps the process of portfolio management relevant, alive, and functioning. Sponsorship creates a final decision-making body for what is going to be done and what is not going to be done. The lack of proper sponsorship aimed at reaching high-quality decisions—rather than allocating the right to make decisions—is by far the greatest barrier to project management success. Good sponsorship supports right decisions, not just decision rights.

The best indicator we have found for the presence or absence of effective sponsorship is *time to decision*, because a key metric for the portfolio process is the velocity of decisions on the projects going through it. Time to decision is an often subjective measure of how long an organization takes to make a decision regarding the scope, schedule, and resources for strategic projects. Slow decisions cost more because the meter on project costs never stops running. As a decision languishes unmade, schedules are slipping, resources are being wasted, and features are at risk because they may have to be cut in order to recover the schedule. If the time to decision is too long, a decision often gets made by default as events begin to encroach on remaining choices and resource availability.

Sponsorship brings critical discipline and support to the process of portfolio management:

- It creates a locus of control, responsibility, and accountability for portfolio-level decisions.

- It coordinates the allocation of resources to the work of portfolio management.

- It establishes decision-making capabilities to adjust the portfolio to fit emerging strategic needs.

A large technology firm we will call Roto Corporation (RC) offers a good example of the difference sponsorship can make. RC grew very quickly and developed a phobia for process: any mention of structured process triggers an immediate flight reaction from people within the company. Taking individual initiative and creating projects without organizational support have long been hallmarks of personal success at RC.

The idea of establishing a portfolio management process to enhance profitability and sustain growth runs counter to RC's structure and culture. Given this freelance entrepreneurial initiative culture, portfolio management is a very difficult thing to get a company like RC to adopt.

The problem stems primarily from the fact that what made RC great today is not what will make RC great in the future. RC's growth pattern is common for young organizations. Their explosive growth curves stem from innovation, and control is the last thing on their mind as they chase the seemingly endless demand curve. But past successes sometimes act as the greatest barriers to success moving forward. At some point, the growth curve begins to flatten, and the behaviors that created their initial success stop working.

To take the next step of growth, RC must move to a new stage of organizational maturity. The company's leaders have used the strategic execution framework to identify a number of critical business processes they need to develop in the value chain. They have clarified each process with a defined start and stop, a set of metrics, and a list of actions that can be taken to improve performance against each metric. They have even assigned project management responsibility for accomplishing several initiatives.

One such initiative deals with order processing. A team of people led by a bright, energetic, and resourceful person has installed a portfolio process that prioritizes projects, gets resources assigned, and determines what will and will not be done. The process is accepted by the organization, and while there is resistance, there is little evidence that people are going around the system. This team's organizational performance is very high.

In another business unit of the same company at the same location, another team has been working to establish portfolio management systems for two years. The second team is led by a bright, energetic, and resourceful person as well. Yet as of this writing, this second team has not made significant progress. The difference? In the first case, there is a strong sponsorship environment: a multitier governance structure with established guidelines for determining which organizational level examines which issues and who provides the multilevel sponsorship needed in RC's matrix organization. There is management agreement and commitment to follow the process of deciding how to decide, deciding, and then demonstrating accountability with regard to the decision. The other organization, in contrast, has no clear commitment to sponsorship.

Both organizations have the technical skill and business process expertise to build and manage the project portfolio. One simply lacks sponsorship. Without the necessary organizational support, the team without sponsorship is relegated to the realm of ineffective overhead spending. Left unresolved, such continued lack of success with portfolio management is worse than an ad hoc process, because cynicism arises when a process that is advertised as creating value instead creates only bureaucracy.

The Key Characteristics of Sponsorship

A well-designed sponsorship system provides senior-level support for project and program managers and creates a forum for the bilingual management conversations that guide the portfolio investment decisions. Sponsors offer invaluable help in terms of the scope, schedule, and resources required to select and manage projects.

Good sponsorship brings vision, commitment, accountability, and empowerment to the project portfolio environment. Some hallmarks of good sponsorship are:

VISION

- Sponsors have a strong vision of the overall strategic importance of the project, portfolio, or program.

- Sponsors monitor the business and political environment and help the project or program adjust, if necessary.

- Sponsors are well enough connected within the organization to understand the decision-making network and to guide decisions and trade-offs among strategic priorities.

COMMITMENT

- Sponsors are fully committed to engaging in the portfolio management process.

- Sponsors are both passionate and objective.

ACCOUNTABILITY

- Sponsors hold the project, program, or portfolio manager accountable for meeting objectives, producing deliverables, conducting reviews, and communicating changes to all affected areas.

- Sponsors also *share* accountability with the project or program manager; if the project or program has problems, the sponsor shares responsibility for correcting them with the project or program manager.

EMPOWERMENT

- Sponsors empower the project or program manager to get the work done.

- Sponsors provide guidance on definition, connections, and resources in the successful completion of project objectives.

- Sponsors have an upward connection to the business, with the ability to influence resource allocation, organizational risk planning, and management, and also to communicate the importance of a project or program across the organization.

"Most Often Requested Items on the Project Managers' Wish List for Effective Sponsors" and "Most Often Requested Items on the Sponsors' Wish List for Project Managers," taken together, go a long way toward describing the ideal project management environment.

Most Often Requested Items on the Project Managers' Wish List for Effective Sponsors

- Translate goals and objectives into understandable and actionable terms
- Support the acquisition and retention of necessary resources
- Help navigate the organizational landscape
- Identify and communicate risk areas
- Make decisions in real time (or just make a decision)
- Be available
- Help with escalation when conflicts arise
- Advocate or help sell

Most Often Requested Items on the Sponsors' Wish List for Project Managers

- Provide clear data with which to make decisions
- Communicate current information
- Offer periodic progress reports
- Take responsibility for day-to-day issue management
- Demonstrate an understanding of larger goals
- Remain responsive to a changing environment
- Identify potential problems early
- Be clear when asking to escalate a problem (tell them what you want them to do)

Identifying Potential Projects

In the introduction, we described a major strategy shift that will change American Power Conversion (APC) from a producer of power conditioning products to a provider of power conditioning solutions. Choosing the right projects for such a radical transformation can be a daunting task. The list of potential projects includes projects for working in, and working on, the existing business, as well as major new projects for transforming the business. There will be alignment projects that reshape the elements of ideation, vision, and nature; infrastructure projects that add, change, or eliminate business systems to support the new strategy; and projects to improve performance on the metrics that drive the new business model. To name just a few candidates:

- Creating a new matrix structure to distinguish the product development from the service delivery organization while leveraging its branding skills

- Designing new HR processes for hiring, development, education, training, career management, and career paths for people in the new solutions business

- Revising and redirecting the internal carriers of culture to fit the new strategy; reshaping the internal brand

- Creating a strategic planning office

- Developing new management information systems to measure performance around a new set of business metrics

- Establishing new product development systems, life cycle management systems, integration test systems

- Installing new customer relationship management systems

- Modifying the sales training program

- Setting up new marketing and branding programs

This partial list illustrates the vast scope of possible investment choices to transform a business or to reach for new performance levels within an existing business. It is easy to see why some organizational change efforts collapse under the sheer weight of all the projects and process work that it takes to sustain the business combined with projects to transform the business. Every investment in a new system to support a new strategy is an investment that is made at the expense of another opportunity. By trying to do it all, the organization goes on overload, and the transformation fails. The only way to avoid project burnout and maintain focus is to clarify the strategy (see "Engaging in the Right Projects: Start by Clarifying Strategy") and prioritize the critical component activities.

Use Strategy Maps to Identify Critical Activities

A strategy or activity map clarifies strategic objectives and helps a company understand which projects are essential for execution. Michael Porter's activity system maps and Kaplan and Norton's strategy maps provide enormously useful ways to depict how a given enterprise creates value in the marketplace.[2] Returning to the example we introduced in chapter 2, figure 4-3 shows Porter's map for Southwest Airlines, one of the rare companies able to maintain profitability almost continuously in a notoriously difficult industry.

This figure shows the array of aligned activities that Southwest performs to generate value in the market. The darker circles represent Southwest's higher-order strategic offering; the others are activities or investments tailored to deliver it. From the founder to the current top management to the

Engaging in the Right Projects

Start by Clarifying Strategy

According to a 2004 study by APQC (American Productivity & Quality Center), about half of all businesses do not have a clear strategy with which to guide product development.[a] Assessing the project investment landscape in 2003, Cathleen Benko and F. Warren McFarlan noted, "Recent estimates indicate that $2.3 trillion is spent on projects each year in the United States, an amount equivalent to one-quarter of the nation's gross domestic product."[b] In 2006, the U.S. GNP reached nearly $12 trillion. Using the 25 percent figure, approximately $3 trillion is now being spent annually on projects. If APQC is correct, that means that up to $1.5 trillion is spent on projects that are associated with no particular strategy whatsoever or an unclear one. Sadly, if only half of all companies have strategies, the maximum number that execute well would be capped at 50 percent! When strategy is unclear, it is impossible to align it to an appropriate project investment portfolio. So, elementary as it seems, a key task of engagement is to get clear on the strategy.

a. Paige Leavitt, Steve Wright, and Marisa Brown, *New Product Development: A Guide for Your Journey to Best-Practice Processes* (Houston: American Productivity & Quality Center, 2004), 1–3.

b. Cathleen Benko and F. Warren McFarlan, *Connecting the Dots: Aligning Projects with Objectives in Unpredictable Times* (Boston: Harvard Business School Press, 2003): 2.

most recent hire, people at Southwest understand how they generate value, and they consistently do so better than their competitors.

When a company has this level of strategic clarity, the choice of projects and programs for the strategic investment portfolio becomes much more obvious. For example, the activity system map immediately tells us what *not* to invest in:

- Do not evaluate in-flight meal service.

- Do not create a seat assignment system.

- Do not work on connecting to other airlines.

- Do not create an incentive system for travel agents.

- Do not contact Airbus to see what competitive aircraft they offer.

FIGURE 4-3

A strategy map identifies key elements of Southwest Airlines' activity system, which translates into potential projects for strategic execution

Southwest Airlines' activity system

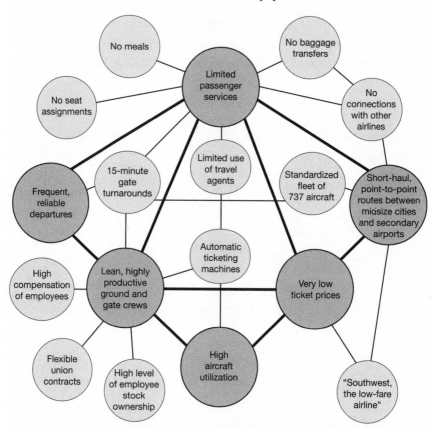

Source: Michael E. Porter, "What Is Strategy?" *Harvard Business Review* OnPoint Enhanced Edition, February 1, 2000.

The map also tells us the sort of things Southwest *should* do. For instance, the airline might invest in projects to enhance:

- Ground crew productivity

- Aircraft utilization

- Turnaround time

- Cost-effectiveness

- Usage of ticket machines and Internet purchase

One measure of Southwest's success is the remarkable lack of trying to be all things to all travelers. This discipline—the ability and willingness to focus on what will and will not be done—helps differentiate Southwest from its competitors.

Translate Critical Activities into Core Objectives and Execution Capabilities

Sayan Chatterjee of Case Western Reserve University made a significant contribution to the subject of strategy maps by overlaying a subtle but crucial distinction between a focus on customer outcomes versus customer needs.[3] Focusing on outcomes generates a different set of questions from a focus on needs. The questions, in turn, identify different objectives that will require different capabilities.

For Southwest Airlines, the customer outcome is the ability to get to a destination faster, cheaper, and with less effort than the alternatives. That customer outcome becomes a competitive objective for Southwest. It drives core objectives such as short flights, frequent departures from lower-cost airports like Love Field in Dallas instead of Dallas–Fort Worth airport, fast turnaround for planes, no meals, and many other elements of the strategy. In contrast, a focus on customer needs rather than outcomes might yield a list of projects addressing assigned seating, passenger comfort, multiple-class service, global coverage and route connections, baggage handling, reservation systems, and airport security.

Figure 4-4 rearranges the Porter activity map to reflect customer outcomes, and adds the implications in terms of objectives and execution capabilities. It shows how Southwest's choice of customer outcomes drives its competitive objectives, which then translate into core objectives and specific execution capabilities.

Any project or program that creates or improves the execution capabilities, or otherwise supports the core objectives, would be suitable to consider for the portfolio. For example, projects to speed boarding procedures or to develop automated ticketing systems would be excellent candidates for the portfolio.

Decide How to Measure Project Success: Link Outputs to Desired Outcomes

Notice the arrow labeled "metrics" at the right side of the chart in figure 4-4. No project or program proposal—no matter how brilliantly conceived, no matter how eloquently presented—should have a chance of

FIGURE 4-4

Translating customer outcomes to potential projects at Southwest Airlines: Consider only projects that support core objectives or improve execution capabilities

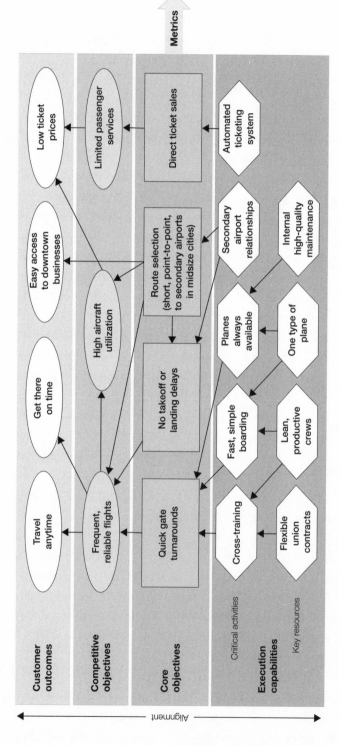

being considered unless it includes a clear statement of its objectives and how they will be measured, and the connection of the project or program to the business metric whose performance the project improves. Every proposal should also include a rough estimate of the resources and time required to accomplish the objectives. The information on objectives, metrics, and required resources and time gives an idea of the potential return on the organization's efforts for each potential project.[4]

Project leaders generally focus on metrics that describe specific *outputs*: systems to design, hardware to build, training programs to develop for defined populations, products to launch, delivery schedules to meet, and so on. Figure 4-4 captures such *project outputs* as the execution capabilities the company intends to create, as seen at the base of the chart.

Strategy makers, on the other hand, usually think in terms of *strategic outcomes* or competitive objectives, as seen toward the top of figure 4-4. One of the biggest challenges of the engagement imperative is to link the project outputs to the desired strategic outcomes. This task is the essence of the necessary bilingual conversations between strategy makers and project leaders.

The appropriate project output metrics represent contemporaneous or leading indicators of strategic outcomes. As we discussed in chapter 2, trailing or lagging indicators such as ROI, earnings per share, and profit margin are far less useful in creating performance than leading indicators. Metrics such as turnaround time of the aircraft, arrival delays, departure delays, and flight cancellations will indicate the success or failure of a project well in advance of the accounting department reports. Moreover, it is very difficult to compute the ROI of a project but easier to compute the net effect of the project on aircraft turnaround time. When the core competitive objectives are clear in a business model, the criteria for designing, measuring, and selecting projects become much easier and more targeted, focused, and effective.

Figure 4-5 charts a process we find useful in choosing metrics that align proposed project outputs with desired strategic outcomes, again using the example of Southwest Airlines. The process translates the desired outcomes into specific objectives and defines the leading indicators that will determine whether those objectives are being met. It then quantifies the desired improvements or execution capacities and finally encapsulates those targeted project outputs in specific initiatives.

This is precisely the process by which strategy-speak gets translated into project parlance. It is a crucial step in choosing the right projects.

FIGURE 4-5

Translating strategy maps into objectives, metrics, targets, and project initiatives

Strategy map: Diagram of the cause-and-effect
relationships between strategic objectives

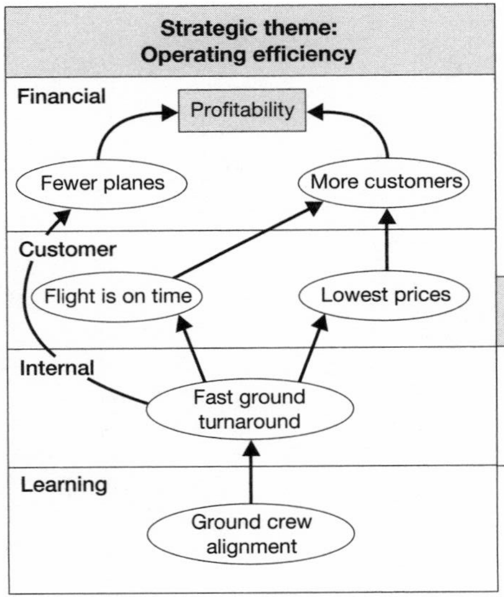

	Objectives	Measurement	Target	Initiative
	Statement of what strategy must achieve and what's critical to its success	How success in achieving the strategy will be measured and tracked	The level of performance or rate of improvement needed	Key action programs required to achieve objectives
	• Fast ground turnaround	• On-ground time • On-time departure	• 30 minutes • 90%	• Cycle time optimization

**Strategic theme:
Operating efficiency**

Financial

Customer

Internal

Learning

Profitability

Fewer planes

More customers

Lowest prices

Flight is on time

Fast ground turnaround

Ground crew alignment

Prioritizing the Project Work: Establish the Criteria

Which is more important: apples or oranges? Neither one. Or both. Or either. Which is more important: product A or product B? There is no way to tell without a structured approach to priorities. First of all, investments fall into categories. R. G. Cooper calls these strategic buckets.[5] Others call them portfolio domains. Whatever they are called, there is no practical way that a company like Southwest Airlines can compare the investment value of projects as different as compliance with FAA requirements versus the implementation of ticketing machines. These two are apples and oranges. Therefore, it is imperative that we sort potential projects into strategic domains or buckets. The process might yield categories of investment such as:

- Regulatory requirements

- Infrastructure

- Product development

- Branding

- Point-of-sale systems

- Hiring, training, and communications

Each of these categories or strategic buckets will have its own criteria. Some, such as regulatory requirements, will have only one criterion: do the required projects. Period. "The Importance of Proper Prioritization: The Odyssey Debacle" describes the disastrously failed Odyssey project at AT&T Wireless, which we mentioned in the introduction. This was a mission-critical program that management failed to prioritize and therefore failed to endow with the resources and the ongoing attention it required.

Other strategic buckets will have multiple criteria that link back to the strategy map. Remember, the strategy map shows how the organization creates value. Thus, the criteria for project selection indicate how each potential project could contribute to the organization's value proposition and set of value-creating activities.

The Importance of Proper Prioritization

The Odyssey Debacle

In early 2003, AT&T Wireless launched a major software upgrade for its customer relationship management (CRM) system. The program was initiated primarily to comply with a Federal Communications Commission mandate specifying that U.S. mobile phone carriers had to enable their customers to switch mobile phone carriers without changing their phone numbers by November 24, 2003.

The company's market position had slipped from market leader to middle of the pack during the previous few years. So in addition to complying with the new regulation, successfully executing the CRM upgrade project was intended to support speedier sign-up and servicing of new customers who were vital to carriers' survival in a rapidly consolidating industry.

The project, prophetically code-named Odyssey, started out looking like a relatively standard system upgrade. However, the number and complexity of new and legacy systems created hundreds of linkages and dependencies that needed to be identified and coordinated. Of these, the Wireless Intercarrier Communications Interface Specifications (WICIS) component proved most critical, as it enables the exchange of customer account information among multiple carriers. Soon after the project launch, all five of AT&T Wireless's competitors selected a vendor with a different WICIS standard from the one in AT&T's system. This greatly increased the complexity of linking AT&T with the competitors—an issue that senior management failed to grasp and the project managers failed to communicate.

When the team began to integrate the various components of the upgrade, they encountered multiple errors that had crept in because of insufficient coordination of the interfaces between modules. As the deadline approached and the internal IT professionals and outside contractors struggled to detect and correct multiple bugs, they relaxed the requirements for freezing of code during testing of individual components. This compounded the number of interface errors, and the project rapidly spun out of control.

A hoped-for postponement of the number portability requirement failed to materialize: the deadline was affirmed by the U.S. Court of Appeals on

October 31. The new system crashed so badly in early November that some team members proposed going back to the earlier version until the upgrade could be stabilized. But since many of the components had not been maintained, this "Plan B" was no longer an option.

As if the technical challenges of this project were not daunting enough, AT&T Wireless executives exacerbated the situation by issuing some excruciatingly ill-timed public pronouncements about their intention to outsource parts of the company's internal IT workforce, and by hiring an outsider with a history of outsourcing IT services at other companies. Eight days before the go-live deadline, a senior executive told industry analysts that the company would lay off almost two thousand workers, and IT managers started telling employees that layoffs would begin in February of the following year.

These pronouncements had a devastating effect on team morale and productivity. Already-stressed IT employees began polishing their résumés and starting to look for other jobs in the final weeks before the project deadline. Once again, management's failure to "understand" and support the project team undermined execution of a mandatory, and therefore mission-critical, activity.

A *CIO* magazine article describes the final stages of the Odyssey program:

> The Odyssey team was still struggling to get the . . . system up and keep it up when, on November 24, customers began trying to port their numbers between carriers. That's when the [WICIS] software for handling number portability crashed. The resulting chaos . . . delayed the delivery of new service to tens of thousands of customers per week. Most gave up the wait in frustration, and signed up with competitors.[a]

Even worse, independent mobile phone retailers, accounting for more than half of all sales in this sector, were similarly unable to access customer records and so began promoting competitors' cell phone services at just the moment when thousands of customers were finally ready to switch carriers without losing their old mobile phone numbers. The result was nothing short of catastrophic for AT&T Wireless. The collapse of the Odyssey CRM program is estimated to have cost the company many thousands of potential new customers and $100 million of potential revenue before customer service once again began to approach minimally acceptable levels late in the first quarter of 2004. This dismal execution failure undoubtedly accelerated the acquisition of AT&T Wireless by Cingular Wireless about three months later, and crippled AT&T Wireless's leverage in negotiating the deal.

What further, or different, investments would it have taken to complete the Odyssey program successfully? Should the project and program managers have done more to warn their seniors of the execution problems? If the same-number account-switching capability project seemed impossible to accomplish with the available resources, should senior management at AT&T Wireless have reconsidered its strategy of addressing this key change in its business environment in conjunction with an upgrade to its Siebel CRM system? We maintain that the single biggest mistake was the failure to prioritize the program as mission critical. This initial lapse manifested itself in a cascade of execution failures, which we will revisit in chapter 5.

a. Christopher Koch, "Project Management: AT&T Wireless Self-Destructs," *CIO Magazine* (April 15, 2004).

The criteria used to prioritize projects in the area of working *in* the business might look very different from those in working *on* the business or *to transform* the business. Criteria to select projects for working *in* the business may be such things as:

- Dollar value of the project (revenue)

- Resources required

- Project risk

- Profit margin

- Growth in market share

- Expansion into emergent market

- Lead time to revenue

- Development of brand

In contrast, criteria for selecting projects to work *on* the business might be:

- Contribution to improvement in key business metrics

- Level of reduction in cycle times

- Level of reduction in process costs

- Amount of improvement to customer service levels

- Improvement in service or delivery quality

- Resources required

New product releases represent a significant portion of projects working *on* the business, and prioritizing them incorrectly can have a dramatic effect on business performance. In a 2005 article from the Product Development and Management Association (PDMA), R. G. Cooper points out that the performance of new product portfolios has deteriorated significantly since 1990. As a percentage of sales, new products fell from 32.6 percent in 1990 to 28 percent in 2004. Profits from new products dropped from 33.2 percent to 28.3 percent over the same time period. The introduction of truly new products is down almost 44 percent.[6]

These figures indicate that product producers have shifted away from innovative products and toward modifications, additions, and improvements to existing products. The problem here is that innovation and business performance are linked: companies that invest more effectively in innovation tend to be those that are the most profitable.

The study also reveals that the portfolio balance in terms of percentage of new products for the "best" company in 2005 was similar to that of "average" companies in the 1990s. This could mean that almost all businesses have made the shift away from innovation, but some have moved away less. Those companies that retained the highest level of innovation are performing the best.

Companies that shift away from innovation and toward minor product improvements may be using the wrong project prioritization criteria. Their selection decisions are characterized by:

- Preoccupation with speed to market

- Focusing on urgent requests at the expense of long-term gain

- Using purely financial criteria such as NPV, payback, and productivity index

Significantly, Cooper found that portfolios driven by pure financial criteria perform the worst. The implication is that selection criteria based on pure financial measures favor quick and dirty project investments that seek low-hanging fruit and short-term gain at the expense of long-term company performance.

Most challenging of all are the criteria for selecting projects that *transform* the business. As we saw in the example of APC, such projects can range from revamping the corporate structure to creating organization-wide training programs to installing new product development systems. These types of projects relate closely to the strategy-making imperatives—aligning the ideation, vision, and nature of the company—as we discussed in chapters 1 through 3.

Decide How to Decide: Build Weighting and Scoring Systems

Recall the clear and focused approach to strategic projects that distinguished ADP from Automation Consulting Services in the examples we cited in the introduction. ADP's selection criteria, though partially based on lagging financial indicators, somehow drove the organization to choose and execute the right projects year after year.

ADP's selection criteria considered only projects that could:

- Bring in at least $50 million in annual revenue

- Achieve a 15 percent compounded growth rate

- Be first or second in the market

- Have mass-market appeal

- Add significant numbers of new clients

- Produce high client ROI

But as ADP knew very well, not all criteria are created equal. Some may have more importance than others. This introduces the concept of weights to the selection process. A weight is a factor placed on a criterion to give it greater or lesser impact on prioritization decisions. For instance, if ADP considered product revenue a more important criterion than market growth, it would place a greater weight on revenue than on growth.

Figure 4-6 shows how an organization might ascribe weights to its project selection criteria. In this case, the company considers market penetration

FIGURE 4-6

Designing the scoring system: Establish criteria, priority weightings, and scoring anchors

Criteria	Market penetration	ROI	Up-front investment	Uses existing technology	Total score	Priority
Weight	(1.5)	(1.0)	(0.5)	(1.0)		
Invention	1	3	2	1	6.5	7
Enter Asia	5	5	1	3	16.0	1
Firewall	1	5	3	1	9.0	6
Upgrader	1	4	1	5	11.0	4
Revamp	1	3	5	4	11.0	4
Innovation	3	5	5	3	15.0	2
Automator	2	5	3	3	12.5	3
Scoring anchors	1 = no new markets 3 = growth in existing markets 5 = intro to target markets	1 = negative ROI 3 = breakeven 5 = positive ROI	1 = exceeds current budget 3 = within current budget 5 = none required	1 = difficult to acquire 3 = easily acquired 5 = no new technology		

1.5 times as important as ROI and the use of existing technologies (both weighted 1.0, compared with market penetration's 1.5), and three times as important as upfront investment (weighted 0.5).

The final piece of prioritization information is the scoring anchor, or the relative value assigned to different project outcomes. The threshold for revenue generation at ADP was $50 million, so if a project did not generate this minimum, it would not even be considered. But if a project generates $150 million, it would score higher in importance on this one criterion than one that generates $75 million. So ADP could set up a prioritization scheme for this criterion that scores a project that generates between $50 and $75 million as a nominal 1, $75 to $100 million as a relative 3, and over $100 million as a 5.

Armed with the right criteria, the right weights, and the right scoring anchors, the portfolio management team can use a model such as the chart in figure 4-6 to make consistent, efficient, and objective decisions about project priorities.

Determining Resource Capacity: Use Systems and Sanity Checks

The prioritization process establishes what we would *like* to do. The crux of engagement lies in connecting that list with the reality of what we're *able* to do. That's why the next step in the engagement imperative is to understand the organization's actual capacity to do the prioritized work.

How can an organization of thirty, three hundred, or three thousand engineers ever know what mixture of projects it can or should accomplish over a specific time period? Even if the company has created strategy maps to determine potential projects, established an effective project management environment to handle the tough decisions, appointed the finest sponsors and project managers, and adopted a portfolio prioritization scheme, it must still learn to identify and assign resources to the projects and programs.

Many organizations have little or no process for determining their true capacity for project execution. Several problems cloud this effort, the trickiest of which center on knowing the real capacity of an individual person.

Spreadsheets and databases have been developed that can calculate the workload of people across an organization and compute to several decimal places the loading of any person, group, or business unit. But such systems are only as good as the underlying assumptions on which they are built and the ongoing status information fed into them. Without the sanity check of actual resource availability, the portfolio reconciliation process remains in the realm of fiction.

Understand Real Capacity and Real Skill Inventory

Real capacity and real skill inventory can massively alter the actual availability of human resources to assign to critical project work. Organizations know how many people they have on the payroll. They also know how many contractors they employ and the costs associated with contract employment. But few truly plan according to the realities of human resource capacity. First, people who work on projects usually have other duties too, which cuts their actual capacity to some fraction of apparent capacity. Most have managerial or administrative leadership demands, or process support demands, or continuous learning demands, or some other form of nonproject work that occupies at least some of their time.

Tom DeMarco and Timothy Lister demonstrated in 1987 that people spend between one and three hours of a nominal eight-hour day doing things that could be considered nonproductive. Things like answering unimportant phone calls, gossiping, taking care of personal matters, and so on. In our experience, people tell us overwhelmingly that the number is more like three hours of wasted time on a good day. More on most days. Given about three hours of wasted time in a day, people have about five hours of productive time per day.[7] The other three hours are spent doing something other than contributing to a project. DeMarco and others have also demonstrated that the productivity of the remaining five hours can vary dramatically because of factors such as:

- Noise and interruptions

- Skill level

- Number of operational contexts

- Length of period of overwork

Noise and interruptions affect productivity in a very distinct way. A person who is interrupted from a task that requires concentration (for example, complex problem solving) may take as long as fifteen minutes to get back the concentration levels that generate peak performance. Severely noisy environments cause major setbacks in concentration levels. Leslie Perlow, in her fascinating book *Finding Time*, chronicles the case of a technology company suffering from a noisy environment.[8] Noise as a performance degrading factor can easily create a 50 percent drop in productivity. More than four severe interruptions per hour will drive productivity below 50 percent. As a running total, our eight-hour day is now 5 divided by 2, or 2.5 hours.

In another experiment, Tom DeMarco gave a group of people a simple task in software creation and measured the time it took individuals to achieve an acceptable level of output. He found that the average person was 2.5 times slower than the fastest and the slowest was 10 times slower than the fastest.[9] If we take this into account, the 2.5 productive hours after interruptions can easily be degraded another factor of 2 by skill level, which could put the effective amount of productive time at 1.25 hours.[10]

Add to the mix the effect of switching context. A 1992 study of one thousand IBM engineers sought to uncover the effect of multiple projects on individual productivity.[11] The study found that when people have one project to work on, their productivity is about 60 percent—about the same as DeMarco's findings. When people had two projects to work on, the reported productivity (time spent contributing value to the project) went up to around 70 percent; however, both projects suffer somewhat from the effect of switching context.

When the project count got to three, productivity dropped to under 50 percent, and for people with more than four projects, productivity was estimated at under 30 percent. So when people have large numbers of projects, many interruptions, and less than average skill, the original five hours of productivity could drop to less than one.

If all this seems a bit extreme, consider the change in the typical working environment since DeMarco's 1987 study. Give all project people:

- A landline phone with call waiting and caller ID

- A cell phone

- A pager

- A BlackBerry-type device

- E-mail with automatic message notification

- A laptop with wireless connection

- Instant message software with pop-up capability

- A cubicle with lots of noise

- Four or more projects

- Minimal training

- Schedule pressure

- Mandatory overtime

- Single-point estimate software

Now consider how many people work with many of the items on the list, and it is not hard to see the difficulty in determining true capacity. Portfolio managers and sponsors must temper their resource planning models with a dose of the factors that affect real capacity. It's safe to say that the real capacity of the organization is not nearly what planners think it is.

Optimizing the Portfolio: Match Projects with Organizational Resources

Optimization is the difficult and iterative process of choosing and constantly monitoring what the organization commits to do. Deciding what actually gets funded is often a volatile area of the business. But remember, strategy is what is done, not what is said. Saying something is in the portfolio while simultaneously starving it for resources is the same as killing the project. In fact, it is worse than killing the project outright—it wastes resources on the way to failure instead of deciding to stop and redeploy resources immediately.

The portfolio optimization process melds two types of information to make the hard decisions about what is and is not going to get done:

- Resource needs and timing for the prioritized projects

- Resource capacity and availability over time

The keys to effective portfolio optimization include:

- A scalable system for project and program managers to feed data to the portfolio process

- An understanding of interdependence in the portfolio

- A computer model to play "what if"

- A means of sanity check

To get started on creating an effective portfolio management process, we counsel companies to start small and use simple tools combined with common judgment.

Start with Small, Scalable Processes

Portfolio management is best implemented in a scaled fashion, starting with the level of information available and working over time to improve it. Project and program managers need a way to interact with the process so that they can see its value without being overwhelmed by its information requirements. Project and program managers stand to gain substantially from the process if it resolves resource issues that they have great difficulty dealing with on their own. But unless they can see such advantages early on, they have little incentive to spend precious time providing the critical information about resource requirements, interdependencies, and availability.

Optimization requires each project or program manager to provide at least the following information for every project and program in her purview:

- Project deliverables

- Success criteria

- Priorities among scope, schedule, and resources

- High-level schedule

- Options for trade-offs among features, time, and cost

- Resources required by skill type and approximate timing

- Interdependencies with other projects and programs

This information can be covered in a short, standard proposal document that is designed as the basis for portfolio management. A standard format will ensure that all the relevant information is included, and will permit easier comparisons than if every project manager creates a unique way of communicating.

Will the process fail if the information is not perfect? No.

Portfolio planning processes often take place with less than perfect data. We can never plan past the horizon of our knowledge; however, we can plan out to that horizon and replan as we gain more information. The limiting factor of the process is the accuracy of the information used. Note that accuracy and precision are two different things. Accuracy gets close, precision gets exact. In a dynamic portfolio management environment, accuracy counts and precision is not worth pursuing. Even rough order of magnitude (ROM) information helps planners find the dividing line between what is achievable with available resources and what is not.

Small portfolios can use spreadsheets to match resource requirements and availability. Large portfolios require more sophisticated tools to compare the demand based on project/program manager input with the capacity model based on available skills. We have found, however, that organizations that attempt to design their systems by first searching for and installing a software tool tend to fail in their initial attempt at portfolio management. The old line says that if a fool is given a tool, what results is a fool with a tool: tools without a contextually relevant process are useless. Lightweight, scalable processes implemented iteratively and reviewed for continuous improvement are more effective than massive enterprise-wide initiatives based on prepackaged systems.

Chapter 5 lays out a "process-light" approach for predicting required resources needed by ongoing projects that meshes well with an agile approach to portfolio planning and replanning in dynamic business settings.

Use Judgment to Avoid Becoming a Fool with a Tool

Sophisticated tools and calculations are useful when applied appropriately, but they do not take the place of considered thought. Some judgment calls are more straightforward than others. For instance, if there are several projects that must work together interdependently, the projects must be evaluated together for a go/no-go decision. If a new data center requires a software project, a hardware project, and a facilities project, either all get done or none gets done. This is what we mean by understanding interdependence in the portfolio.

Another, more delicate type of judgment call takes place at the dividing line between what is done and what is not done. The highest-priority project that falls just under what is affordable is usually cause for argument. Portfolio optimizers must consider all projects close to the dividing line with a critical eye to make sure they are setting the right priorities. This is where sponsorship becomes critical because a governing entity must make the tough call. People with emotional investment in the projects may be unable to make a decision in the gray area at the dividing line and may need strong leadership to move forward. The spreadsheets get organizations close; the remainder is fact-based decision making and quality thinking in the face of uncertainty. In combination, seasoned calculation or risks versus rewards and fact-based decision making are far superior to guessing.

A word of warning on using judgment, however. Any strength used to excess is a weakness. In one company we studied, a CEO agreed to a set of criteria for the portfolio on at least two separate occasions. But after three runs of the portfolio calculations, the CEO still insisted on moving projects that ended up at the bottom of the priority list to the top. In a case like this, the process has lost its credibility—and hence its value. Criteria cannot be so far off that they completely miss the real priorities three times in a row without a serious disconnection in the model development. So where there is excessive bottom-line shuffling, it is cause for alarm because something has come unplugged. Some companies have gone as far as listing both the calculated priority and the enforced priority simply to make this gaming of the portfolio visible.

Much has been done in recent years to refine the means by which portfolios of projects and programs can be evaluated for what is loosely termed "balance." Although such tools lie outside the scope of this book, they include:

- Number of projects that are the work of the organization versus the number that improve the organization's ability to do work, versus the number of projects that are aimed at transforming the business to the next level[12]

- Number of projects or percent invested in developing systems most critical to lowering the strategic execution risk via systems risk assessment[13]

- Bubble diagrams that show risk versus reward and relative project size[14]

- Level of investment in innovation versus iteration in product development[15]

Mastering the Portfolio: Review, Revise, and Realign

The engagement imperative is not an event. It is a process. In the financial world of portfolios that include a mixture of stocks, bonds, futures, commodities, antiquities, art, real estate, race horses, stamp collections, coins, and anything else that could be construed as an investment, there are two kinds of investors: passive and active.

Passive investors are those who put their money in various things and then come back in twenty-five years or so to see what has transpired. They seldom make adjustments and either remain static or at least let someone else do the work of figuring out what to do with the money. Brokers love them because they are low maintenance. They are also most susceptible to the brokers' making unwarranted changes in the portfolio for the sake of commissions. This process is referred to affectionately as "churning and burning."

In contrast, there is the active investor. These individuals are constantly looking, analyzing, calculating, and adjusting their investments. Some are compulsive about the real-time micromanagement of assets. We have come across people who modify their stock portfolio several times per day.

Neither the passive nor the active approach is necessarily wrong, but the fact is that either hyperpassive or hyperactive investors exhibit extreme behaviors that reduce the effectiveness of the portfolio process. Hyperpassive portfolio management occurs when the development and periodic update cycle of the portfolio is much longer than the cycles of significant change in the external environment. ("Iridium-Type Failures: The World Turns While the Project Churns" describes the extreme example of Motorola's spectacular but ultimately doomed investment in Iridium.) This is the case in some organizations that are still stuck in the annual budgeting cycle while the external markets evolve on a daily basis.

Hyperactive portfolio managers are just the opposite. If they are a product firm, they tend to chase the latest shiny object in the market. The symptoms

Iridium-Type Failures

The World Turns While the Project Churns

Motorola, the company that spawned Iridium, has a long and distinguished history of creating industry-leading products with breakthrough technological sophistication. Motorola's special niche was one- and two-way wireless communication. The company invented and delivered the first affordable car radios in the 1930s, supplied rugged walkie-talkie handheld two-way radios to the military during World War II, and manufactured the first portable televisions. However, even measured by the yardsticks of Motorola's strong wireless communications capabilities, Iridium was a bold venture.

In 1987, spurred by the limited geographical coverage of early analog cell phones, three engineers at Motorola developed the concept of launching a network of seventy-seven (later reduced to sixty-six, although the project's name came from the element iridium's atomic number, 77, on the periodic table) low-Earth-orbit (LEO) satellites to provide line-of-sight mobile phone coverage everywhere on the planet for executives traveling to remote locations. The only existing competitor used a small number of geostationary satellites orbiting at high altitudes. The power needed to communicate with these high-altitude satellites necessitated large, unwieldy phones and introduced quarter-second voice latencies that irritated customers. The LEO satellites proposed in the Iridium program would solve both of these technical shortcomings.

The technological challenges and risks of launching sixty-six satellites, and creating switching hardware and software to reroute calls among the fast-moving LEO satellites and their terrestrial gateways to existing telephone networks, were truly staggering. Understandably, the team's managers originally nixed the project. Undeterred, the team floated the idea higher in the corporation until it was finally picked up by the chairman, Robert Galvin, who gave his OK for the project to proceed.[a]

In 1991, Motorola created a separate limited liability company, Iridium LLC, in which it was the major investor, to develop the $5 billion project. Iridium then contracted back with Motorola for satellite design, launch, and system operations and maintenance. Thus, Motorola remained heavily involved in the project and had an important financial stake in Iridium's continuation as a contractor, aside from its shareholder's stake in the project's eventual success.

Iridium IPOed at $20 per share in June 1997, and as late as May 1998, the stock was selling above $72 per share. By the end of 1998, Iridium's total market capitalization stood at $5.6 billion.[b] Confounding the legions of technological naysayers who asserted that Iridium would never fly, the Iridium team executed this incredibly complex program successfully, launched all sixty-six satellites, and began offering its global mobile telephone service in November 1998—eleven years after the project had first been proposed and seven years after the formation of Iridium LLC.

When the Iridium service launched, its handsets weighed three pounds, were roughly the size of a brick, and cost $3,000. Telephone calls on the service were billed at $3 to $8 per minute, and connections could only be made from outdoors with a clear line of sight to the orbiting satellites. So the Iridium telephones might be useful to mineral prospectors, explorers of remote lands, and rich, adventurous backpackers—or fictional characters like Dirk Pitt.[c] But by 1998, Iridium had little to offer its primary target customers—globe-trotting executives who could now do business in most parts of the world on multiple alternative wireless phone services. A global network of terrestrial cell phone operators, whose services were far less expensive and more convenient, had sprung up while the engineers at Iridium were developing their technological marvel.

The dismal market uptake for the Iridium service should have come as no surprise in the changed environment. By August 1999, after signing up less than 40 percent of the customer base required to meet its loan covenants, Iridium defaulted on $1.5 billion of loans. Two days later, on August 13, 1999, Iridium filed for Chapter 11 bankruptcy.

How could this have happened? Did no one at Iridium—or at Motorola, which launched the program—notice that Iridium's proposed service had become a white elephant?

In contrast to the Odyssey project described in "The Importance of Proper Prioritization: The Odyssey Debacle," Iridium was managed extraordinarily well. The project implementers developed, tested, and fielded breakthrough hardware and software systems required to reroute satellite telephone calls dynamically through the network of satellites and ground stations, exactly as planned. They revised their initial technology requirements (from seventy-seven to sixty-six satellites), managed interdependencies in their projects and programs, worked with outside vendors, and executed virtually all aspects of this extremely ambitious program on schedule and on budget.

Iridium's project investments were initially flawlessly aligned with its strategy. However, technology and markets had shifted dramatically from the time the project was conceived until the service was first offered to paying customers. The company's downfall was in ignoring the necessary periodic realignment of strategy to external reality. This was certainly an executive failure—but was it also a project management failure?

Iridium's project teams were working long hours, heads-down, to accomplish the technological goals of this extraordinarily challenging program. Yet at least some of them seem to have realized that the world had changed around them. A former HP employee who served on the team that partnered with Iridium provides a particularly revealing insight into the fiasco. She recalled that in the later phases of the project, "We were killing ourselves to put the system up, and we knew it didn't have a chance to compete against cell phones."[d]

At senior levels, Motorola executives who might have sounded the alarm about the continued viability of this project were caught in their own trap of escalating commitment. Public commitment to the goals of the project by Motorola's leaders, and the fact that Motorola was being paid significant fees by the joint venture project, made it psychologically and politically difficult for these executives to press their representatives on the Iridium board to modify or cancel the Iridium project "in spite of known and potentially fatal technology and market problems."[e]

a. Theodore B. Kinni, "A 'Ma Bell' for the Space Age: Motorola Inc. Plans the Iridium Project for Satellite-Based Phone services," *IndustryWeek*, March 21, 1994, 71.

b. See http://www.thunderbird.edu/pdf/about_us/case_series/a07000025.pdf.

c. Clive Cussler, *Flood Tide* (New York: Simon & Schuster, 1997), 42.

d. Private conversation with author, September 2005.

e. Sydney Finkelstein and Shade H. Sanford, "Learning from Corporate Mistakes: The Rise and Fall of Iridium," *Organizational Dynamics* 29, no. 2 (2000): 138–148.

of a hyperactive organization are that priorities are shuffled faster than a corresponding reaction is possible in the organization. The result is mass chaos followed by lack of performance. When an organization is turned too often in too many directions, its people become numb to change. Somewhere between the lethargy of the hyperpassive investor and the frenetic pace of the hyperactive is the best balance of realigning the portfolio to the external environment.

Companies can take steps to help find the right balance between hyperactivity and hyperpassivity. For one thing, they can integrate the portfolio reviews with the business performance reviews. For another, they can create decision points inside project and program proposals to review and revise the plan. The periodic portfolio reviews ensure that the organization continues to do the right projects. The project and program checkpoints ensure that it is doing the projects right. Successful portfolio managers conduct both types of reviews to adjust the portfolio as a dynamic, real-time alignment to the strategy and the environment.

Integrate Portfolio Optimization and Business Reviews

In many organizations, the project portfolio is created, approved, and reviewed as a separate process from business performance review. This may be a relic of the preoccupation with lagging indicators such as profit, revenue, return on investment, and other accounting data. As we noted in chapter 2, lagging indicators evaluate the *results* of previous portfolio investment decisions. In contrast, the current project portfolio lies ahead of the business. It is the carrier of future results.

An active investor manages the content and progress of the project portfolio. A passive investor makes demands relative to lagging indicators and lets the organization figure out the portfolio. A passive investor reviews the portfolio on an annual basis as a means of setting budgets. An active investor reviews the portfolio quarterly or at other regular intervals and makes adjustments to align to strategy.

Passive investment may work in very stable market conditions where strategic execution is well understood and expertise in delivering to the strategy has been created over a long period of time. Fast moving, highly competitive, relatively ambiguous market circumstances require more active investment.

Does Anyone Ever Get This Right?

There is light at the end of the tunnel, and it is not a train headed your way. Many companies have developed working investment systems and continue to improve their ability to target, align strategy, and invest accordingly. One such company is eBay, the world's largest online auction house. Some indicators of eBay's success as of 2006 are:[16]

- 233 million registered users

- At any given time, there are approximately 100 million listings worldwide, across more than fifty-thousand auctions and sales categories

- Gross merchandise volume (GMV), the total value of goods and services traded on eBay worldwide, of more than $52.5 billion ($1,664 GMV per second)

- A global presence in thirty-six international markets accounting for 53 percent of the company's total GMV during the fourth quarter of 2006

- Net 2006 revenues totaling $5.97 billion, a 31 percent increase over the $4.55 billion in 2005

- More than 1.3 million people worldwide use eBay as their primary or secondary source of income

- More than 4 billion feedback comments posted by eBay members regarding their eBay transactions

Information technology is eBay's business—not just an aspect of its business, it is the business itself. Everything revolves around the information technology. There are almost infinite possibilities to expand and change the information systems that drive eBay. However, only a small subset of those possibilities can be taken on as projects at any one time. The portfolio process at eBay benefits from the following conscious choices:[17]

- Budgeting is done annually.

- A clear funding model is in place for who sponsors what.

- Prioritization is done twice per year.

- A portfolio process runs on a quarterly basis.

- Technology is reviewed once per year.

- About 180 to 200 projects are completed per year.

- About 20 projects per quarter are changed, modified, deleted, or substituted.

- Resource loading determines what is done, not done, or purchased as a service.

- Prioritization is driven by strategy and associated business objectives.

- Projects are accomplished in a shared services model that serves multiple business units.

- Tools are homegrown and heavily customized to eBay processes.

The result? A growth curve that puts eBay's growth relative to start-up ahead of these much-admired organizations:

- Dell

- Microsoft

- Starbucks

- Cisco

- Yahoo!

- Wal-Mart

- Nike

Some organizations that are in explosive growth areas question whether portfolio processes are overly restrictive and a significant barrier to growth because of the apparent "controls" involved. EBay offers a striking example of how controls and growth are compatible. In fact, eBay's remarkable portfolio management controls help fuel its spectacular growth performance by providing strategic clarity and focus. "The Project List for Building Stronger Engagement" offers a list of potential project investments that could help your organization achieve similar results.

The Project List for Building Stronger Engagement

Companies attempting to achieve the engagement imperative—engage strategy through the project investment stream—may need project investments to develop their capacity to choose and endow the right projects. These critical investments might create such capabilities as the following:

- Selection criteria development
- Scoring model development
- Prioritization process design
- End-to-end portfolio governance design
- Strategic execution office
- Resource pool creation
- Enterprise-level portfolio process design
- Enterprise planning processes
- Portfolio management education at the executive level and below
- Creation of a project registry
- Education at the executive level on execution
- Tools, templates, and processes

Rate Your Organization on the Engagement Imperative

How do you know whether you need to work on your ability to achieve the engagement imperative? Perhaps your organization has never before established a formal link between strategy making and project leadership. If so, you may need help in getting started. Perhaps you have advanced project management capabilities but lack a system for choosing which projects to undertake. We offer the following rating instruments to help you decide how important it is for your company to invest in developing your performance in the engagement domain.

Measuring Strategy in Engagement

On a scale of 1–10, 1 = seldom true, 5 = sometimes true, 10 = almost always true.

TABLE 4-1

Measure your organization's strategy in engagement

	Rating (1–10)
We know what investments to make in support of our strategy, and we focus on strategic fit in making investments.	
We have a disciplined process for evaluating proposed investments, and we follow the process.	
Management and leadership in the organization support decisions made in the investment process.	
We have information systems that pinpoint the investments to be made and their relative benefit.	
We translate strategic language into investment criteria.	
We prioritize among various aspects of our strategy.	
We consciously restrict our investments to avoid attempting to become all things to all people.	
	Average score:

➤ Interpretation of average score:

➤ Below 3: Strategy is largely smart talk.

➤ Between 3 and 6: Some investments are on track.

➤ Above 6: Strategy is getting engaged.

Measuring Portfolio in Engagement

On a scale of 1–10, 1 = seldom true, 5 = sometimes true, 10 = almost always true.

TABLE 4-2

Measure your organization's portfolio in engagement

	Rating (1–10)
Our portfolio process links projects to strategy via weighted selection criteria and a scoring model, and reconciles resources necessary at the project and program level.	
We follow an established process for managing the portfolio of projects and programs; changes to the priorities of the business are systematically reflected in the portfolio and communicated to the organization.	
Managers and leaders support and follow the portfolio process decisions.	
Our systems provide the information needed to make informed decisions in the portfolio management process.	
We have relative balance between working *in* the business, working *on* the business, and transforming the business.	
Our portfolio does not overtax the organization's resources.	
Private agendas are kept out of the portfolio process.	
Portfolio processes are part of the management process of governance.	
	Average score:

Interpretation of average score:

➤ Below 3: The portfolio is running amok.

➤ Between 3 and 6: Investment is occurring by getting lucky.

➤ Above 6: The portfolio is getting engaged.

Five

Synthesis Imperative

Monitor and Align Project Work

The best-laid schemes o' mice an' men gang aft agley.

—Robert Burns

THROUGH THE FIRST four imperatives, we have focused on choosing and engaging in the right portfolio of strategic projects. In this chapter we make the connection between *doing the right projects* and *doing the projects right*. This requires continuous, two-way synthesis and alignment between the *planned portfolio* of the engagement domain and the *actual portfolio* of ongoing projects and programs in various stages of execution. The strategic project organization must monitor both the outside environment and the internal activities to make certain that the portfolio remains right and that the projects are being done right.

Accomplishing these twin tasks requires nimble, rapid-response approaches for checking key external indicators of strategic relevance for each program or project, and for planning, validating, executing, and tracking the portfolio of projects and programs. These two steps maintain the necessary alignments in the *synthesis* domain. Taken together, they help avoid both the Iridium-type failures and the Odyssey-type failures we described in chapter 4. This is the work of the *synthesis imperative: monitor and align the project work.*

What makes the synthesis imperative so challenging is that both the planned portfolio and the actual portfolio are constantly changing in today's business world. As discussed in chapter 4, the planned portfolio must be managed actively (but not hyperactively) to accommodate changes in the organization's strategy as it responds, in real time, to a variety of external contingencies. And the actual portfolio is constantly changing as one or more of the organization's active projects and programs go awry—or, sometimes, as they go better than expected.

On the one hand, organizations want to plan and execute those projects and programs that make the largest contribution to achieving their strategic goals and metrics, subject to limits on the available resources. At the same time, as things go awry in the execution of the actual portfolio, the available resource base can change dramatically. The synthesis imperative requires continuous feedback about the actual current status of projects and programs in the portfolio, so that the portfolio management team can inject extra resources into critical but lagging projects, cancel ongoing projects whose goals have become irrelevant or infeasible, and initiate new projects to address emergent strategic objectives.

Figure 5-1 illustrates the key alignments of projects, programs, and portfolio in the synthesis domain, and the connections with the other domains. It shows how the conversations of the strategy-making domains—ideation, nature, and vision—cascade through the engagement domain to the project leadership domains—synthesis and transition—and back, in a dynamic, ongoing two-way dialogue. As we discussed in the introduction, this requires a conscious commitment to *bilingualism*, so that the strategists and portfolio planners truly understand—and truly *value*—the input from project managers, and vice versa.

This chapter is not about the details of how a project manager should conceive, plan, execute, and close out a project. Instead, it covers the more nuanced issues of continuously aligning the set of project and program priorities in the organization's strategic portfolio to its evolving strategy while maintaining the necessary internal alignments among the projects and programs themselves. ("Odyssey-Type Failures: Things Go Awry" revisits the Odyssey endeavor we introduced in chapter 4, which failed at both these tasks.)

Achieving the synthesis imperative is a project in itself. It requires investments to develop planning and tracking processes for project and program managers, who must keep the ongoing projects and programs aligned with the periodic updates from the portfolio planners in the engagement domain. These processes should be "light" and simple to use, and should provide a realistic assessment of the remaining resources and time that will be required to achieve the current projects.

FIGURE 5-1

The synthesis imperative: Monitor and align the project work

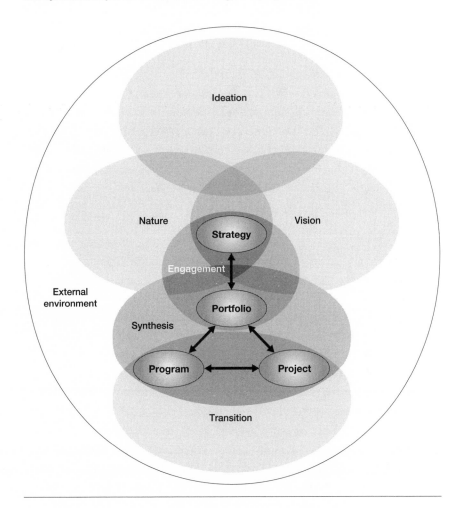

That information must then roll back up to the portfolio level, where it helps recalibrate resource availability for the planned portfolio. This enables the portfolio management team to reevaluate project and program priorities against realistic estimates of available resources in the next portfolio cycle, so they can reallocate the organization's investment resources among the right strategic projects.

In addition, program managers must identify all the critical interdependencies or "white spaces" between the projects that make up their programs, and ensure that team members or groups responsible for each pair of interdependent tasks communicate and coordinate appropriately.

Odyssey-Type Failures

Things Go Awry

The Odyssey program at AT&T Wireless, described in "The Importance of Proper Prioritization: The Odyssey Debacle" in chapter 4, suffered from flawed prioritization in the engagement domain, which led to failed co-ordination in the synthesis domain. Changes or setbacks from an almost in-finite variety of internal and external causes directly affect the time, cost, and scope outcomes of individual projects. Worse, they tie up scarce finan-cial and, especially, human resources that were budgeted for other pro-grams and projects in the portfolio. So it is important to validate the pro-posed project schedules and resource budgets very thoroughly when they are initially considered for investment, and then to track the ongoing per-formance continuously and proactively, to detect and mitigate emerging problems before they become severe enough to impact the entire portfolio.

AT&T Wireless had just a single, very risky plan with no fallback posi-tion for the vital Odyssey project. The outcome requirements remained fixed in place—uncomfortably so, because the hoped-for postponement of the completion deadline would have provided some relief to the belea-guered project team. Meanwhile, numerous small and large management errors compounded the technological risks and undermined the motiva-tion and morale of team members at critical junctures.

Odyssey's project managers failed to grasp—and therefore to commu-nicate to the leadership at AT&T—the difficulty of developing, integrating, and testing a project with hundreds of complex, interdependent, new and legacy software components, on a highly concurrent, fast-track schedule. For their part, the leaders apparently failed to master the language of

Aligning Projects, Programs, and Portfolios

As we have noted, a *project* is simply a defined set of deliverables that will be accomplished by a defined set of tasks to which resources and time have been allocated. Think of projects as the "atoms" of strategic execu-tion. They are the low-level, well-defined packages of work that enable strategic execution.

project management enough to understand the scope of the impending disaster. Neither leaders nor managers seemed to grasp the serious implications of changes in the external environment, especially the competitors' choice of WICIS standard. And the unyielding deadline left no time to recover from these mistakes.

In our view, the Odyssey project began to flounder when the actual projects and programs veered off course from the planned portfolio. The project managers were caught by a market and technology change that they failed to detect, and so they did not replan the portfolio to accommodate it. When the new standard emerged, its incompatibility with AT&T's standard became a critical barrier to exchanging data with other carriers. The project was doomed by the failure to realign the strategic project portfolio and to reevaluate the resources required for completion.

These mistakes cascaded through the project organization as the team struggled to meet the looming deadline. The processes and planning systems were weak and lacked adequate mechanisms for identifying and coordinating technical interfaces or for tracking progress. AT&T Wireless failed to identify, prioritize, and invest in the projects necessary to synthesize all the necessary work and to support its timely transfer back to operations.

Compounding the planning and management errors, senior management's public announcements about outsourcing IT services created dissonance for key contributors about the value of their work and seriously compromised their capacity to finish the project. Essentially, this amounted to the management team's striving for maximum efficiency while misunderstanding minimum viable product delivery requirements. In project-speak, it's called trading scope for cost that is not in alignment with the realities of stakeholder needs.

In many cases, a cluster of related projects must be performed in close coordination, often sharing some key resources, in order to accomplish a strategic goal. This cluster of interdependent projects is called a *program*. The Odyssey and Iridium examples from chapter 4 were both programs involving multiple, tightly coupled projects with dozens or hundreds of technical and organizational interfaces between the projects sharing key resources. Think of programs as the "molecules" of strategic intent, in which specific clusters of project "atoms" are tightly bound to one another by technical and organizational bonds to yield higher-level strategic deliverables.

Projects and programs can be very small initiatives involving just a handful of individuals for a few days or weeks, such as a small software debugging project. Or they can be large, bet-the-company initiatives with thousands of people assigned to a complex series of interdependent tasks for ten or more years, as in the Iridium example. One of the major thrusts of the business process reengineering landscape over the past twenty years has been to organize smaller and smaller packages of work—for example, a single insurance claim or loan application—as projects, in order to obtain the benefits that projects offer in clarifying task assignments and accountability for deliverables.

The *planned portfolio* is simply the complete set of projects and programs that have been selected to execute an organization's strategic intent. The current status of the organization's set of ongoing projects and programs represents its real, on-the-ground portfolio. In the unlikely event that all projects and programs are proceeding exactly as planned, the real portfolio of ongoing projects and programs is identical to the planned portfolio. In practice, the real portfolio always diverges from the planned portfolio to a greater or lesser extent.

Aligning Projects: Use Nimble, Proactive Processes

The philosophies, processes, and tools for planning and tracking projects were developed—and are therefore most mature—in the traditional project industries: construction, defense/aerospace, and pharmaceuticals. In each of these industries, individual projects are typically large efforts involving hundreds or thousands of workers over durations of many months or years. During the 1960s—when critical-path planning tools, work breakdown structures, and many of the well-known project definition and planning tools were being developed—the business world changed slowly, if at all, over the lifetime of a particular project. The unstated but deeply embedded philosophy behind all these tools was that a carefully worked-out task breakdown, budget, and schedule for the project was likely to be a good plan, and it would remain a good plan for the duration of the project.

In this traditional management-by-exception world of projects, the primary role of a project manager was to make sure that actual work hewed as closely as possible to the original "good plan" for that project. The actual costs and schedules for tens of thousands of individual activities and sub-activities were constantly monitored and compared with their planned budgets and schedules. Any variance in an activity's cost or schedule from what was budgeted or scheduled was viewed as an aberration that needed to be corrected. New kinds of project professionals—"project schedulers" and "project cost engineers"—arose to meet the challenges of managing these oceans of historical information. A project that delivered its origi-nally defined scope within its assigned budget on or before its planned completion date was viewed as successful. Any other outcome was viewed as a failure of project execution.

The program plans for large constructed facilities such as nuclear power plants or for defense programs to develop new submarines or airplanes can involve hundreds of thousands of activities, organized in a hierarchy that roughly corresponds to the organization structure for executing it. Even in mature industries, as the world turns and as things go awry, these programs often need to be redirected. For example, nuclear power plant programs of the 1970s and 1980s were bombarded with frequent regula-tory changes from the Nuclear Regulatory Commission, requiring both changes in designs and demolition and reconstruction of already com-pleted parts of the facility, such as pipe hangers, whose specifications had been upgraded.

Updating a project schedule containing hundreds of thousands of activ-ities, without violating any of the thousands of logical constraints embed-ded in the original schedule, is a truly challenging task, even for large teams of skillful project schedulers and cost engineers. The elaborate proj-ect schedules and budgets became virtual balls and chains around the ankles of the nuclear plant construction project schedulers, as they strug-gled to revise their schedules to accommodate each new set of regulatory changes. The electric utility clients for these projects eventually came to understand this and ultimately converted their fixed-price engineering and construction contracts to cost-reimbursable contracts, for which less de-tailed planning and budgeting were acceptable. The planning tail was truly wagging the dog for these programs.

Contrast that with the majority of today's projects in both private and public organizations. First, businesses are managing smaller and smaller ini-tiatives as projects, so many companies have hundreds or even thousands of projects and programs in their strategic portfolio. Just composing and maintaining the list of all projects is a significant task. Breaking each project up into thousands of activities for tracking is unimaginable. Moreover, the world is turning much faster relative to the duration of significant strategic initiatives. Yesterday's alliance partners become today's competitors in a heartbeat. Rapid cycles of product development change the market landscape from week to week. And fluctuating interest and currency exchange rates, energy prices, availability of scarce commodities such as steel or cement, and other environmental variables require many organizations to rethink their strategies and planned portfolios from month to month. Clearly, today's project managers must use a more nimble approach for planning, tracking, and redirecting their large portfolios of rapidly evolving projects in something less than geologic time—something like the approach Rich Grimes adopted at AT&T Wireless in the 1990s.

AT&T's Los Angeles Wireless Rollout Project

The Wireless Infrastructure Division of AT&T Wireless, the same company whose IT division so badly botched the Odyssey project, developed an extremely effective "process-light" planning and tracking process for an earlier series of projects designed to extend its wireless network infrastructure across the Los Angeles region during the 1990s.[1] Wireless telephone regulations, markets, and technologies were all changing very rapidly as this multiyear project proceeded. So, instead of using traditional project management approaches of detailed planning and process-heavy status reporting and control, project manager Rich Grimes held "replanning" sessions every six weeks in which the team focused on assessing the current environment (goals, technologies, and available resources) and on replanning the high-level set of tasks and deliverables for the next six weeks.

Grimes didn't choose the six-week replanning interval at random. For one thing, he wanted to minimize the need for status reporting, which siphons off significant managerial effort that would be better spent on directing and controlling project tasks. He felt that the length of time over which significant external changes might occur for these wireless infrastructure projects was about three months. Control theory suggests that a process should be sampled twice as frequently as the frequency with which it might move out of alignment, in order to keep the process under control. Grimes calculated that sampling the project every six weeks (twice per quarter), and intervening as needed to bring it back under control, would achieve this objective.

This wireless infrastructure rollout was a fast-track project with multiple interdependent tasks to be carried out in parallel. Changes in one task could require compensating changes in schedules or deliverables for multiple parallel tasks. The volume of information to process a fast-track project like this can easily overwhelm the upper levels of a project organization. So Grimes's major concern over the course of the project was how to allocate his time as project manager most effectively over each successive six-week period.

He made several investments in developing innovative work processes and tools to support this challenging project. First, he brought in a consultant to help him use modern project work process and organization simulation tools to model the key, high-level tasks and available resources in the project organization for each six-week period.[2] Rather than investing in traditional project scheduling tools and analyses to predict and track the performance of thousands of individual tasks, Grimes chose a few dozen high-level activities and used the rolling six-week simulation to predict and manage their performance. This allowed him to adjust the project proactively in terms of schedule, cost, quality, and work process metrics, and assured him that the project team could achieve its scope, schedule, and cost objectives for each successive six-week period while maintaining strategic focus.

In addition, Grimes used the same proactive simulation model to predict the expected backlogs for all key managers on the project. In each six-week period, he then invested his time and attention selectively on working closely with key managers in AT&T Wireless and its partner organizations for whom the simulations predicted high backlogs during the following period.

Research has shown that fast-track projects with multiple interdependent tasks carried out in parallel generate huge volumes of information to be processed by project and functional managers.[3] This "hidden work" for managers can become so onerous in fast-track projects that it easily overwhelms the managers. Excessive backlogs for managers lead to delays and cost overruns in the tasks that they supervise, and even more significantly, they can trigger coordination or supervision failures that result in disastrous quality meltdowns such as the Odyssey failure at AT&T Wireless.[4]

To combat such risks, the managers for specific tasks used traditional project planning and scheduling tools such as Microsoft Project or Prima- vera to develop detailed work plans and task assignments for each upcoming six-week period. They were encouraged to focus their planning efforts on evaluating the work remaining to be done during the next period, given current project goals and updated estimates of available resources.

Grimes made no attempt to review, monitor, or track these detailed work plans for components of the project, nor were they discussed in detail at project meetings. Project meeting discussions focused on major changes in the status of key, high-level milestone events that affected multiple partici- pants; on technological changes that might impact decisions already made in the project (to avoid the kinds of technological incompatibilities that occurred with the WICIS component of the Odyssey project); and on any changes in regulatory requirements that might impact the project.

Table 5-1 highlights the differences between this kind of forward- looking replanning and the traditional backward-looking approach of managing variances.

The forward-looking, decentralized approach is much more compatible with the requirements of a large, fast-moving, highly concurrent strategic project than a traditional rearview-mirror project tracking approach. In the Los Angeles wireless rollout, using this process-light, forward-looking ap- proach yielded outstanding results. All the infrastructure rollout programs finished on time and within their budgets, often with major changes in scope having been smoothly integrated during the course of the program.

Replan Projects Proactively

The implications of this successful experience are clear. If the world turns faster than the project churns, it is essential to replan the project

TABLE 5-1

Traditional versus new approaches to project management

Traditional approach	New approach
Rigid	Nimble
Retrospective	Forward-looking
Managed by exception	Managed by rapid response
Process-heavy	Process-light

proactively and frequently at a high level, rather than tracking project activities retroactively in great detail against baseline schedules and budgets. The frequency of project replanning should be set at double the expected frequency of major changes. If the frequency of major changes is difficult to estimate, then replanning sessions can be held whenever a major change in the project's task environment is detected, rather than replanning at fixed intervals.

Six weeks seems to be about the right interval for replanning many of today's typical large projects with durations of twelve months or more. More focused projects that run for six to twelve months can be replanned every three weeks. Even shorter projects can be replanned weekly, daily, or even more frequently. A very short but critical project to install new uninterruptible power supplies and a series of hardware and software upgrades at the Los Angeles transaction processing facility operated by a major commercial bank was scheduled to be completed in four hours between midnight and 4:00 a.m. on a Sunday. This project was replanned every thirty minutes using two-way radios, through status updates and forecasts submitted directly to the project planning team by workers located all over the facility.

One advantage of a three- or six-week replanning interval (versus a weekly, monthly, or quarterly interval) is that it separates and distinguishes the forward-looking strategic planning and replanning process from various kinds of retroactive financial or regulatory reporting that are typically required to be carried out weekly, quarterly, or monthly. This helps managers maintain a high-level and forward-looking perspective in reassessing the next six weeks and designing ways to accomplish the goals for that period. Proactive planning turns out to be a much more useful approach for continuous replanning in a fast-moving environment than analyzing what went wrong during the previous six-week interval.

Aligning Programs: Manage the White Spaces

A NASA Mars probe failed in 1999 because the units of measure used by two of its subsystems were incompatible. Data for one subsystem were expressed in metric units and data for the other in imperial units.[5] How could such an obvious incompatibility have fallen through the cracks?

We defined a *program* as a cluster of tightly coupled projects, in which significant interdependencies exist between the projects, often including the need to share scarce human, equipment, and other resources. Most program managers understand that there can be constraints in sequencing individual tasks across multiple projects. A task in one project may create a deliverable that is a required input for a task in another project. However, a pair of tasks within or across two projects can be interdependent with one another in multiple ways, each requiring a unique kind of coordination.[6] The existence of different kinds of interdependency is a poorly understood element of program management that has been the source of many failures in recent programs. Managing the "white spaces" between a set of interdependent projects in a larger program is a critical skill in mastering strategic execution.

Many catastrophic project and program failures have been directly linked to the organization's failure to manage the interdependencies between tasks on a single project or between projects in a multiproject program. Project and program managers need a richer way to think about managing these white spaces in the synthesis domain, to ensure reliable, high-quality outcomes for strategic projects and programs.

We will discuss four kinds of interdependency: *pooled*, *sequential*, *reciprocal*, and *rework*. All four must be identified and coordinated for a program to be successful. However, each type of interdependency arises for a different reason and requires a different kind of coordination.

Pooled Interdependency

Any two tasks in a project or program must be completed for the project to be deemed complete. So any task that contributes a critical physical or information output to a project has at least *pooled interdependency* with all other tasks in the project and program. An example of this would be the task to design the headlights and the task to design the rearview mirror for an automobile. Both design tasks contribute to the overall design of the automobile, and both are required for its complete design. However, the tasks do not depend on each other in any additional ways, so they have only pooled interdependency with one another.

Rules and standards are the most efficient coordination mechanism for coordinating pooled interdependencies. For example, an automobile manufacturer that purchased these two components from vendors might impose the rule and standard that both be dimensioned in metric units, and both be represented using the CATIA CAD system, Version 7.0. NASA failed to impose, or at least failed to monitor compliance with, this kind of rule and standard for coordinating the pooled interdependency of the components in its failed Mars mission. Airbus encountered a similar coordination breakdown regarding the true dimensions of wire harnesses to be installed in the fuselage of its ill-fated Airbus A380 aircraft when the divisions assembling different parts of the fuselage in its plants in France and Germany used different release versions of CATIA CAD software that were not backward compatible.

Sequential Interdependency

In addition to pooled interdependency, two tasks may need to be performed in a given sequence. For example, the structure of a building cannot be erected before the foundations have been completed. So we would describe the interdependency between the task to construct the foundations and the task to erect the structure as a *sequential interdependency*.

This is the best-understood type of interdependency in projects and programs. Since the 1950s, project managers have modeled and tracked sequential interdependency using "critical path" or PERT precedence diagrams in which they define the sequential constraints between all project and program tasks and then calculate the longest or "critical" path through the network of tasks. The critical path of sequential tasks that runs through a project or program determines the earliest project and program completion dates. Activities on other paths are said to have *float*—that is, they can be delayed by some amount of time without delaying project completion.

If all tasks on a project could be started and completed according to the original "good" project schedule, all that would be required to coordinate sequential interdependency would be to issue start times to the workers involved in each task. However, since something always goes awry on even the simplest project, tasks start later or run longer than anticipated—or, occasionally, they complete early. Changes in a task's completion date trigger changes in the start and finish times for subsequent tasks that cascade throughout the entire project and program network. So project managers need to track all these changes and issue instructions to downstream workers to delay or advance their start times or to accelerate their rates of progress in order to make up lost time, as needed, to meet the project goals.

This is a relatively well-understood aspect of project and program management and is well supported by a variety of scheduling tools running on PCs, and even personal digital assistants, that can be used to organize project and program tasks hierarchically and produce exception reports and summaries at various levels of detail. A number of project scheduling tools now also exchange information over the Internet to facilitate scheduling and tracking of distributed tasks. Project scheduling applications are power tools in the toolkit of the traditional project manager.

Traditional project scheduling tools do a good job of capturing sequential dependencies and facilitate management-by-exception tracking and control. What scheduling tools fail to capture, however, is all the managerial decision making and exception handling that arise in revising project schedules. In extreme cases, neglecting this "hidden work" can be the cause of project failure. Two additional, often ignored types of interdependency—reciprocal and change/rework—trigger the most serious hidden work of managerial decision making, exception handling, and peer-to-peer coordination.

Reciprocal Interdependency

In the program planning stage, managers typically break down the overall program goal into a series of finer-grained goals for individual projects. Each project's objectives are then typically broken down into a series of intermediate milestones associated with major deliverables, each of which requires one or more tasks to complete it. Each task will have a set of strictly required or desirable technical, cost, and schedule subgoals that the individual task managers will attempt to accomplish. Ideally, there would never be any conflict between the subgoals of different tasks. However, in many cases, one or more of the subgoals of a particular task conflict with the subgoals of another task.

For example, the designer of an automobile door might be attempting to achieve the subgoal of protecting passengers from side impacts. The designer's solution to optimize this subgoal might be to insert a heavy steel reinforcing beam in the door. At the same time, the designer of the automobile's engine might be attempting to achieve a subgoal of maximizing fuel economy. For the engine designer, minimizing the weight of the car body helps optimize this subgoal. This creates a conflict in subgoals between their two tasks that must be negotiated and mutually adjusted to come up with an optimal door design that trades off side impact safety versus fuel economy goals. Alternatively, this negotiation and mutual adjustment process might lead to the choice of a lightweight door that favors the fuel economy goal and the development of a workaround for the side impact safety goal, such as installing side-curtain airbags. This type of subgoal conflict between two tasks is called *reciprocal interdependency*.[7]

A few other examples help illustrate reciprocal interdependency. The designer of the screen for a laptop computer is attempting to optimize readability and brightness. This may increase the power demand of the screen. The motherboard designer has the subgoal of maximizing the computing power for the laptop. This indicates a faster cycling microprocessor, again increasing power demand. Power is a scarce resource on a laptop computer. The battery designer is struggling to provide adequate power for a six-hour cross-country flight within specific size and weight constraints. In this case all three designers need to negotiate and make mutual adjustments, with the involvement and approval of the laptop's overall design manager. The same kind of subgoal conflict occurs for the architect and structural engineer of a building. The architect would like to have unrestricted column-free floors to maximize architectural flexibility, and the structural engineer would prefer to have closely spaced columns to minimize the depth, and hence cost, of the beam-and-slab structural systems for the building.

Reciprocal interdependency requires negotiation and mutual adjustment between two or more project and program participants and often requires project and program managers to mediate the deadlocks that arise. So it is the most costly kind of coordination to manage and the most vital function for program managers. Effective program managers make sure that the team spends enough time to identify all the important interdependencies and white spaces between projects and across tasks within each project. Experienced project managers can often catch and resolve reciprocal interdependencies within their own projects in team meetings or in separate discussions with individual task managers. But when reciprocal interdependencies cut across projects, there is significant risk of their falling through the cracks unless the program manager makes a systematic effort to identify them.

Project and program managers often fail to detect all reciprocal interdependencies, resulting in programs with components whose interfaces have not been adequately coordinated. Individuals and organizations do learn from their experience, albeit imperfectly. Reciprocal interdependencies that arise frequently between components or subsystems eventually get resolved by developing standard interface solutions to resolve the predictable interdependencies.[8] Thus, reciprocal interdependence usually turns out to be less of a problem for projects and programs that involve relatively mature products and technologies.

But working on an innovative product or a relatively mature product that is being updated to incorporate one or more emerging technologies, program managers must take great pains to be sure that their project team leaders spend enough time early in the program to identify all the key reciprocal interdependencies between critical subsystems. As work on the program proceeds, the program manager must be sure that the people involved in developing each subsystem communicate frequently with one another and understand that they need to escalate any interface conflicts or deadlocks rapidly for resolution.

Change/Rework Interdependency

Time-to-market pressures challenge managers to complete projects in less time but without any reduction in quality. Especially when the goal of the project is a new product introduction, time to market has important strategic implications for competitive positioning and the company's revenue stream. Some examples help illustrate its importance:

- For products like high-end microprocessors, the value of early market revenue can be as high as $1 million per hour, 24/7, with gross margins exceeding 50 percent. And market windows can be as short as three months, until a competitor—or the manufacturer itself—introduces an even faster microprocessor, so that prices need to be cut by 30 percent or more, eliminating most of the early gross margin.

- For an offshore oil platform in the North Sea, the "weather window" for installing the platform during a given summer is typically just a few weeks. Miss that window, and a year's revenue from the platform—hundreds of millions of dollars—is forfeited!

- Being first-to-market in consumer products confers a different kind of advantage. Aside from early market revenue, successful buyer experience with a novel product—such as the first fluoridated toothpaste or the first cholesterol-lowering statin drug—allows the producer to capture precious market share that can persist for years.

Faced with these overwhelming benefits of rapid time to market, managers often opt for fast-track project designs. In a fast-track approach, many design and implementation tasks that were previously performed sequentially are scheduled to be performed concurrently, so that project completion time can be drastically reduced. For example, a manufacturer might place orders for long lead-time manufacturing equipment before completing full-scale consumer testing to speed up time to first product. If problems arise in consumer tests that require changes in product design, there may be costly implications for the prepurchased but now inappropriate manufacturing equipment. Product managers often knowingly trade off increased development cost for faster time to market, even though they find it difficult to quantify the trade-off or identify the risks. "Lockheed's First Commercial Satellite Launch Vehicle: Fast Track to Disaster" offers the dramatic story of a failed fast-track program to help illustrate this dilemma.

Three compounding effects cause exponential increases in the hidden work of coordination and supervision in fast-track projects:

- First, increased staffing levels required to accelerate completion of individual tasks increase managers' workloads exponentially. Incremental workers are likely to be less skilled and/or less experienced than those already in place, so that they will encounter more frequent "exceptions"—situations in which they lack some of the information or knowledge required to complete their task.[9] These additional exceptions need to be handled by more experienced colleagues or supervisors, thereby increasing their workloads. For complex hardware and software projects, adding workers after the project has begun can actually slow the overall progress of the project.[10]

- Second, overlapping interdependent activities that were previously executed in parallel compound this problem. It leads to higher levels of reciprocal interdependency between tasks. Higher levels of reciprocal interdependency result in the need for increased coordination between workers performing interdependent tasks, generating additional information processing load for already stretched workers and their managers.

- Third, as the number of team members on a project increases to accelerate its completion, spans of control for first- and second-level managers tend to increase. Supervising larger numbers of workers who are performing simultaneous (versus sequential) tasks increases the rate at which the manager must process exceptions, even if all workers are equally skilled—and, as we have pointed out above, extra workers hired to accelerate the project are almost always less skilled.

Lockheed's First Commercial Satellite Launch Vehicle

Fast Track to Disaster

The U.S. military has long encouraged commercialization of many of its aerospace technologies and systems. In 1995, Lockheed won the rights to commercialize the design of a missile launch vehicle it had initially developed for the navy. The company found a commercial customer that agreed to use the adapted missile launch vehicle to carry a telecommunications satellite payload on the first flight test. Thus, one goal was to develop a new, commercial version of the military product that would work perfectly the first time. In addition, Lockheed needed to reduce development and production costs substantially to counter Russian, Chinese, and French competitors in the commercial satellite launch vehicle marketplace. One way the company attempted to reduce costs was by outsourcing the design and manufacturing of several of the launch vehicle's components. In particular, the design and manufacturing of the cable harnesses that connected all the communication, propulsion, and control systems on the launch vehicle was outsourced to an East Coast vendor.

But the biggest challenge, by far, for the managers of this commercial satellite launch vehicle project was to shrink the design and development period radically in comparison with their previous practice. The navy had given the company five to seven years to deliver each new version of the missile launch system that it had developed over the past twenty-five years—but all the prospective customers for the company's commercial satellite launch vehicles were demanding delivery in one year!

To accelerate the schedule, the project managers adopted an aggressive, fast-track program for all design and manufacturing tasks. This created myriad new reciprocal interdependencies across tasks that required extensive coordination between the responsible team members and much higher levels of supervision by managers at all levels. In the company's long experience in developing each new launch vehicle in five to seven years, these tasks had been carried out sequentially with relatively simple hand-offs of information from predecessor tasks to successor tasks.

Many aspects of the design could be readily adapted from previous missile launch vehicles. But semiconductor-based technologies for the avionics system that computed the position and planned the trajectory of the launch vehicle were changing relatively rapidly during the mid-1990s. Changes in the avionics system from previous missile launch vehicles necessitated corresponding changes in the propulsion and control systems. These changes, in turn, required changes in the design of the launch vehicle's structure and in the specifications for the thousands of cable harnesses that provide electrical power and instrumentation connectivity between all major subsystems. Anytime the design of an avionics, propulsion, or structural component changed in any way, the number and type of wires, their lengths, terminals, and bundling in one or more cable harnesses needed to be changed accordingly. Given the extraordinarily high reciprocal interdependency of the cable harness tasks with other concurrent tasks, this was probably the worst possible subsystem to have outsourced, in retrospect.

All these tasks were being carried out concurrently by separate project teams to meet the one-year launch schedule. So changes began to ricochet around between project teams in the program organization, with the outsourced cable harness group being particularly hard-hit. The cable harness contractor's backlog of unanswered requests for coordination and of changes that had not yet been implemented mounted steadily over the duration of the project. The launch vehicle company eventually dispatched some of its own engineers to the cable company's East Coast location to help the company cope with the backlog.

Result: in spite of heroic efforts by program team members, the launch date slipped past its one-year target date, and the vehicle was finally launched almost four months late. Upon launch, the vehicle and its payload almost immediately "departed controlled flight" and had to be preemptively detonated by the mission safety officer, destroying both the $100 million launch vehicle and its $300 million commercial satellite payload.

The company's published analysis of telemetry data from this failed launch vehicle identified the most likely cause of the failure to be a cable harness that had been misrouted too close to a high-temperature source, causing its insulation to melt and the wires to short-circuit—a literal "quality meltdown." As one manager of the company put it, "Everything was insured except our company's reputation!"

How could a leading company from a mature project management industry like aerospace so badly miscalculate the resources and time required to execute a program to develop a product for which it had twenty-five years of development experience? The answer is the hidden work caused by fast-track concurrent development of programs with significant degrees of reciprocal interdependency across the component projects. Accelerating project completion for reciprocally interdependent tasks increases the hidden coordination and supervision work for managers, and for technical workers who must coordinate multiple reciprocal interdependencies with colleagues engaged in concurrent tasks. As the degree of concurrency of interdependent tasks increases beyond some minimal threshold, the increased workloads for both workers and managers begin to overwhelm key team members in the organization, leading to delays, cost overruns, and, in the worst cases, quality meltdowns such as the one that occurred for this launch vehicle.

As individual tasks accelerate, team sizes increase, and previously sequential tasks overlap, backlogged participants on information overload tend to focus on completing their own work, so they begin to underemphasize coordination, failing to reply to requests for information, skipping meetings, and so on. Coordination failures frequently result, leading to increased numbers of downstream errors, more rework to address those changes or errors that are detected, decreased subsystem and system-level quality, and missed deadlines. Employee burnout of overstressed team members is another frequent consequence of such projects.

When projects involving relatively immature technologies with high levels of reciprocal interdependency are subject to aggressive fast-track scheduling, the result is often an explosion of changes and rework from one task to another. We refer to projects like this as having high levels of *rework/change interdependency* and correspondingly high levels of hidden work for workers and managers. Such projects must be planned in a completely different way from conventional projects. But over and over, companies fail to recognize the risks and adapt their processes. "Lockheed Launch Vehicle Redux: The 2006 Airbus A380 Delay" describes another such mishap at Airbus—and we'll revisit the Airbus story in our concluding chapter.

Lockheed Launch Vehicle Redux

The 2006 Airbus A380 Delay

In June 2006, the European consortium Airbus SAS shocked airlines and investors when it announced a second delay of six months, until 2009 for many customers, in its plans to deliver the A380, the world's largest passenger plane. European Aeronautic Defence and Space Company (EADS), which owned 80 percent of Airbus, admitted that its $300 million (£160 million) double-decker A380 was far behind schedule, entailing at least €2 billion ($2.5 billion) in penalty clauses and extra costs over the next four years. The delay placed several already booked orders in jeopardy and sent EADS shares in Paris and Frankfurt plunging as much as 34 percent. Commentators described it as Airbus's worst manufacturing crisis in years.

In Airbus's head-to-head competition with Boeing for supply of commercial airplanes to the rebounding airline industry, this additional six-month delay was an unmitigated disaster, just as sales of Boeing's smaller, fuel-efficient Dreamliner airplane were taking off dramatically. In the two weeks following the announcement, three senior executives resigned or were dismissed, including Gustav Humbert, president and chief executive officer (CEO) of Airbus SAS, and "Monsieur Airbus," Noël Forgeard, the cochief of EADS, whose position in EADS' bipartite management structure had appeared unassailable. Three months later, with no solution to this problem in sight, the new chief executive, Christian Streiff, left Airbus.[a]

What went wrong with what should have been a routine, semicustom manufacturing operation for this mature aerospace company? Once again, the problem turned out to be a combination of fast-track "concurrent engineering" without adequate consideration of the hidden work caused by interdependencies among subsystems. And as with the Lockheed launch vehicle, wiring was the highly interdependent subsystem that triggered the schedule and quality meltdown. A *Wall Street Journal* analysis described the problem:[b]

Wiring is an increasingly significant part of new aircraft, as electricity replaces clunky mechanical systems. New computers and entertainment systems also need wiring.

continued

The Airbus wiring problems started about two years ago, when Airbus factories began assembling A380 parts before wiring plans were complete. Building airplane parts while designs are being finalized is a standard practice called "concurrent engineering" and is aimed at saving time. But the design was fluid as the A380 was being built, because of tweaks by engineers and because of customization requests by airlines. When the plane started flight tests in April 2005, for example, engineers discovered that certain antennas needed to be shifted.

Clear signs that the rewiring process was proceeding more slowly than expected emerged in April of this year [2006]. Airbus managers noticed a backlog of fully built A380s sitting on the assembly line waiting to be wired, according to Mr. Fehring. Airbus engineers thought the situation was controllable. It was several weeks later, after a further analysis aided by management consultant McKinsey & Co., that the extent of the rewiring problems emerged. "The number of small changes we have to apply to the number of aircraft built has caused the delay," Mr. Fehring said.

In this case, the challenge arose from the fact that each airline uses somewhat different cabin layouts with different kinds of in-seat passenger entertainment systems. These require significant amounts of custom wiring to be designed and installed in each airline's fleet, on top of the already complex wiring for the fly-by-wire electronic controls and avionics systems on the Airbus A380. The decision to begin assembling aircraft parts (through which wiring would have to be routed) before completing the design of the entertainment systems, and while Airbus engineers continued to "tweak" the core control and avionics systems, generated unprecedented requirements for coordination between design and manufacturing. And it resulted in large amounts of difficult and costly rework when backlogged middle managers proved unable to provide the unanticipated coordination.

The same kind of overlooked hidden work resulting from rework dependence in a fast-track, concurrent project had caused the failure of the Lockheed launch vehicle (see "Lockheed's First Commercial Satellite Launch Vehicle: Fast Track to Disaster") and had caused production delays for Airbus in the past. Yet Airbus A380 managers once again failed to predict and manage it. Worse, in September 2006 the company's new CEO, Christian Streiff, was forced to confirm rumors of yet another delay.

a. Ambrose Evans-Pritchard, "Airbus Troubles Deepen as CEO Streiff Quits After Three Months," *Daily Telegraph* (UK), June 16, 2006.

b. Daniel Michaels, "Airbus Scrambles to Fix the Wiring on Its A380 Jets," *Wall Street Journal*, June 26, 2006.

Use Simulation Tools to Predict Hidden Work and Potential Backlogs

Why do sophisticated companies like Lockheed and Airbus so often fail in executing strategic projects, and how can anyone avoid a similar disaster? When companies are considering fast-tracking a project or program, it becomes critical to assess whether high levels of reciprocal interdependency exist between project subsystems or components. If so, then aggressive fast-tracking will cause exponentially increased workloads for both workers and managers. Direct and managerial staffing requirements will increase accordingly, yet many planners grossly underestimate the project staffing challenge. It may be possible to shrink the duration of a project by about 10 percent with 10 percent more workers and managers. But shrinking the project duration by 50 percent may take three times as many direct workers and five times as many middle managers. The span of control for managers (the number of workers reporting to each manager) must be reduced to allow for the extra hidden supervision work, especially if incremental workers with potentially lower skills or experience are brought in to increase staffing levels.

Some experienced project leaders effectively use judgment and intuition to make allowances for extra workers and managers when planning fast-track projects. This is certainly better than assuming that linear increases in the numbers of full-time equivalent direct workers and managers will permit corresponding degrees of fast-tracking. However, as Rich Grimes demonstrated in the AT&T Wireless rollout, new kinds of modeling and simulation tools are available to model the work process and organization for a fast-track project or program.[11] These approaches and tools can predict with considerable accuracy task-, project-, and program-level outcomes related to time, cost, and process quality. Moreover, they can predict in advance which workers and managers in the program team will be most heavily backlogged for a given configuration of a fast-track work process and the performing organization.

These modeling and simulation tools can help program planners explore and assess the implications of different degrees of fast-tracking, different numbers and skill sets of managers in key managerial positions, and other attributes of the organization structure, such as the degree of centralization of decision making, formalization of communication, and matrix strength (as discussed in chapter 3). Once they can roughly predict project- and program-level outcomes, managers can intervene proactively to avoid bottlenecks and simulate multiple alternative scenarios by adjusting aspects of the work process, organizational configuration, or both, until a project plan is developed or they determine that no acceptable plan can be found that meets scope, schedule, and resource requirements. It is obviously far preferable to discover this in an exploratory computer model than to invest an organization's resources and its reputation in what is doomed to be a failed project.

In contrast to the fifty-thousand-activity critical-path models for power plants and other large facilities that can easily wallpaper an entire conference room, this approach to designing a project or program organization typically models a large project or program with a few dozen "actors"—individuals or subteams—and fifty to one hundred tasks. So these models can be developed in hours, the project or program can be replanned in minutes, and the work process and organization can be visualized on a single screen for discussion with project executives, clients, and others.

The members of a program team involving multiple organizations with different work practices and values may have quite different views about the scope of the program and how their part of the program fits in with other parts. In programs like this, involving representatives from all key participating organizations in the process of modeling and simulating their shared project or program—what Michael Schrage calls "serious play" and what we call "flight-simulating projects and programs"—can be enormously valuable.[12] First, the ability to visualize the work process and organization of an entire program on a single screen helps the team develop a shared mental model of the program and its component projects with all their interdependencies. Second, the ability to propose a change in the planned work process or organization, model the proposed change in minutes, and then immediately see the implications of the proposed change on project outcomes transforms ego-based conflicts about which approach is more "beautiful" into rational and level-headed discussions about the implications of each proposed intervention.

One of the authors used this kind of "program flight simulation" to help guide the program management team of a leading consumer products company. This company had brought two of its divisions together to create a breakthrough new product combining elements of technology and manufacturing expertise from each of the divisions. This costly and strategic product development program was falling behind schedule, and the company was concerned that a competitor might beat its product to market. Each of the two divisions had developed its own proposed strategy for accelerating completion of the program. One division's strategy involved early ordering of long–lead time manufacturing equipment, which carried the risk of incurring extra costs if changes to the equipment were subsequently required as a result of customer feedback from the final phase of consumer testing. The second division's strategy involved curtailing the amount of consumer testing before releasing the first version of the product, and addressing customer feedback through a second version of the product to be released six months later.

After almost two weeks of fruitless discussions among managers from each of these divisions about which of the two proposed acceleration strategies to use on this program, we were asked to facilitate a two-hour "project flight simulation" meeting of managers from the two groups. A colleague "piloted" a laptop computer with a SimVision model of the project that could be projected onto a screen in the conference room for all to see and that could then be simulated in real time to show the group the implications of the two proposed approaches and any other approaches that the group developed through the discussion.

The collaborative flight simulation radically transformed the interpersonal dynamics between managers from the two divisions about how they should accelerate the program. Focusing on the predicted outcomes of each of their proposed solutions, they immediately began debating the trade-offs between the risks of delayed time to market versus the risks of incurring equipment change costs by ordering manufacturing equipment before consumer testing had been completed. By the end of two hours of "serious play" with the project model, the managers of the two divisions agreed on a hybrid approach that involved splitting the final round of consumer testing into a series of shorter and more specific consumer tests, scheduling the ones that they collectively felt had the greatest potential to require changes in the manufacturing equipment first.

Aligning the Planned Portfolio with the Real Portfolio

It is important to remember that even with the most sophisticated approaches to project and program planning, things will go awry. This inevitable reality is the reason we need to replan projects and programs frequently in dynamically changing environments. Thus, the synthesis imperative requires keeping the ever-changing real portfolio of ongoing projects and programs as closely aligned as possible with the planned portfolio, which is itself in a state of flux based on the organization's dynamically changing strategy.

Failure to align the *real portfolio* of projects and programs with the *planned portfolio* will result in one of two outcomes, both of which compromise the success of strategic execution:

- The first kind of misalignment occurs when one or more major projects or programs is running late and consuming more resources than planned. In this case, the planned portfolio may be perfectly aligned with the organization's *strategy* in the *engagement* domain, but the planned portfolio has no chance of being fully implemented, because resources that were being counted on to implement other projects and programs in the portfolio are no longer available. This results in overpromising and underdelivering on strategic execution—an outcome that has career limiting implications for all of the managers involved.

- The second kind of misalignment occurs in the happy event that one or more major projects or programs are proceeding much better than expected and consuming fewer resources, but the planned portfolio has not been updated to recognize this. In this situation, the project and program managers of the successful initiatives are viewed (and should be rewarded) as heroes, but the organization is not taking full advantage of the resources released by those projects and programs to implement other strategic initiatives that would have been in the planned portfolio, but were postponed or canceled due to inadequate resources. So the organization as a whole suffers the opportunity cost of failing to implement the additional initiatives.

Strive for More Reliable Forecasts

Every executive knows how department or division managers attempt to hoard resources in conventional budgeting processes, in which future budgets are based on current expenditures. Why should project or program managers be any different? Senior managers should keep in mind that the first situation described above—missed project and program deadlines and budgets—traditionally causes heads to roll at the program and project manager level. So project and program managers will often be reluctant to reveal that their projects are going better than expected, hoarding their resources for future use in case things should begin to go awry later.

How can an organization avoid this kind of pessimistic forecasting and hoarding of resources by managers of projects and programs without taking away their incentives to manage their projects and programs for the best possible outcomes? For one thing, it is important to make sure that senior managers do not scapegoat managers whose projects and programs end up being behind schedule or over budget. Keep in mind that even when managers forecast reliably, they are likely to overrun schedules and budgets about half the time. The answer is to set up "honesty reward functions" that reward managers for making honest estimates that they will only achieve about half the time, rather than making pessimistic estimates that they can easily beat.

Of course, managers need to be held accountable for the success of their projects and programs and rewarded when they succeed. The key is to obtain reliable current forecasts of the true state of ongoing projects and programs, so that the organization can maximize the results of its investment decisions, given the changing state of key strategic drivers in the outside world and of project and program execution by the organization and its delivery partners.

Real-Time Portfolio Management: Viabene

A start-up biotech company we'll call Viabene developed an exciting new product that involved delivering influenza vaccinations through a spray inhaler rather than by injection, which is anathema to parents of small children needing to be vaccinated. The program to launch this drug in the United States during the late 1990s involved a series of projects across facilities in the United States and Europe to complete the final phase of FDA Phase III testing, develop full-scale manufacturing facilities for the inhaled vaccine, and develop a marketing and sales program for the vaccine. There was no systematic planning process in place for these projects, but there was a general sense among senior managers in the company that the *planned portfolio* was not realistic. A team of external consultants was brought in to review the plans and schedules for the projects in the company's portfolio as a sanity check for senior management. A high-level, forward-planning process revealed that many of these projects were planning on using some of the same scarce human resources in this small company simultaneously. For example, some of Viabene's senior scientists were allocated to more than ten projects in multiple time zones.

The external consultants reported that the portfolio had virtually no chance of succeeding, and that the company needed to obtain extensive additional resources to have any chance of accomplishing this planned rollout by the beginning of the northern hemisphere winter of the year when the vaccine had been projected to be approved and released. Missing this deadline would result in the loss of one year's early revenue for the company—a serious setback.

It turned out that it was too late to turn the ship around. As predicted, the company failed to complete its Phase III testing successfully, so the revenues from the planned first year's flu season were lost. Early the following year, the company was acquired by a larger pharmaceutical firm that released the product one year later. If this company had engaged in realistic project portfolio planning from the beginning so that it could react in time, it might have been possible to avert this unfortunate outcome.

The way to balance the need for accountability with the need for reliable forecasts of projects and programs is to insist on frequent, forward-looking planning and replanning processes for all projects and programs and to link resource allocation in each replanning period to realistic, cur-

The Project List for Building Stronger Synthesis

Project management as an organizational capability can turn into a discussion of the chicken or the egg: which comes first—the ability to manage projects or the ability to manage a project to improve project management? We call this the *self-referential* nature of project management. If strategic execution is blocked by insufficient project management performance, then we need project management to install project management. This may be a great place to get some outside help. In our experience, attacking the first three of these suggested project investments concurrently is the best approach to building a synthesis capability:

- Project, program, and portfolio management process development
- Project, program, and portfolio management training
- Sponsorship training
- Program and project forecasting and tracking systems
- A program management office (PMO)
- Executive training in how to leverage program and project management
- Leadership development for project, program, and portfolio managers

rent, forward-looking plans. Getting reliable forecasts from frequent replanning is the key to aligning the *real portfolio* of projects and programs with the *planned portfolio* in the *synthesis* domain. "The Project List for Building Stronger Synthesis" lists some of the project investments that can help your company achieve the synthesis imperative.

Rate Your Organization on the Synthesis Imperative

Whoever said that when all is said and done, there is more said than done, must have been talking about synthesis. If you were given a list of things to do and told that they were all equally critical, and you quickly realized that you could not get them all done, what would you do? Perhaps spend a large amount of time discussing alternatives. Perhaps go from the top of the list to the bottom, perhaps bottom to top, perhaps start all of them and complete none but get all to some level of completion. This would be a synthesis failure. Synthesis demands the real-time setting, resetting, and adjusting of priorities as a result of strategic demand. It also requires information flow from project and program levels to balance demand with capacity. Last, synthesis demands that programs and projects deliver the value committed. Here are some ways you can get a sense of your ability to synthesize.

Measuring Portfolio Synthesis

On a scale of 1–10, 1 = seldom true, 5 = sometimes true, 10 = almost always true.

TABLE 5-2

Measure your organization's portfolio synthesis

	Rating (1–10)
Programs and projects are managed under a well-defined process that establishes priorities and allocates resources accordingly.	
We follow the output of a portfolio process and make changes only in concert with overall organizational priorities.	
Managers and leaders support decisions made in the portfolio process and provide resources to support the decisions.	
We have systems in place to base our portfolio on credible program and project resource demand.	
Program management processes operate under the priority set identified in the portfolio process and deliver according to specific agreed-on objectives for time, cost, and deliverables.	
Project and program managers understand the priorities of the organization and how their project or program relates to those priorities.	
	Average score:

Interpretation of average score:

➤ Below 3: Organizational priorities do not drive work directly, and decision quality may be at risk.

➤ Between 3 and 6: Organizational priorities drive some work, but there is still a great deal of adhocracy.

➤ Above 6: Priorities are used effectively to drive work.

Measuring Program Synthesis

On a scale of 1–10, 1 = seldom true, 5 = sometimes true, 10 = almost always true.

TABLE 5-3

Measure your organization's program synthesis

	Rating (1–10)
There is a clear definition of programs and projects that clarifies the differences between them.	
Hiring, staffing, training, and promotion take into account the difference between programs and projects.	
Program management processes operate under the priority set identified in the portfolio process.	
Programs are managed by a well-established process that is designed to identify and manage the interconnections/white spaces between projects.	
Our information systems track project and program interfaces to facilitate real-time decision making.	
	Average score:

Interpretation of average score:

➤ Below 3: Program and portfolio processes do not work together, risking large amounts of waste, poor delivery performance, and confused priorities.

➤ Between 3 and 6: Program and portfolio processes work together in some cases, but waste is still an issue.

➤ Above 6: The organization is beginning to leverage synthesis to its advantage in getting priority programs executed.

Measuring Project Synthesis

On a scale of 1–10, 1 = seldom true, 5 = sometimes true, 10 = almost always true.

TABLE 5-4

Measure your organization's project synthesis

	Rating (1–10)
Our project management process is consistent and scalable to fit the size of the projects we manage.	
Project management processes operate under the priority set identified in the portfolio process and deliver specific agreed-on objectives for time, cost, and deliverables.	
Our shared project management processes make integration of projects into programs easy.	
Managers and leaders in the organization support projects and provide resource commitments, clear direction, and sponsorship when needed.	
Our information systems track project progress proactively and provide the forward-looking information project managers need to make real-time decisions.	
Average score:	

Interpretation of average score:

➤ Below 3: The building blocks of strategic execution are missing at the project layer.

➤ Between 3 and 6: Strategic execution is hindered by hit-and-miss performance at the project layer.

➤ Above 6: Project management is becoming a competitive strength.

Six

Transition Imperative

Move Project Outputs into the Mainstream

However beautiful the strategy, you should occasionally look at the results.

—Sir Winston Churchill

T HE 2004 U.S. WOMEN'S 4x100 track team consisted of what many considered the four fastest runners in the world in combined individual 100 meter races. They appeared to be sure winners in the final race—except for one disastrous thing. The second handoff failed when the runners passed the window of opportunity for transition before the baton changed hands. No gold medal, no silver, no bronze: four years of preparation for naught. Similar mishaps occur too often with strategic projects and programs. Even if you have star project managers in your organization and they have fantastic teams, it will do no good if they fail to accomplish the transition to operations.

Transition is the crucial final step in realizing the benefits of strategic projects and programs. Transition can free up resources, or it can leave the organization mired in unfinished projects, unable to operationalize its strategic intent. The *transition imperative* guides the handoff between the strategy carrier (project or program) and the ongoing organization. This includes translating and connecting program and project outputs into ongoing operations to achieve the tangible outcomes the projects or programs were designed to create. It requires completing the programs and projects to free up scarce resources needed for the next strategic endeavor. In short, the transition imperative asks us to *move project outputs into the mainstream to reap the strategic benefits and redeploy the resources where the portfolio says they should go next.*

Projects have a finite useful life. They are like the forms around a concrete structure: once the concrete has set, they are dismantled, leaving behind the shape they gave it. The work of the transition imperative maintains the shape of the concrete, allowing it to harden; identifies the right time to dismantle the form; and then dismantles it to prepare for the next set of strategic activities. This takes place at the interface between project/ program management and operations process management, as shown in figure 6-1.

Successful transitions create seamless and timely handoffs from the project management organization to the ongoing operations. As we shall see, this requires strong sponsorship, especially to combat last-minute creep at the time of handoff, and also in the earliest stages of embedding the project benefits in the operations. In addition, the prelaunch commissioning and testing phases of complex projects or programs require significant centralized coordination to integrate and test subsystems or components of the product or service offering.

Finally, to reap the full magnitude of strategic benefits for the organization, there must be feedback from the ongoing operations to the strategic planners regarding the actual ongoing results of all the projects and programs in the portfolio. Figure 6-1 diagrams this feedback in the two-way arrows that connect operations to project, program, and portfolio management and from there to the strategy itself. These two-way arrows represent the critical bilingual conversations that connect strategy makers with project leaders—the very conversations that guide the conversion of strategy into action.

This crucial feedback serves as a perpetual monitor of the organization's performance in bringing strategy to life. On the one hand, it forces project sponsors and strategy makers to review whether the strategy being enacted is still the correct strategy in the evolving context—whether the organization is doing the right things and maintaining all the right alignments.

On the other hand, the feedback requires project leaders and sponsors to evaluate whether the actual project portfolio still aligns with the planned

FIGURE 6-1

The transition imperative: Move project outputs into the mainstream

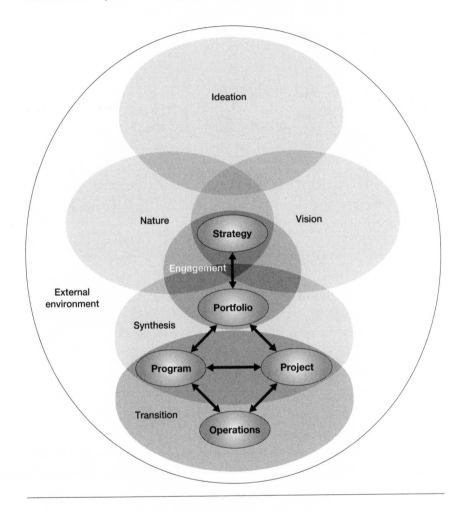

portfolio, and to make the continuous, inevitable adjustments in deploying the organization's resources. At the same time, these two-way conversations strengthen the organization's ability to learn from its experiences with every strategic project and program it undertakes.

Organizations that fail to accomplish the transition imperative are unable to move forward with their strategies. Their projects and resources get "stuck" on incomplete tasks and are unavailable for the next important activity. This effect almost always leaves strategy makers unable to account for the resource shortfall in their portfolio resource allocation. The only solution to this typical execution problem is to be vigilant in managing the transitions.[1]

Choosing the Right Time for Handoffs

Handoffs present some of the most difficult challenges of strategic execution. The first such challenge may be learning to recognize when a project is *ready* for transition—when to take the forms off the finished concrete. By the time we reach the transition imperative, the program is ready for deployment—or it should be. But often at this stage, new questions or observations come up:

- Opportunities exist for significant improvement in the thing we have built, because the world has changed or we just have a clearer—and potentially different—view of reality now.

- The players have changed and see things very differently from those who signed off on the original deal.

- Customers have modified their view of the world and request a few features they would like us to squeeze in "while we are at it."

- The competitive landscape has changed.

- New technology has changed the shape of the solution.

- A few undocumented features showed up that our supplier did not completely detail for us up front.

- The project team has taken the liberty of coming up with some great new add-ons and is excited about building them in.

- We just realized that maintenance of the system will need some costly ongoing support after program completion.

Each of these common realizations—and a hundred or more similar ones—creates the potential for large-scale creep that will necessitate more time and resources. When this happens, the transition imperative forces us to cycle back to the portfolio process in order to align end-of-project decisions with the best interests of the organization. Among other things, this entails understanding the difference between outputs and outcomes.

Distinguish Outputs from Outcomes

You may wonder why we raise this challenge as part of the transition imperative and not in synthesis. After all, defining project outputs and clarifying outcomes is part of the program and project management process in the synthesis domain. Yet at transition, the world may be very different than it was when we put our plans together. It is also possible that outputs and outcomes were never defined well in the planning of the project or program. The smooth transition of projects and programs relies heavily on the alignment of outcomes and outputs to the original business case plus changes that have become necessary during the duration of the project or program. Whether we are validating, reevaluating, or creating from scratch, how we manage the definition of outputs and outcomes will determine whether we finish now, invest more to improve the product or service being delivered, or pull the plug to cut our losses.

It is always fascinating to ask a group of people in a project workshop to focus on the outcomes the project is intended to create. This seems like such a simple request: all it requires is to fast-forward to the end of the project and name the outcome or the tangible impact the project should yield. Remember, the project itself is only a means toward an end. It would seem only reasonable to expect the project team to describe the end result of their project. Yet far too often, the first blank looks turn to utter frustration when the group members realizes that they have no idea what their intended outcomes should be.

Typically, a project team gets chartered to create what in one company is referred to as a BFI. No, this does not stand for what you think it does. It is also not the initials of Browning Ferris Industries, which handles solid waste (garbage). It stands for big fuzzy idea. Many projects start with a big fuzzy idea that somehow is supposed to congeal at the project layer. We have seen project teams languish for months in this space as they grapple with the question of what the project is really intended to create, for whom, by when, and for how much.

In our experience, the process of getting this definition in place should take no more than three days. But many organizations seem quite content to let it drag out over months of wasted meetings, e-mails, voice mails, and phone conferences. Even a luxurious off-site session can't jump-start a team that is suffering from this malaise unless it focuses on a common underlying issue: the lack of basic understanding of the difference between an output and an outcome.

Outputs are the tangible things a project creates:

- Systems

- Hardware

- Software

- Processes

- Documentation

Outcomes are the results that the outputs create for the customer, the customer's customers, or the organization itself:

- Greater productivity

- Better performance through innovative product features

- Faster response time

- Enhanced ease of use

The project's completion date is associated with completing the *outputs*. Benefits realization is based on the *outcomes*, which may come much later. In fact, there may be a significant delay between the delivery of outputs and the ability to detect outcomes. Where there is no direct relationship between the project outputs and the desired outcomes, transition runs into a serious problem. The project team has created something to "specification," but the customer is dissatisfied with, or no longer interested in, the outcomes (see "The Iridium Syndrome: Emphasizing Outputs over Outcomes")—or the internal organization fails to capitalize on its newly created capabilities.

Apple Computer made this sort of mistake with the Newton, which ended its short life as a product failure. The original intent was to design a general-purpose handheld computer that could learn how to read any

The Iridium Syndrome

Emphasizing Outputs over Outcomes

Motorola's Iridium project, described in chapter 4, delivered its hugely ambitious outputs as chartered: on time, on budget, and on scope. On the outcome front, Iridium was not so good. Eventually, Iridium was sold for pennies on the dollar as the outcomes simply did not meet the needs of the marketplace. Motorola's CEO, John A. Richardson, explained after taking over as interim CEO of Iridium in 1999, "We're a classic MBA case study in how not to introduce a product. First we created a marvelous technological achievement. Then we asked how to make money on it."[a]

Iridium's classic mistake was emphasizing outputs over outcomes. Earlier we discussed the difference between a "make to offer" company and an "offer to make" company. Iridium's leaders were so focused on "make to offer" that they forgot to monitor the evolution of the marketplace in which they would offer their complex telecommunication solution. So Iridium suffered from a disastrous misalignment between the project outputs and the evolution over time in desired customer outcomes. By the time the project was ready to deploy, users demanded small, cheap, and efficient mobile communication. Iridium met its original output goals to provide line-of-sight satellite uplink communications capabilities for its mobile telephone users worldwide, but its product was neither small nor cheap nor efficient.

When outputs no longer align with outcomes, the issue becomes whether to launch as is, spend more resources on revising the system to fit the reality of the marketplace, or pull the plug. Perhaps you have small-scale "Iridiums" in your organization—projects and programs that will reach transition and without clear transition processes, will continue to take up resources that are needed elsewhere as teams wrestle with how to realign outputs with outcomes.

a. Mark Leibovich, "A Dream Comes Back to Earth: Missteps, Shortfalls, Glitches Have Iridium Scaling Back Expectations for Its Satellite Phone Service," *Washington Post*, May 24, 1999.

user's unique handwriting. The output of a personal digital assistant (PDA) with a freehand data entry system was severely misaligned with the required customer outcome of "easy to use." In contrast, Palm Computing developed a handheld PDA a few years later with a limited set of the most useful personal organizer capabilities (calendar, phone list, to-do list, and memos), able to synchronize with the most widely used desktop PC organizers, and with a standardized alphabet for pen-based input ("Graffiti") that users could easily learn.

Palm required its users to learn the Graffiti input format, which was close enough to standard block printing that it turned out to be easy for users to do. In contrast, Apple tried to have the handheld organizer learn to decipher the user's handwriting, which the Newton never succeeded in doing at acceptable levels of accuracy. Ironically, doctors in clinics were an early target market for the Newton—and we know how difficult their handwriting is to read, even for humans! The Newton failed; the Palm Pilot was an instant success. "Apple iPod: Matching Project Outputs to Desired Customer Outcomes" describes the alignment of outputs and outcomes for Apple's iPod, which fortunately fared much better than the Newton.

Project handoffs should take place when the outputs reach the scope definition that was used to justify and charter the project in the beginning. If outputs are aligned with outcomes, and the definition of the deliverables stays stable at the end of the project, then the time is ripe for transition. If not, or if the project schedule starts to creep, it is time to manage trade-offs.

Manage Trade-offs

When project creep threatens, it is important to recognize that various stakeholders will perceive differently the value of potential outputs and their expected outcomes for the organization. Consider the scenario in figure 6-2, where a strategic project has been designed to deliver a faster production process and also reduce the manufacturing loss ratio.

Beneficiary A is eager to capture the time savings and speed the products to market, for an additional $20,000 per week, or $40,000 total. Beneficiary B, on the other hand, wants most to implement the features that will reduce the loss ratio by 5 percent, for a total savings of $500,000. Both beneficiaries stand to gain significant advantage from the proposed project, but beneficiary B receives the bulk of the benefit.

Apple iPod

Matching Project Outputs to Desired Customer Outcomes

The Apple iPod represents a perfect alignment between output and outcome. As a project output, the iPod is:

- Small and battery operated
- A music and video player
- Black or white

In terms of customer outcomes, the iPod is:

- Cool and fashionable
- Contemporary (the latest thing)
- A way of taking one's music—which is a powerful symbol of personal identity—anywhere and everywhere; something of a portable ego
- A way of enjoying music and podcasts while doing other stuff like walking, jogging, biking, flying—ah, the joy of multiplexing!

According to *USA Today*, Apple could not project when iPod capacity would meet demand.[a] A nice problem to have, but when it arises, project resources can still get stuck and unable to move on to the next innovation.

a. Jefferson Graham, "Apple's Record Fourth Quarter Called 'Disappointing,'" *USA Today*, October 12, 2005.

In the course of completing the project, the project manager is likely to face many a challenge in delivering the outputs as originally planned. For example, at some point it may become obvious that the features and functions that deliver the minor share of benefit (the time savings) are in conflict with the overall delivery date. By cutting them from the scope of the project, the project manager can deliver the bulk of the benefit (the decreased loss ratio) on schedule.

Beneficiary A is not likely to agree to such a change, nor is beneficiary B likely to volunteer to give up some benefit in order to accommodate beneficiary A. Conflict emerges. The project manager cannot get the parties to

FIGURE 6-2

Desirable outputs reside in the eyes of the beneficiaries

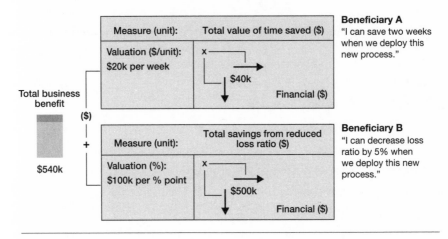

agree. When this happens—and it happens very often, in our experience—the project manager needs support in the form of a decision among the various options the project manager is able to propose. The conflict-resolving decision must come from the realm of sponsorship.

Strengthening Sponsorship Through to Project Handoffs

In chapter 4 we explored the importance of sponsorship in establishing the right portfolio management environment. The lack of appropriate sponsorship is one of the most often cited causes of project failure. Sponsorship also figures prominently in the literature on success or failure in executing organizational changes. In fact, as we have argued throughout this book, organizational change *requires* projects and programs, so it is impossible to accomplish one without the other. And the ultimate responsibility for the changes that convert strategy into action lies with the sponsors.

As we discussed in chapter 5, managing critical interfaces is key to effective execution. And transition—the handoff of outputs from the project portfolio to the ongoing operations—represents a crucial interface in the life of a new strategy. So sponsors must stay engaged through project handoffs and through the earliest stages of embedding project benefits in ongoing operations. They also must resist becoming part of the problem of project creep.

Sponsors must remain plugged into the project until:

- Stakeholders' expectations have been managed.

- The project finishes cleanly without "creep."

- Project managers are extracted from being swallowed by the process.

Beware of Project Creep: Stakeholders and Portfolio Decision Processes

Resolving conflicts in the transition domain may mean sorting through the different needs and perceptions of a large number of stakeholders. An Oracle or SAP installation may have hundreds, if not thousands, of potential beneficiaries, each with specific—and sometimes conflicting—expectations. In an Oracle implementation at Stanford University, the project outputs were optimized for some stakeholder groups at the expense of others. For example, while university administrators stood to benefit from additional controls, the delays caused by adding those controls would cause extreme frustration for faculty members eager to be able to enter travel reimbursement requests, get contract approvals, and track commitments against project research budgets with the new system.

Similarly, in the implementation of an accounting system, sales may want revenue recognition when the contract is signed, finance may insist on tying revenue recognition to invoices, while Wall Street may expect revenue to be reported on the basis of Generally Accepted Accounting Principles (GAAP), and the IRS might require yet another specific set of rules—for example, to spread the revenue from software sales over the life of the related maintenance plan. This is not to debate the right answer for such a conflict. The point is that a given project cannot serve mutually exclusive outcomes.

This sort of conflict is best handled in the early stages of planning, as part of the engagement imperative. However, even if the early decisions are clear, it is not uncommon for the original definition of the project to morph over time to the point where the project managers have no way to satisfy all stakeholders. Everywhere the project managers turn, they get new demands, with no leverage to decide among mutually exclusive outcomes. If they hang on to the full scope of the project, they will overrun the budget and schedule. If they meet the schedule and budget, they may have other unhappy stakeholders on their back. Something has to break the logjam.

If the project team gets stalled, the results will include:

• Countless meetings that take up valuable time to finish the project

• E-mail and voice mail traffic that takes up still more time

• Project team time to research alternative solutions

When the project hits such an impasse, a sponsor must make a decision so that the project team can get back to productive work. In these cases, the sponsor's incremental, logjam-breaking decisions are actually strategic portfolio management decisions. Any decision that directs additional time and resources to an ongoing project is a decision that delays or eliminates a future project. Any decision that redirects project efforts or revises target outcomes actually reflects a real-time change of strategy, whether the sponsor realizes it or not.

Technical change logs have been part of project management for decades. Sometimes, changes to projects are seen as revenue opportunities because they give the supplier an opening with its customer to add value and cost to a project. Sometimes they are even used as a mechanism to reset a bid that was intentionally low to get the business, knowing full well that the change order would come along and afford the opportunity to reprice.

But that is just the point. Changes come at a price. Effectiveness in converting strategy into action is based on the ability to match the demands of the portfolio to the capacity of the organization. If resources are being drained into changes, modifications, and additions, the real capacity of the organization can be far less than what it appears on paper. Every time a stakeholder gets something added that was out of scope, it subtracts from the organization's capacity to do other projects. So saying yes to changes is saying no to something else in the portfolio. That is the price of change.

What makes this difficult is that the decisions are seemingly so small and so distributed that taken individually, they may seem almost trivial— until they add up. In fact, some very large portfolio decisions seem deceptively small when they're being made.

Small changes in a person's diet over time can create a large change in waistline. Small change, large impact. In the case of companies, if the portfolio consists of one hundred projects and each project accepts a 5 percent change in resource utilization, it effectively eliminates five projects from the portfolio in a given time period.

So the Answer Is Always "Yes, If . . ."

We coach project managers not to say no. We recommend that they adopt a "Yes, if . . ." approach. Yes, if the costs and benefits are acceptable to the business. Yes, if the investment in the change is the best investment, on balance, that we can make on the basis of the best data available. Eliminating five projects, as in the simple example above, may be a great trade-off. It might be catastrophic. Who is to say? The portfolio process should provide the answer through continuous two-way feedback in the project leadership domains.

Part of a portfolio management system's value lies in the ability to decide how to decide. If the portfolio management system is strong and well understood at the project management level, project managers can help make decisions. In some cases they can make decisions on their own that are completely consistent with the portfolio. But the risk of having project managers make a portfolio decision unilaterally is that their purview may not encompass as much as a sponsor's and could therefore be off target. To minimize the risk, any significant addition to, change to, or deletion from a project is best a joint decision between the sponsor and the project manager.

Sponsors and project managers must work actively together to make these joint portfolio management decisions. Both have distinct roles to play. Sponsors must know the business and the strategic project portfolio. Project managers must understand the project requirements, and when potential conflicts arise, they must consult with the sponsors. These conflicts and trade-offs rear their heads especially high in the late stages of projects, when overruns against schedule and cost targets become evident and require tough choices about whether to relax scope, schedule, or resource constraints.

Create Three Options for Sponsor Trade-off Analysis

When project managers are facing an impasse (i.e., the needs of various stakeholders are mutually exclusive and the project manager is not in a power position to make a decision without support from a sponsor) or a potentially significant change, we recommend that project managers create and submit at least three options for the sponsor to consider. Offering three options allows the sponsor to decide which would be good, better, and best. Sponsors' perspectives are critical because their understanding of the overall business is much more comprehensive than that of the project manager. The project manager has far better grasp of the details of what will work and what won't work. So when the project manager develops at least three viable options from the broad range of potential solutions, the sponsor's decision-making capability combines with the project manager's on-the-ground intelligence to yield an optimum decision. Within each option, the project manager must analyze benefits and trade-offs so that the sponsor can make the right portfolio management decisions.

This process, which we call *sponsor trade-off analysis*, converts the impasses and arguments to a true collaborative decision-making process between the sponsor and the project manager. It encompasses the vast range of elements that constitute good portfolio decisions in the strategic execution framework, including:

- Strategic fit

- Brand consistency

- Goal alignment

- Metric alignment

- Cultural fit

- Organizational design

- Portfolio fit

- Stakeholder balance

- Long-range implications

Many of the items in this list are not typically used as decision-making criteria. However, they are important in making trade-off decisions because they allow all six imperatives to figure in, either at a cognitive level or, when the elements of each domain are fully ingrained, subconsciously.

Combat Last-Minute Sponsorship Blunders

As we noted above, the lack of strong sponsorship is a major cause of failure in project management, program management, and organizational change management. Given the statistics on decision making, this is not surprising.

As Paul C. Nutt notes in *Why Decisions Fail*, more than 50 percent of all decisions fail; they are quickly abandoned, only partially implemented, or never adopted at all. Not only that, 81 percent of managers and executives pushed their decisions through persuasion or edict.[2] And only 7 percent of decisions were made using long-term priorities. Despite these rather sobering statistics, 91 percent of the managers in Nutt's study rated themselves as exceptional decision makers![3]

One common barrier to optimum sponsorship decisions arises when the sponsors themselves initiate last-minute change. When this happens, sponsors actually *cause* the scope creep. Sponsors tend to be more closely associated with the strategy of the organization and more attuned to fast-paced changes in the external environment. As a result, many are tempted to mirror the speed of change in the competitive environment with change in the project environment. When this happens, the rate of change of a project's direction becomes so rapid that the project team cannot respond quickly enough. Changes often come to project teams so fast and frequently that the next change happens before the last change is implemented.

To combat the chaos, sponsors must strike a balance between the need to remain flexible and adaptive to the external environment and the reality of what the team can produce given the state of flux in the project. Too much change stalls the project when project team members no longer can commit themselves entirely to getting work done because they know most of that work will be scrapped to make way for the next change.

Strengthen Centralized Controls During Commissioning and Start-up

The coordination needs of a project change dramatically over its life cycle. In the early stages, small groups of experts from each relevant discipline or function meet frequently to resolve reciprocal interdependencies and define the scope, boundary, and interface requirements for each of the project's subsystems. Once subsystems, boundaries, and interface requirements have been identified, a larger number of team members can work in parallel in a more decentralized way to flesh out the details of their own subsystem or components.

Toward the end of a project, reimposing a more centralized structure is often necessary to pull together all the final details associated with component testing and quality assurance, system integration, and system testing. In addition, end users often must be involved during the later stages of a project so they can learn how to operate the new hardware or software created by the project team members. This is especially true for projects with many moving parts, such as an airplane, a factory, or even a modern office building with complex security, fire safety, energy control, and other active systems.

Moving from the decentralized project work to this commissioning or start-up phase requires a significant change in organization structure. Not only must decision making be centralized, it must coordinate across the subsystem or functional groups within which the project components were designed and manufactured. This requires a new dimension of strong matrix structure, in which the systems integration, testing, and start-up personnel are made more powerful than subsystem managers or functional managers. This can be done using the levers and dials for moving power between managers that we discussed in the weak versus strong matrix organization section of chapter 3.

For example, the team involved in designing and creating a new piece of semiconductor manufacturing equipment includes multiple hardware, software, and control engineers who will be involved in testing and integrating all the subsystems and components in the commissioning phase. During the transition to start-up, a manufacturing systems engineer must move into a position of authority, with enough power to direct all participants through the processes of subsystem build-out, quality assurance and testing, systems integration, and further testing of higher-level subsystems all the way up to the completed manufacturing system in the plant setting.

A similar testing and integration process is required to close out and hand off any complex information technology implementation involving networking hardware and software infrastructure, middleware, platforms, and the hardware and software associated with a variety of end-user applications. In parallel, members of the client's IT department may need to be trained to set up and maintain all these hardware and software systems.

One of the challenges during the often frenetic project-commissioning phase is to limit design changes to those that are absolutely essential to basic system functionality. Several experienced system integration companies have evolved rules to limit late changes. For example, a major petrochemical engineering and construction company has developed a rule that any changes requested by the client after the 85 percent completion point are held off until after the system is up and running, and then implemented as retrofits. This kind of "design freeze" helps avoid the coordination overload problems that Airbus experienced on the A380 project that we described in chapter 5.

Close Out Projects Crisply and Unambiguously

In facilitating workshops to help organizations assemble a registry for all their ongoing projects, we have repeatedly observed managers who are amazed to learn that multiple projects they thought had been shelved were still actively absorbing people's time and other scarce resources. The resources being frittered away on strategically irrelevant and unproductive "immortal projects" are thus being denied to more strategically relevant projects that may have critical needs for them.

Projects that are paid for by external customers are generally relatively straightforward to close out. Resources used in such projects are typically billed to an external account, usually controlled by the project manager in a strong matrix organization. At a certain point, the client accepts the completed work product, the project leaders no longer have a budget to pay for additional work, and so the resources on the project must be reassigned to other projects or released if there is no project to which they can be assigned.

Closing out a project is not nearly so straightforward or crisp when human resources that are "owned" by cost centers are used to create projects for internal customers who do not "pay" for them. In these situations, a project can often acquire a life of its own, and people who find the project goals to be exciting—or who have not been clearly informed that the project has been canceled—may continue to work on the project for weeks, months, or even years, even though managers consider it canceled.

The way to avoid this immortal-project syndrome is to put in place a clear process for terminating projects that have been completed or canceled. When a project has been completed or canceled, the project or program manager should fill out a project closeout report that lists the disposition of all of the project assets, including any intellectual property that was developed in the project, and that lists the new assignments of all personnel who had been involved in the project (which may involve their reassignment back to a departmental resource pool, or layoffs in some cases). The organizations that are most successful in closing out completed projects often have a clear career path for project managers, giving them interesting and exciting options for life beyond the current project.

To complete the transition, it is valuable to organize a victory celebration for each successfully completed project and a "wake" for each canceled project. This helps people deal with the very real emotions of pride, joy, disappointment, and sadness that they feel when a project is closed out as either a success or a failure and the team, which may include new or old friends, disbands. Absent a decent burial accompanied by a celebration or wake, projects tend to be immortal.

Realizing Benefits

Benefits are the project outcomes expressed in terms of advantages for the organization. They come in various shapes and sizes but generally show up in a finite number of tangible ways. For example:

DECREASES IN

- Development or operating cost

- Time to market

- Time to benefit

- Product cost

- Product failures

- Service delivery cost

INCREASES IN

- Revenue

- Productivity

- Profit

- Capacity

- Speed

- Flexibility

- Market appeal

Regardless of the way the benefit is expressed, the organization needs a system for ascertaining whether the expected benefits remain the right ones to focus on—as Motorola neglected to do for Iridium—and whether these benefits actually occur after the project outputs begin to be folded into ongoing operations. In other words, it must evaluate whether each project and program in the portfolio contributes successfully to the current strategy—and if not, to understand why not.

Benefits realization does not require a costly, long-drawn-out initiative. Benefits realization could start off with simply looking at the last ten projects the organization has undertaken and comparing the actual results and outcomes with what was expected when the projects were initiated. Rather than institute a large spreadsheet- or database-driven application, a more practical first step—and one that can be taken immediately—is to begin by looking even subjectively at the results created by recent projects.

Dave Kelly at IDEO Corporation has instilled in his organization a commitment to "fail often to succeed sooner."[4] In terms of benefits realization, this translates to evaluating a small sample of results of recent projects to get a better idea of what further steps may be necessary and how large an opportunity benefits realization represents for the company. After taking small steps to evaluate even at a high level what results are being generated relative to initial projections, the organization can put a more elaborate system in place to track portfolio management decisions through to project outcomes, introducing a more rigorous system for benefits realization. The important thing is to start, start soon, and start with information that is readily available.

Close the Loop

Benefits realization begins with the choice and design of projects in the engagement domain and ends with the verification of outcomes in the transition domain. But a continuous learning loop must also exist so that portfolio managers and project managers alike can consciously study the results of their work—and thereby improve future outcomes throughout the project and portfolio life cycles. This means that transition is not complete until benefits realization has closed the loop.

In an open-loop system, benefits are not fed back to the strategy-making level of the organization. The difficulty with open-loop systems is that decisions are made at the strategy level without the benefit of supporting information to confirm or deny the viability of underlying assumptions. If the outcomes of projects launched in the distant past on the basis of the best reasoning at the time are not checked for current validity, the organization fails to learn. It simply cranks out another set of decisions and hopes for the best. Too often, this lack of learning causes firms to waste significant investment money and time.

In a closed-loop system, benefits are used as a continuous cross-check for future decisions based on the efficacy of former decisions. Figure 6-3 contrasts the failures of open-loop systems with the advantages of a closed-loop benefits management system.

FIGURE 6-3

The advantages of a closed-loop benefits management system: Checking actual project outcomes against strategy makers' expectations to drive organizational learning

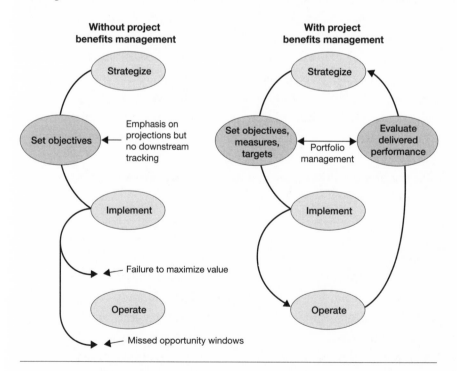

Closed-loop benefits management and benefits realization must be part and parcel of the overall management of projects. Of the many models of project management created over the last several decades, the one we find most useful has been proved over more than fifteen years. It summarizes the steps in benefits management as they occur in the life cycle of a project, as illustrated in figure 6-4.

The Project Management Body of Knowledge (PMBOK), created and maintained by the Project Management Institute, classifies the necessary stages as initiate, plan, control, execute, and close.[5] Other models use other names for the stages, but most fail to include the crucial, loop-closing far-right column, "Assess business results." The final box at the bottom of this column—"Publish benefits realization report"—may seem unnecessary and bureaucratic, but in fact it embodies the essential learning loop back to decision making at the strategy level. Managing the organization's ever-expanding body of knowledge about benefits realization is a critical skill. Unfortunately, very few companies have learned to do it effectively. Worse, most don't even try.

Shift Metrics and Incentive Systems from Output to Outcomes

To close the loop from operations to strategy and from there to goals and metrics, organizations need to take a close look at how the operating incentives connect to the strategy once the project work becomes embedded in the ongoing organization.

At transition, the performance metrics shift from those of project management—scope, cost, schedule—to those of ongoing operations. This is the transition that turns project outputs into strategic outcomes and that drives the entire organization's ability to realize its strategic intent.

For example, when the tunnels in Boston's "Big Dig" were built to carry traffic underground, the projects themselves were measured on cost, scope, and delivery schedule. On an ongoing basis (after completion of the tunnels), the aspects of maintenance costs and durability come into play as outcomes. In the case of the Boston tunnels, the now famous problem of tile falling from the ceiling of the tunnel may not have anything to do with project output but has everything to do with project outcome.

In other cases, such as the baggage system at Denver International Airport (DIA), the performance characteristics of the original design had to be

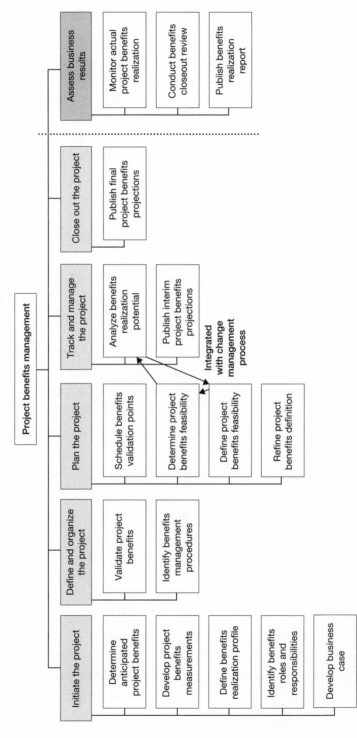

FIGURE 6-4

Stages of project management: Don't neglect to assess actual results and capture the lessons learned

Project benefits management

Initiate the project
- Determine anticipated project benefits
- Develop project benefits measurements
- Define benefits realization profile
- Identify benefits roles and responsibilities
- Develop business case

Define and organize the project
- Validate project benefits
- Identify benefits management procedures

Plan the project
- Schedule benefits validation points
- Determine project benefits feasibility
- Define project benefits feasibility
- Refine project benefits definition

Track and manage the project
- Analyze benefits realization potential
- Publish interim project benefits projections

Integrated with change management process

Close out the project
- Publish final project benefits projections

Assess business results
- Monitor actual project benefits realization
- Conduct benefits closeout review
- Publish benefits realization report

Source: Stanford Advanced Program Management, Financial Mastery of Projects

altered to transition the project into operations, and even that was a severely scaled-back version. Ultimately, the system was scrapped because it
was unable to deliver on the outcomes. The cost of the transition in a case
such as DIA is part financial and part reputation. The cost of the baggage
handling system disaster was over $200 million—while the reputation of
the supplier was a near complete loss.

"The Project List for Building Stronger Transition" lists some of the project investments that can help improve your performance on the transition
imperative.

The Project List for Building Stronger Transition

Your organization may need a significant tune-up on how programs and
projects are introduced into operations. Resources may be getting stuck.
Some of the problem may be governance. Some of it may be project and
program management process. If you're struggling with the transition imperative, consider the following project investments as a way to start getting back on track:

- Program and project closeout processes
- Technical change approval processes
- Change review using portfolio processes for decision making
- Sponsorship education
- Decision-making processes to support right decisions versus
  decision rights
- Benefits tracking systems
- Knowledge management on program completion learning
- Program and project manager reward systems
- Design-review and stage-gate processes, including outcome
  analysis requirements

Rate Your Organization on the Transition Imperative

Chances are that move-in day was more exciting than move-out day, strategy planning was much more fun than the sweat of making it work, and the concept discussions were much more entertaining than fixing the bugs. The tasks of transition may not be all that glamorous, but they are the only way to reap the full benefits of the project work and redeploy resources to the next strategic endeavor. Here is a simple questionnaire to help you rate your organization on the transition imperative.

Measuring Program and Project Transition

On a scale of 1–10, 1 = seldom true, 5 = sometimes true, 10 = almost always true.

TABLE 6-1

Measure your organization's program and project transition

	Rating (1–10)
Programs are developed, executed, and delivered to the organization in such a way that the transition to operations causes little to no disruption.	
The transition of program output and outcome to operations is executed in a predictable, repeatable, and orderly process.	
Management and leadership ensure support for smooth implementation of program outputs based on stakeholder needs.	
Changes in programs are treated as portfolio decisions. Sponsors closely monitor changes and deletions in program transitions.	
Systems are in place that provide benefit realization data and information for programs.	
Projects are developed, executed, and delivered to the organization in such a way that the transition to operations causes little or no disruption.	
The transition of project output and outcome to operations is executed in a predictable, repeatable, and orderly process.	
Management and leadership ensure support for smooth implementation of project outputs based on stakeholder needs.	
Changes in projects are treated as portfolio decisions. Sponsors closely monitor changes and deletions in project transitions.	
Systems are in place that provide benefit realization data and information for projects.	

	Rating (1–10)
The operations segment of the organization plays an integral role in the selection, oversight, and implementation of project and program outputs.	
Changes to operational processes due to project and program outputs are part of a disciplined process of change management.	
Sponsor and project leaders maintain continuity throughout the early phases of project implementation in operations to ensure that early issues are handled.	
Information is readily available for the measurement of project and program implementation effectiveness (benefits realization).	
Project and program completion are made clear (we know when we are done).	
Rewards for project and program management and team are designed to reward outputs as well as outcomes.	
	Average score:

Interpretation of average score:

➤ Below 3: Project and program transition is at high risk of robbing capacity from the organization to execute.

➤ Between 3 and 6: Transition is creating some level of waste and lowered capacity versus planned capacity.

➤ Above 6: Transition moves programs and projects into operations with minimum waste. Planned and actual capacity are very close.

Conclusion

Executing Strategy by Doing the Right Things Right

If pathfinding identifies a path, aligning paves it.
Organizations are perfectly aligned to get the results
they get. Think about that. If you are not getting the
results you want, it is due to a misalignment somewhere
in the organization and no pushing, pulling, demanding,
or insisting will change a misalignment.

—Attributed to Stephen Covey

MANAGERS AT ALL LEVELS with whom we have shared these six imperatives for strategic alignment want to understand how they can begin to apply them in their own professional and personal spheres. Knowing the six domains, translating the pieces in the domains into the imperatives of execution, and hearing compelling examples about how all those elements work together—or, in some cases, don't work together—differ from actually applying that knowledge in your own life, in your immediate organization, or in an overall enterprise. So where should you start?

The first step may be to acknowledge that every use of time, energy, or other resources is actually a strategic investment. We have emphasized that strategic project portfolio management is *always on*. Whether individuals or organizations recognize it or not, every investment leads somewhere, even if they never bother to define where they want that somewhere to be. Our goal is to help readers make conscious investment choices that will lead them toward the purpose and the goals they desire. Addressed consciously, systematically, and comprehensively, the six imperatives of strategic execution offer a road map that anyone can follow.

As we stated in the introduction, all six domains must fit together—and all six imperatives must work together—for an individual or organization to *do the right things right*. When the domains are aligned and working together, they unleash tremendous energy for the organization. Alignment is the most important message of the overall strategic execution framework (SEF), shown in figure C-1.

FIGURE C-1

The strategic execution framework

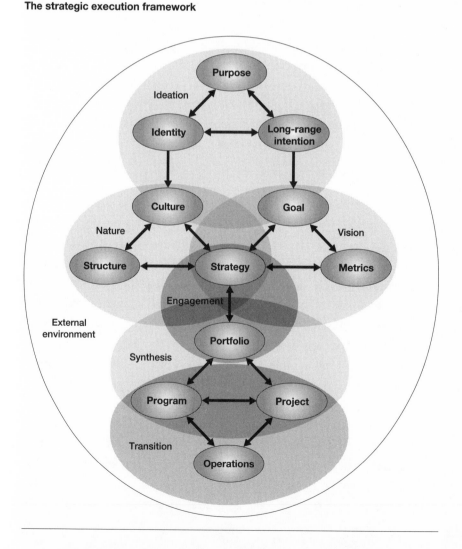

The SEF depicts the multiple moving parts of strategic execution and highlights the essential connections among them. We have emphasized throughout this book that *it is how the elements work together, how they are fused, that propels the organization toward its goals.* The six imperatives, recapitulated in table C-1, guide the work of creating the key connections. So one good way to get started is to see how well you're doing on each of the six imperatives.

You or your organization may not need to address every imperative, nor is there a necessary order in which you should address the domains most in need of alignment. The rating instruments at the ends of chapters 1 through 6 should provide the best indication of which of the imperatives are most in need of attention and, hence, where to start. One note of caution, however: if the strategy-making domains and incentives lack clarity and coherence, no amount of work on the project leadership domains can bring the organization into alignment.

Sometimes, what seems to be an execution problem actually marks a deficiency in the strategy-making domains. "Airbus Reconsidered: The Perils of Misalignment" reexamines the example of the Airbus A380, where we believe the wiring problems (which we described in chapter 5 as a failure in the synthesis domain) actually stemmed from much broader systemic misalignments in all the other domains. So the SEF could help an organization like Airbus figure out how to get back on track. And when used proactively

TABLE C-1

INVEST: Six imperatives of strategic execution

The strategy-making imperatives

The **ideation** imperative: Clarify and communicate identity, purpose, and long-range intention

The **nature** imperative: Align the organization's strategy, culture, and structure

The **vision** imperative: Translate long-range intention into clear goals, metrics, and strategy

The project leadership imperatives

The **engagement** imperative: Engage the strategy via the project investment stream

The **synthesis** imperative: Monitor and continuously align the project work with strategy

The **transition** imperative: Transfer projects crisply to operations to reap the benefits

Airbus Reconsidered

The Perils of Misalignment

Let's revisit the wiring problems that caused such disastrous delays in delivering the Airbus A380 to an eagerly awaiting market. The repeated setbacks, which we described in chapter 5 in "Lockheed Launch Vehicle Redux: The 2006 Airbus A380 Delay," cost several executives their jobs and lost billions in sales for the company. Airbus's many stumbles in delivering the A380 superjumbo jet reflect multiple, severe misalignments in its strategic execution framework.

First, Airbus's *ideation* was never a conventional corporate ideation. Airbus viewed its *identity* as a pan-European counterweight (with units in Germany, France, Spain, and the United Kingdom) to the strong U.S. commercial aircraft industry. Airbus's complex corporate governance system and dual management structure were designed with the *purpose* not of maximizing revenue or even job creation but rather of allocating whatever jobs and revenue it could generate equitably among the countries that owned it—particularly Germany and France. So while Boeing has shrunk its workforce 40 percent and outsourced many aspects of its production to lower-cost manufacturing locations, Airbus employment has grown 25 percent across Europe. Yet Airbus espoused a distinctly business-oriented *vision*—to compete head-to-head with Boeing in the hypercompetitive commercial aircraft marketplace, in which existing and new carriers and aircraft-leasing companies carefully evaluate each new aircraft, using metrics like fuel consumption and operating cost per passenger-mile, and make long–lead time purchase commitments accordingly.

Compounding Airbus's political ideation versus business vision misalignment was a *nature* domain misalignment. Both France and Germany have *cultures* that support strong labor unions that watched closely over decisions about where to manufacture particular aircraft or aircraft com-

to create and maintain the right alignments, the framework helps guide individuals and organizations to do the right things right every time.

We dedicate part of this closing chapter to two shining examples of the concepts behind the SEF in action. One features a large public organization, the Singapore National Library Board (SNLB). The other is the story

ponents. This led to the disastrous *structure* misalignment, in which the decision was made to separate highly interdependent aspects of A380 design and production. The design and manufacture of the electrical wire harnesses and the rear section of the fuselage were allocated to Hamburg, Germany, while the main part of the fuselage would be assembled in a plant in Toulouse, France. The rear section of the fuselage would then be transported from Hamburg to Toulouse to be mated with the main fuselage section, and the wire harnesses originating in the rear of the fuselage would have to be threaded into the main section upon final assembly in Toulouse.[a]

Variations in the configuration of in-seat passenger entertainment systems sold to different customers made the design of each set of A380 wire harnesses a highly customized process, involving a reciprocal interdependency (as discussed in chapter 5), requiring a great deal of coordination and checking. Further compounding the key misalignments in the ideation, vision, and nature domains, Airbus designers in Hamburg used an earlier version of the CATIA CAD software than the fuselage assembly team in Toulouse did—a serious misalignment in the *synthesis* domain, since CATIA files were not backward compatible across release versions. So, when workers in Toulouse attempted to install the wire harnesses in the main section of the fuselage, the harnesses simply would not fit! The resulting chaos around redesigning and reinstalling the wiring destroyed any hope for crisp project closeout and timely *transition* to operations. By early 2007, the two-year delays and multiple order cancellations were estimated to have cost Airbus over $6 billion in lost sales.

In March 2007, the Airbus A380 program received yet another body blow when UPS canceled its order for ten A380s, which did not even require passenger entertainment systems. Severe misalignments within and across multiple SEF domains had derailed the execution of Airbus's business-critical A380 program.

a. Carol Matlack, "Airbus: The Ride Just Got Bumpier," *BusinessWeek Online*, October 10, 2006.

of Lance Armstrong and his small team. In each of these cases, we can see how a systematic, comprehensive approach manifested itself in the achievement of extraordinary results.

Both cases describe instances where people and organizations *intuitively* fulfilled the six imperatives, as successful individuals and organizations often do. In fact, our work over seven years with the SNLB and in similar undertakings for other organizations gave us the impetus to codify its intuitive success patterns in the strategic execution framework and the six imperatives. Whether consciously and systematically adopted or instinctively applied, the six imperatives work for individuals, teams, business units, overall enterprises, government agencies, and—as the SNLB example illustrates—entire populations.

We then look at some of the ways that individuals, teams, local organizations, and overall enterprises can begin to employ the underpinning principles that the imperatives represent. We conclude with a plea for the role of alignment in creating better workplaces, and our own answer to the question, What now?

Creating the Right Alignments: Singapore National Library Board

Among the most difficult strategic execution challenges in the world is causing a government agency to effect significant organizational change. The long-standing, sometimes rigid culture and the hierarchical, sometimes messy structure of government agencies tend to limit the chances of getting substantive change to happen in real time. Aggressive goals, clear metrics, and executable strategy are often obscured in such organizations by long-standing tradition, entrenched thinking, and a lack of clarity about purpose, identity, and long-range intent that develops over long periods of complacency.

The Singapore National Library Board is a notable exception. In its case, since documented in a Harvard case study, the leadership of the organization brought about substantive change in a relatively short time and created outstanding operational results.[1] This case illustrates the power of the strategic execution framework in aligning all the necessary forces to effect practical change on a large scale.

In May 2001, Christopher Chia, chief executive of the Singapore National Library Board, summarized the results of his organization's massive transformational effort for the new millennium:

> In six years we quadrupled the visitorship, tripled the collection, and doubled the membership and the physical space. We increased our loan rate from 10 million to 25 million books without a corresponding increase in staff, and generally reduced queues from 60 minutes to 15 minutes. Four times more people walk around a space not more than

twice the size, yet libraries feel more spacious. No jobs were lost. 800,000 members joined the library during the first 35 years of the library system compared to one million in just the last five years.[2]

These are the results of six years of dedicated effort. Strictly speaking, these are operational outcomes. How did they happen? Was Chia simply lucky? Was this serendipity? We don't think so.

From a statement printed in the library report of 2000, it becomes apparent that the SNLB built toward operational outcomes using a comprehensive approach that integrated every domain from ideation through transition. The 2000 report includes the following powerful statement: "Our purpose is . . . to support the advancement of Singapore."[3]

The title of the report, *Investing in a Learning Nation*, is most telling. The SNLB considered the transformation of the library as an investment—an investment with a purpose. George Yeo, the minister for information and the arts, further elaborated on purpose in the 2000 report: "My ministry borrowed its mission from the BBC—'to inform, educate, and entertain.'"[4]

Minister Yeo set up the Library 2000 Review Committee—a structural move—in order to gain clarity around long-range intention. The committee, in turn, settled on a long-range vision for Singapore to become a "first league developed country in terms of economic dynamism, quality-of-life, national identity, and global reach." Thus the SNLB achieved alignment in the ideation domain by establishing a purpose to support the advancement of Singapore; an identity as a place for people to learn, explore, and discover; and a long-range intention of making the citizenry information-literate. Those three elements taken collectively formed the basis for all actions moving forward. They were further reinforced and repeatedly emphasized by the actions and statements of the library's leaders.

For example, Yeo explained, "Libraries had to change as technological advances were affecting the way users obtain information and knowledge. The library function has a national competitiveness dimension as well as a quality-of-life dimension."

Some organizations are puzzled by their inability to effect change. One source of that inability, in our experience, comes from leaders failing to articulate purpose and intention as coherently as Yeo does in the above statement. And of course, articulating your purpose and intention is a continuous task: Yeo needed to reinforce the statements in the review committee's report with his every activity and utterance.

The SNLB focused on three dimensions that represent a somewhat unusual combination in today's business strategies:

- Organizational leadership

- Technology

- Human resources

Of course, attacking the problem from three fronts simultaneously is not an appropriate strategy for every organization. It worked for the SNLB, though. The following quotation offers further insight into Chia's systems view of strategic execution: "In a transformation you have many things start at once. About one third of what you try will fail, but that is the cost of change. We felt that the first three years would be key. Everything is interrelated. We could not introduce change in small bite sizes one at a time. Every change had an impact on other changes. [W]e had to coordinate and move simultaneously on all fronts."

In the area of organizational leadership, the priorities were to build a management team capability that would boost staff confidence, reduce resistance to change, and support a flexible structure and effective management system. So the first projects that the SNLB team took on aimed to focus on the responsibilities of leadership in accomplishing these objectives. This is highly unusual. Most strategy-making teams do not accept such accountability for project leadership, nor do they see accountability as strategic in any way, shape, or form. And flawed incentive systems typically reflect and reinforce this flawed mind-set.

The strategy for technology focused on streamlining and improving service delivery and increasing efficiency of library services. Significantly, the SNLB approached technology as a servant, not a master—that is, it used technology to serve the strategy, not to drive it.

The human resources aspect of the strategy focused on changing the hiring process, building a flexible organization, implementing standards and training, and introducing performance evaluation and recognition. Notice that two-thirds of the strategy revolved around people: developing organizational leaders and developing people capability across the enterprise. And the technology aspect was designed to serve the human organization.

Chia provided a clear, concise, and straightforward expression of the SNLB's approach and set the tone for decision making. He elaborated on the role of technology: "The message was that the library's transformation is first about people and new services, not new gadgets and the latest technologies. Technology should be seen as an enabler."[5]

Along with the alignment of ideation, the SNLB made some clear choices about how to structure itself as it approached its strategic agenda. In the following quotation, Chia lays out how structure and strategy were aligned and made to work together: "We realize that a hierarchical structure is good for stability, but not good if you want to make a lot of changes happen quickly. So we try to encourage teamwork. We said that we will try things; if they work, we will quickly enhance and spread them around. If they don't we will retire them and look for alternatives."[6]

This is a clear demonstration of what it truly means to set cultural tone, structure, and strategy in alignment with one another. A flat, team-oriented structure, a strategy that encourages and adopts a portfolio of experiments, and a no-excuses, no-blame culture emerged in the library and acted to its benefit.

Since the library oriented its ideation toward users and user outcomes, it is not surprising that the measures used to gauge success aimed at transforming the user experience, as monitored along four key metrics:

- Time to market

- Time to shelf

- Time to checkout

- Time to information

These metrics served to drive the strategy. They also helped optimize the selection of investments in the project portfolio. By using these metrics to track progress toward clearly defined goals, the SNLB aligned strategic vision with strategic engagement in an appropriate portfolio of projects and programs.

Many organizations experience tremendous difficulty in aligning this critical interface. They struggle, or perhaps neglect, to determine which metrics to associate with which goals, and which projects to undertake to accomplish each goal. Absent these alignments, organizations are unable to show the causal relationship between the work going on in the organization, its contribution to key metrics, and therefore the linkage to organizational objectives. Because this critical linkage typically does not exist, most organizations find themselves unable to determine where they stand on the path to strategic execution, since there's no way to tell which project is doing what work, associated with what goal, driving what performance along what metric.

Most strategic execution failures stem from this sort of ad hoc, unorchestrated, and chaotic approach to measuring and rewarding progress toward outcomes. In contrast, the SNLB's coherence in managing to these metrics internally resulted in significant bottom-line results. The membership target of 1.5 million reached a 2.2 million actual in 2003. Walk-in visits, targeted to be 18 million, rose to 32 million in 2003. Books and CD-ROM loans reached 32 million against a 27 million goal. Digital searches skyrocketed to 11 million against the 2 million goal. Collections rose from 3.4 million to 9.3 million, compared with the original 11.4 million goal.[7]

The 2003 results speak for themselves. In every area except for collections, the SNLB far exceeded its original goals. Along the way, the ratio of compliments to complaints went from 1:4 to 22:1.[8]

Accomplishing the work that generated these results entailed investing in and managing a rich portfolio of projects and programs:

- Training over two hundred people in project management methodology

- Training selected people in program management

- Providing coaching for project and program managers

- Setting up a program management office

- Establishing discipline for technical change management

- Using workshops for mission-critical SNLB projects

- Implementing a portfolio management system

The SNLB provides a prime example of what happens to operational results when organizations take a comprehensive approach to aligning ideation, nature, vision, engagement, synthesis, and transition. Though the SNLB did not consciously adopt the strategic execution framework, its work and its outcomes clearly show that it fulfilled all six imperatives.

The strategic execution framework is an outgrowth of our on-the-ground observations of what actually works (including what worked for the SNLB), not what theoretically works. Some organizations understand many of the imperatives but may address only one or two of them. Some may excel in vision but not in engagement. Some are operationally efficient but build the wrong thing strategically and therefore suffer poor performance. The SNLB example shows leaders and managers working in sync to accomplish all six imperatives and deliver extraordinary performance for a large governmental agency.

Tour de Lance

Or was that Tour de France? From the mid-1990s through 2005, it was hard to tell. Lance Armstrong and his U.S. Postal Service team, followed by Lance Armstrong and his Discovery Channel team, won the most difficult athletic encounter in the world for an astonishing seven straight years. The Tour de France bicycle race takes place over approximately three weeks of racing, averaging six to eight hours a day over ever-changing and often grueling terrain. It has no equal in terms of a physical endurance challenge.

The Tour is a team sport. Lance Armstrong and his team have set a standard that will be very difficult for another individual and team to equal. It will now take the better part of a decade of continuous winning to surpass the record Armstrong and his team created. So the questions are the same for Armstrong as for the SNLB. Was it luck? Was it a weak field of competitors? Was it superior technology?

Or was it drugs? We don't think so. Long before Armstrong ever set the record for consecutive wins, he was the subject of a video titled "Who Says We Can't Do It?"[9] He also wrote a book (with Sally Jenkins) called *It's Not About the Bike* and, later, another, *Every Second Counts*.[10] The video and the books offer numerous clues as to how Armstrong and his team accomplished their now legendary results. Without ever using our domain names, Armstrong orchestrated the six imperatives—from ideation right through to transition—at a masterful level. We will examine each one of them in order.

Armstrong and the Ideation Imperative

When Armstrong was a young man, by his own admission he had what he considered fair athletic talent but never made the most of it. He experimented with several sports before settling on bicycle racing. In his documentary, he relates that he raced as fast as he possibly could without much thought toward strategy. He became somewhat successful by his now global standard in doing so. Given his level of physical talent, operating without clear strategy was working at least on some level for him.

Then came cancer. Armstrong was diagnosed with testicular cancer that spread to his abdomen, to his lungs, and eventually to his brain. He endured long months of treatment and his prognosis was bleak. But somehow he triumphed over the cancer and it went into remission.

Still having some passion for cycling, Armstrong got back on the competitive circuit. But the enjoyment was no longer there. In the middle of a race in France called Paris–Nice, Armstrong stopped. He simply pulled over to the side of the road, got off his bike, and quit. His teammates thought that he was through forever, that he would never return to cycling. Armstrong went back to Texas, where, by his own account, he experienced a feeling of being lost. But that lost feeling ended in a most unusual fashion.

Armstrong went on a bicycling trip to North Carolina. The weather was cold, rainy, and gloomy, yet somehow during that trip he regained his passion for racing. For him it was a tipping point. In his video he describes falling back in love with what he did for living and, in his words, "what I was probably *supposed* to be doing for a living."[11]

This statement reveals a very strong sense of purpose. Whether Armstrong recognized it at the time or not, he had just reached clarity of purpose, identity, and intent. Somehow the experience with cancer and the subsequent soul-searching had acquainted Armstrong with his lifelong purpose. Whether we choose to view his identity as a bicycle racer, a cancer survivor, a cancer survivor advocate, or a cancer research fund-raiser is more or less immaterial to the fact that Armstrong found his ideation and therefore his sense of drive.

Armstrong made his video after his first Tour de France victory, and even at that time, his coach and his sponsor recognized that it wasn't just about the bike. In the video they both describe Armstrong as responding to a higher calling, and they acknowledge that in the grand scheme of things, working toward curing cancer is a higher priority for Armstrong than racing bicycles. However, racing bicycles provides him with the recognition or brand equity, the portfolio choices, the funding, the visibility, and the networking with which to explore his larger agenda of finding a cure for cancer and supporting people who have cancer. Armstrong's sense of drive, determination, and dedication emanate from this deep-rooted sense of ideation.

Armstrong and the Nature Imperative

Culture, structure, and strategy: the three elements of the nature domain. How does a bicycling team make use of the idea of hierarchical versus flat structures? What does strong matrix versus weak matrix structure mean for their work? Does it matter whether a bicycling team adopts a control culture or one that emphasizes competence, cultivation, or collaboration?

As it turns out, culture, structure, and strategy were crucial to Armstrong and his team. Armstrong used a flat structure without much discernible hierarchy in order to accomplish his goals, his team's goals, and his sponsor's goals. Armstrong himself was clearly the focal point of the team. All team members were selected specifically to fill certain roles in accomplishing the goal of getting Armstrong across the finish line first. Thus, the culture of his organization was extremely collaborative. All team members knew the role they played and how their role contributed to the overall performance of the team. Certain team members were recruited for flat stages of the race. Others were chosen specifically for hill climbing.

The basic strategy as embodied in the team culture and structure was to place specific people in specific roles during specific stages of the race in order to support Armstrong's overall speed. Some team members worked on blocking other teams. Others worked on creating draft to reduce air resistance for Armstrong to keep him as strong as possible throughout the race and as fresh as possible at the end. So Armstrong's organization consciously took a strategic view of structure and culture. The team's alignment among culture, structure, and strategy became a significant competitive weapon. Lance Armstrong and his team brought the ability to create competitive advantage through culture, structure, and strategy alignment to a new global standard.

Armstrong and the Vision Imperative

When it comes to racing bicycles or winning the Tour de France, it may not seem immediately obvious that goals, metrics, and strategy are as critical to Lance Armstrong and his team as they are to Southwest Airlines, IBM, Capital One, or Ford Motor Company. But a closer look at what made Armstrong and his team effective reveals that goals and metrics figure prominently in the way they prepared, the way they executed, and therefore the way they performed.

In fact, the team relied heavily on numbers to prepare for the Tour. The main variables in the ability to win the race are the weight of the bike, the weight of the body on the bike, and the power of the legs that propel the two. As the weight of the body decreases and the power of the legs increases, the total power available in the system increases. So Armstrong and his team operated from several different kinds of goals and metrics. One set was built around body weight, leg strength, and bicycle weight—but that was only one set.

Another entire set of goals and metrics applied for time trials and individual stages of the Tour. In the months before each race, Armstrong rode almost every segment of the Tour. In planning his overall race strategy, he set goals for which stages were a must-win and by how much. By assigning priorities for various stages and setting goals and metrics for each one, Armstrong was articulating strategy. That's one of the ways that it's possible to know when goals and metrics align with strategy. When strategy, goals, and metrics can all be used in coherent sentences, chances are that there is an alignment among all three.

Most organizations are nowhere near as clear as Armstrong's team in articulating goals, metrics, and strategy. It is much more common for a leader to say something like "Our strategy is to be a world leader in our field and earn greater than average profit." There's nothing wrong with that sort of statement—except that it's not specific enough to be actionable. Armstrong and his team knew exactly which races or segments they had to win and understood the target time margins for each intermediate victory. They also knew which races or segments were less important, and consequently they knew where to put their focus as a team.

Armstrong and the Engagement Imperative

The engagement domain offers an opportunity to examine strategy from yet a third point of view. It is the view of strategy as linked to portfolio management. The engagement imperative requires making portfolio investments that are coherent, consistent, supportive, and enabling to the strategy.

Regarding the goals and metrics of body weight, for example, certain portfolio decisions are consistent with that goal and that metric, and some are not. Certain types of foods translate into caloric intake, fat intake, salt intake, and so on that are completely consistent with the goals and metrics. Other foods do not. Armstrong and his teammates couldn't consume unlimited amounts of carbohydrates and alcohol and still achieve their objectives. So their choice of nutrition during training offers an example of a portfolio decision. The team's menu, exercise routine, sleep habits, where they trained, when they trained, with whom they trained, who was on the team, and how much time they spent with the press, in team meetings, on race strategy, or on reviewing maps all factored into their overall success—and every one of these choices was a portfolio decision.

The same set of portfolio decisions is available to all teams racing in the Tour de France. However, Armstrong and his team were clearly better than their opponents at aligning goals, metrics, culture, structure, strategy, and portfolio decisions.

Armstrong and the Synthesis Imperative

After all is said and done about using a very strong sense of ideation to formulate strategy and align goals, metrics, culture, structure, and portfolio investments, winning or losing comes down to synthesis. Armstrong and his team had to perform to their goals and metrics. They had to prioritize and invest in every time trial and stage as a strategic project. Taken together, the projects formed a portfolio of programs.

The Tour de France, in a sense, is a program. It was not the only race that Armstrong and his team took on every year—so they had to synthesize and monitor their investments in all the races, segments, and other activities they undertook each year. In Armstrong's case, the larger purpose of supporting cancer research added a whole range of other projects and programs to the portfolio. Each piece was critical. Success depended on the accumulated effect of all the projects being completed as planned.

But sometimes things don't go as planned. A stage is not won, a time trial is lost, a margin of victory is not attained—or perhaps a potential fund-raising appearance conflicts with the training schedule. When any of those things happened, Armstrong and his team had to reevaluate their portfolio decisions and revise their strategic decisions in order to win. This underscores the dynamic nature of portfolio management. Armstrong and the team learned to adjust midrace to unforeseen outcomes. They couldn't wait until the end of the race to look at lag indicators and then make a change and still win the race. They had to replan in real time.

Armstrong and the Transition Imperative

The U.S. Postal Service racing team, which became the Discovery Channel racing team, was almost a pure project organization. Every race was a project. Every prep day was a project. Practically every activity was time bound, scope bound, and resource bound. That made every activity essentially a project. Transition, which is the interface between project management and operations, operated in a unique way for Armstrong. What happened in a race or on a practice day became an opportunity for learning to improve performance during the next project. So what the team learned each day became part of the preparation for the next day's race.

In relating Lance Armstrong to the transition imperative, the key thing to remember is that the ongoing operation of a race essentially is project management: there's no way to separate Armstrong's project management from Armstrong's operational management.

Deciding Where to Start

The examples of the Singapore National Library Board and Lance Armstrong demonstrate how the overall framework of strategic execution works and how the imperatives operate both at organizational levels and for individuals and smaller teams. But understanding an example in someone else's world does not necessarily translate to the ability to execute in our world. As Clayton Christensen points out in *Seeing What's Next*, best practice is often what used to work in someone else's context.[12]

Just because something worked at Singapore National Library or for Lance Armstrong does not necessarily mean it will work for anybody else. The strategic execution framework offers a systematic, integrative approach for choosing the right projects and implementing them in the right way. It does not provide the answers themselves. But it does offer a plan for converting strategy into action. Every individual, team, division, business unit, or overall organization must decide where best to embark on the journey through the six imperatives. Fortunately, there are tools and questions that can help determine where to start.

Consider the Framework from a 30,000-Foot View

Look at the overall framework. Consider the challenges, the obstacles, and the frustrations that your organization experiences today. Chances are that without delving into months of tedious data analysis, you will see some relatively obvious leverage points even from a helicopter view. Remember that most of the risk of strategic execution comes from the interfaces, or the arrows in the model. It is not goals per se, or metrics per se, or strategy per se; rather, it is how the three are aligned or misaligned that matters most.

Hovering at 30,000 feet, select one of those arrows that seems to be the most problematic; then zoom in and explore what generates the misalignment and what could be done about it. Engage a team of people early in the process. It is far better to involve a team in a meaningful conversation about generating the right questions than to have lots of answers to the wrong questions. Recognize that your judgment is probably as accurate as reams of analysis at this stage.

We have observed over and over that people are extraordinarily perceptive in pinpointing where fundamental misalignments occur when they engage in thoughtful dialogue using the framework as a basis for discussion. Don't worry about being too precise or about getting exactly the right entrance point to strategic execution. The entire system is connected, so no matter where you enter it, you will eventually find the misalignments if you approach it systematically.

Go Fast, Go Ugly

This is not about perfection. It is about excellence. Analysis paralysis does not lead to better strategic execution. Any incremental improvement in getting goals to line up with metrics, metrics to line with up the strategy, structure to line up with strategy, and so on is a step in the right direction. Certainly, a comprehensive approach is beneficial, so long as that comprehensive approach doesn't turn into another endless debate, a series of high-level meetings and off-sites with no results, or a 50-pound plan that nobody ever executes.

Lance Armstrong does not have a three-thousand-page run book. Nordstrom has only one operational rule: "Use your good judgment in all situations. There will be no additional rules."[13] So getting started is not about adding complexity. It's about finding clarity.

Don't Wait for a Miracle from Above

Small teams can work miracles. In one organization that we work directly with, we discovered a hero who transformed her area of the business against some large odds. This person took on the task of implementing portfolio management in an organization that by its own admission was extremely process averse. The organization had operated over a long period of time with very little fiscal accountability and process control. But eventually, the strategic direction of the organization made portfolio management an imperative. What this person did was to start with a small group of people and design a system for portfolio management that gained immediate governance support at the highest levels in the organization.

The team's smartest move was to make sure that the processes they were designing did not receive a global high-level announcement. The process began operation without any official fanfare. The benefits to the organization soon began to become evident, and overall organizational acceptance of the portfolio management process gradually and almost imperceptibly took hold. Eventually, the process of portfolio management began to be valued and widely emulated across the company instead of being resisted.

The organizational engineering demonstrated by the person orchestrating this change was nothing short of masterful. The processes have become so strong that even high-ranking people cannot circumvent the system. This was tested when a senior executive attempted to go around the system, only to find that the executive management team would not support any project request that did not go through the process.

This example demonstrates that organizational change can originate at any level. It is true that executive support and executive sponsorship are crucial. But executive sponsorship is not necessarily the origination point. A small team of people can create a significant revolution. Waiting for a miracle from above via edict, executive order, or divine intervention is not the most productive way to generate change. Small teams working on focused actions are more often the key to creating real improvement in organizations.

Ask the Acid Test Questions

Many people simply want to cut to the chase to determine where their organization stands relative to alignment. In addition to the rating instruments in chapters 1 through 6, there are some simple high-level questions whose answers give a reasonably clear indication of where the opportunities lie. The following six questions cover the overall framework and the six imperatives.

- *Question 1—Ideation strength:* Are the reason the organization exists, the internal and external branding, and the long-range intention clear enough and compelling enough to attract the right people and energize them to perform at their very best on a daily basis?

- *Question 2—Vision clarity:* Are the goals, measurements, and reward systems designed so that people at all levels know exactly what to do to meet their own and the organization's goals and metrics?

- *Question 3—Structure and culture alignment:* Is the enterprise structured in a way that makes its work easier to accomplish, and does its culture support the types of working relationships the strategy requires?

- *Question 4—Engagement effectiveness:* Can the organization trace the connections between its portfolio of project investments and the strategic goals that the investments are intended to achieve?

- *Question 5—Synthesis effectiveness:* Do the project and program investments support each other and truly reflect the espoused strategy of the organization?

- *Question 6—Transition effectiveness:* Do the project outputs translate rapidly and seamlessly into the intended tangible benefits for the ongoing operations?

By starting with such targeted and focused questions and constantly refining them to fit the organization's reality, individuals and teams can begin to find the right traction points among the elements inside each of the domains. The right answer to the wrong question is useless. Even a marginal answer to the right question is more useful.

The most useful questions come from integrative thinking. Disintegrative, parochial thinking produces narrow, piecemeal questions rather than the broader kind of inquiry that is necessary for generating effective action to create better alignment and better performance. The value of better questions and better-aligned enterprises is better performance and a better life experience.

Getting Alignment Right to Create a Better Workplace

In the 1950s and 1960s, when technological advances, work-saving appliances, and new gadgets of every kind began to explode in availability and popularity, the conventional wisdom projected that our biggest problem around the turn of the millennium was going to be how to deal with all the extra time on our hands. In our travels and in our experience, this problem does not seem to have materialized. With cell phones, pagers, PDAs, BlackBerrys, and wireless technology, we are now capable of working 24/7, globally, 365 days a year.

This poses a significant problem with regard to humanity in the workplace and quality of life overall. The constant push for availability to the

Toward Humanity in the Workplace

The transformation of work in the twenty-first century is, in many respects, a call for humanity—the new consciousness that suggests more than simply trying to strike a balance between our work and our personal life. It is a call to honor our own individuality and fully engage our human spirit at work—whatever that may be. While this idea of empowering workers in body, mind, and spirit is not new, actually putting it to work is new. In some ways, our technological advances have redesigned work to better accommodate human factors. What we need now is a way to elevate the human spirit at work.[a]

It is difficult to tell which comes first: great performance or employees' perception of a great working environment.[b] In fact, the best-aligned companies can strive for both simultaneously: perform better and become a better place to work at the same time. The six imperatives offer a guide for formulating the actions necessary to accomplish just that. As the baby boomers reach retirement age and the gap for knowledge workers widens, competition for top performers will increase. Misaligned organizations are at a disadvantage in attracting the skills necessary to compete effectively. Organizations that offer a better-aligned place to work will enjoy a significant advantage in their ability to recruit and retain the kind of talent that generates outstanding performance.

Which of the following two company descriptions is most likely to attract and maintain an outstanding performing work force that would vote it "best"?

- *Company A:* purposeful, well branded, well intended, goal oriented, streamlined, fiscally disciplined, persistent, intellectually curious, successful

- *Company B:* purposeless, aimless, without goals, directionless, unmeasured, unfocused, fickle, underperforming

boss, to the customer, and to the family is bringing about a new set of challenges people must overcome to retain their sanity. It is highly unlikely that the pressures of professional life are going to subside. However, fully aligned organizations can offer better balance in the workplace and in workers' broader lives. This is a quest well worth striving for, as described in "Toward Humanity in the Workplace."

The message is obvious. Very few top players want to work for company B. Most top players want to work for company A. That could be why long lines form whenever Yahoo!, eBay, Google, Southwest, or IDEO announce job openings. People like to compete. People like to win. People like to be successful. It's all part of humanity—and company B could be characterized as an inhumane place to work.

One way to summarize this in terms of the imperatives is:

- Ideation drives motivation.

- Nature aligns the wind, waves, and currents of strategy, culture, and structure for smooth sailing.

- Vision gives people a destination to aim for.

- Engagement connects knowing with doing.

- Synthesis helps people work together on doing the right things right.

- Transition embeds project learning, improves sustainability, and creates pride of ownership.

Together, the six imperatives enable companies to create more humanity in the workplace. Doing the right things right enhances the quality of working life and increases performance simultaneously. It is the most important I-N-V-E-S-T-ment an organization can make.

---

a. Alex Pattakos, *Prisoners of Our Thoughts: Viktor Frankl's Principles at Work* (San Francisco: Berrett-Koehler, 2004), 6.

b. As Phil Rosenzweig points out, people ascribe the title of being a "best" company to work in largely on the basis of the organization's overall success; see Philip M. Rosenzweig, *The Halo Effect and Other Business Delusions: Why the Experts Are So Often Wrong—And How to Get It Right* (New York: Free Press, 2007), 61–64. In other words, the knowledge of good performance drives the impression of being a great place to work.

What Now?

This book is a starting point, not an end point. It is the beginning of what we hope will be a rich, ongoing dialogue. Already we see many topics on the horizon to be addressed. For example:

- More integrative thinking about how the six imperatives can be better linked and aligned

- Better business processes to help create better linkage end to end from ideation to transition

- Communities of practice to promote better alignment among the six imperatives

- Integrated tools to create scalable governance processes for linking and managing strategic projects from concept to reality

- Better ways to incorporate leading practices, because best practice is what used to work for someone else in their context, not what will work for us in our context in real time

- Better ways to generate situational awareness, or an understanding of where we are relative to where we want to be

- More research on metapatterns

- More thought and research on the connections between strategy making and project leadership

- Better integration of decision-making models

- Broader development of organizational engineers

- Better connections between visual planning tools and linear tracking tools

When strategy makers and project leaders truly work together to convert strategy into action, they create organizations that outperform others and are attractive places for people to invest their productive energy. In these great companies, we suggest that the role of CEO would be better described as chief *execution* officer. After all, *executive* and *execution* differ by only two letters—and leaders can excel only if they master strategic execution.

As authors, educators, and consultants, we dedicate a significant portion of our lives to helping organizations achieve better results through the six imperatives. But the job of generating alignment extends far beyond any small group of people. We look forward with eager anticipation to feedback from readers of this book that will help us create new tools, new processes, and new insights into all the ways the six imperatives can improve performance for individuals, teams, and organizations of all sizes.

Notes

Introduction

1. Jeffrey Pfeffer and Robert I. Sutton, *The Knowing-Doing Gap: How Smart Companies Turn Knowledge into Action* (Boston: Harvard Business School Press, 1999), 1–2.

2. Walter Kiechel, "Corporate Strategists Under Fire," *Fortune*, December 27, 1982, 38. See also Ram Charan and Geoffrey Colvin, "Why CEOs Fail," *Fortune*, June 1999, 69–78; this article reports a similar failure rate, of 70 percent. Both articles are discussed in Robert S. Kaplan and David P. Norton, *The Strategy-Focused Organization: How Balanced Scorecard Companies Thrive in the New Business Environment* (Boston: Harvard Business School Press, 2001), 1.

3. Cathleen Benko and F. Warren McFarlan, *Connecting the Dots: Aligning Projects with Objectives in Unpredictable Times* (Boston: Harvard Business School Press, 2003), 3.

4. As an example of someone who gets it, the CEO of Southwest Airlines, Gary Kelly, recently has been pondering whether to add assigned seating to the mix of services within Southwest. The project would represent roughly a $5 million investment for Southwest. According to *USA Today* (Dan Reed, "Southwest Closer to Assigned Seating," June 21, 2006), the CEO was holding that decision pending a review of the return on investment from implementing such a system and how it would really contribute to the service offering. An investment of $5 million is small for a company the size of Southwest. But given the strategic importance of the passenger boarding process to Southwest Airlines' business model, it is clear why the CEO is involved in the decision of whether to implement assigned seating. This is a case of an executive who doesn't consider making project and program portfolio decisions and being involved in execution as beneath his "pay grade."

5. Robert L. Simons and Antonio Davila, "How High Is Your Return on Management?" *Harvard Business Review*, January–February 1998, 71–80.

6. Ibid., 73.

7. Jeffrey Pfeffer and Robert I. Sutton, *Hard Facts, Dangerous Half-Truths, and Total Nonsense: Profiting from Evidence-Based Management* (Boston: Harvard Business School Press, 2006), 156.

8. Michael E. Porter, "What Is Strategy?" *Harvard Business Review*, November–December 1996, 61–78.

9. Ibid., 64.

10. Lawrence Hrebiniak, *Making Strategy Work* (Upper Saddle River, NJ: Wharton School Publishing, 2005), 11.

11. Geoffrey Carr, "A Survey of the Brain," *Economist*, December 23, 2006. Carr offers this example of a patient whose corpus callosum has been severed: "Sometimes the two

hemispheres have completely different personalities, and where that happens the individual's behaviour does change—indeed, he ceases to be an individual as the hemispheres fight for control of the body. The conflict often manifests itself in the person's hands, each controlled by a different hemisphere, trying to do opposing things. One hand may try to put on a piece of clothing, for example, while the other tries to remove it." Seldom have we seen a more fitting metaphor for an organization whose executive strategy makers behave as if they have no connection with the people who must implement the strategy. In such an organization, the old saw applies: the right hand doesn't know what the left hand is doing.

12. We describe both Iridium and Odyssey in detail in chapter 4 and revisit Odyssey in chapter 5.

13. *Webster's Dictionary* defines *ideation* as "the process of forming ideas or images."

14. A further note on these domain names: we intentionally chose words that are not all common entries in the business lexicon. This helps us avoid falling into the trap of using what Dilbert creator Scott Adams calls "weasel words"; see *Dilbert and the Way of the Weasel* (London: Pan MacMillan, 2003). *Mission*, for example, is glaringly absent from the strategic execution framework, and for good reason. Its meaning has become so muddied that Adams developed a "mission statement generator" that assembles meaningless buzzwords in random combinations to create equally useless mission statements. Adams, who is nowhere near as recognizable as the iconic Dilbert, has gone so far as to run fake half-day meetings, posing as a consultant to help executives create mission statements that he later reveals as hollow weasel-word drivel; see Scott Adams, The Official Dilbert Web Site, Mission Statement Generator Page, http://www.dilbert.com/comics/dilbert/games/career/bin/ms.cgi. Not the best use of the executives' time, but a rather pointed, if painful, lesson to learn about language and meaning in business.

Furthermore, we believe there is too often a disconnect between the words that strategy makers use and the words that project leaders use. Thinking about meanings in a new way will help both groups engage in the kinds of conversations that are essential to strategic execution.

15. We are indebted to one of our Stanford Advanced Project Management course participants, Peter Tapscott, for bringing this example to our attention. See also Robert Collier, "Behind Toyota's Hybrid Revolution: Automaker's Successful Gamble with Prius Fuels Its Image as a Trendsetter," *San Francisco Chronicle*, April 24, 2006, http://www.sfgate.com/cgi-bin/article.cgi?f=/c/a/2006/04/24/MNG3JIE6DK1.DTL&hw=toyota&sn=002&sc=410 (and other references).

16. The description of Wipro draws on personal interviews and the Web sources http://en.wikipedia.org/wiki/Wipro and http://www.wipro.com.

17. "Creating a World Class Cadre," internal presentation at Wipro, Bangalore, India, May 2006.

Chapter 1

1. Sharon Beder, "BP: Beyond Petroleum?" http://www.uow.edu.au/arts/sts/sbeder/bp.html.

2. William Maclean, "BP Goes Greener with 'Beyond Petroleum' Rebrand," Planet Ark, July 25, 2000, http://www.planetark.org/dailynewsstory.cfm?newsid=7577.

3. Kenny Bruno, "BP: Beyond Petroleum or Beyond Preposterous?" December 14, 2000, http://www.corpwatch.org/article.php?id=219; Paul K. Driessen, "BP: Beyond Petroleum—or Beyond Probity?" 2002, http://www.cdfe.org/driessen.htm; Andrew Gumbel and Marie Woolf, "Beyond Petroleum, or Beyond the Pale? BP Left Out in the Cold," January 23, 2003, http://www.globalpolicy.org/security/natres/oil/2003/0219bp.htm; and see, for ex-

ample, "About BP: Renewable and Alternative Energy," http://www.bp.com/sectiongeneric article.do?categoryId=22&contentId=2006538, and related links.

4. The company's reaction to a tragic 2005 accident that killed fifteen workers and injured a hundred more at a Texas refinery serves as a more positive example of a response that aligned BP's actions with its identity. Lord John Browne, by then chairman, flew from London to Houston the next day to explore and intervene personally, sending a strong message about how deeply the company was concerned about breakdowns in safe operating procedures. Such visible executive statements and actions often embody and reinforce a company's choice of identity—but only if they are sincere and backed up by the company's subsequent behavior.

5. Sources for this description include "Toyota Prius Chronological History," Toyo-Land Page, http://www.toyoland.com/prius/chronology.html; "Prius History," http://john 1701a.com/prius/prius-history.htm; and Robert Collier, "Beyond Toyota's Hybrid Revolution: Automaker's Successful Gamble with Prius Fuels Its Image as a Trendsetter," *San Francisco Chronicle*, April 24, 2006, http://www.sfgate.com/cgi-bin/article.cgi?f=/c/a/2006/04/24/MNG3JIE6DK1.DTL&hw=toyota&sn=002&sc=410.

6. Jeffrey K. Liker and David Meier, *The Toyota Way Fieldbook: A Practical Guide for Implementing Toyota's 4Ps* (New York: McGraw-Hill, 2006), 8.

7. Some accounts of the Prius's history state that Toyota began the project after being rebuffed (as a non-U.S. company) by the Clinton administration's Partnership for the Next Generation of Vehicles (PNGV), intended to promote research into "developing family sized vehicles that could deliver 80-mpg efficiency." (See, for example, http://john1701a.com/prius/prius-history.htm.) The U.S. manufacturers, at first, were remarkably uninterested in participating. The Bush administration discontinued the PNGV in early 2001 (ibid).

8. See "Vision: Principles and Policies," Toyota Motor Corporation, http://www.toyota.co.jp/en/environment/vision/policies/index.html.

9. "Prius History."

10. "Toyota Prius," Wikipedia, http://en.wikipedia.org/wiki/Toyota_Prius#Sales; and "Honda Insight Sales Statistics," InsightCentral.net, http://www.insightcentral.net/KB/sales.html.

11. James B. Treece and Lindsay Chappell, "Honda Kills the Insight," *AutoWeek*, May 17, 2006, http://www.autoweek.com/apps/pbcs.dll/article?AID=/20060517/FREE/60517001/1041.

12. Michael E. Porter, *Competitive Strategy: Techniques for Analyzing Industries and Competitors* (New York: Free Press, 1998), 36.

13. Geoffrey A. Moore, *Living on the Fault Line: Managing for Shareholder Value in Any Economy*, rev. ed. (New York: HarperBusiness, 2002).

14. Quoted in Collier, "Behind Toyota's Hybrid Revolution."

15. Clayton M. Christensen, Scott D. Anthony, and Erik A. Roth, *Seeing What's Next: Using the Theories of Innovation to Predict Industry Change* (Boston: Harvard Business School Press, 2004), xxii.

16. Douglas K. Smith and Robert C. Alexander, *Fumbling the Future: How Xerox Invented, Then Ignored, the First Personal Computer* (New York: William Morrow & Co., 1988), 13, 19.

17. Louis V. Gerstner Jr., *Who Says Elephants Can't Dance? Inside IBM's Historic Turnaround* (New York: HarperBusiness, 2002), 106.

18. Stephen R, Covey, *The 8th Habit: From Effectiveness to Greatness* (New York: Simon and Schuster, 2004), 2.

19. Joe Calloway, *Becoming a Category of One: How Extraordinary Companies Transcend Commodity and Defy Comparison* (Hoboken, NJ: Wiley, 2003).

20. Ibid., 11.

21. Ibid., 34.

22. A student of both Freud and Adler, Frankl went on to develop a third school of Viennese psychotherapy that he called logotherapy. Like the word *logo*, logotherapy stems from the Greek *logos*, or meaning. Essentially, Frankl helped people with their psychological problems by connecting them to their sense of meaning.

23. Viktor E. Frankl, *Man's Search for Meaning: An Introduction to Logotherapy*, trans. Ilse Lasch, 4th ed. (Boston: Beacon Press, 2000).

24. Ibid., 66.

25. Ibid., 58–60.

26. See, for example, Paul A. Eisenstein, "1999 Volvo V70 XC," The Car Connection, http://www.thecarconnection.com/index.asp?n=157,181&sid=181&&article=610&article =792.

27. See Robert F. Bruner's case studies and videotapes examining the Renault-Volvo alliance. Case studies: "Volvo AB/Regie Nationale des Usines Renault," Case UVA-F-1088, and "Volvo/Renault: The Contest for Corporate Control," Case UVA-F-1089, both reprinted in Mark Eaker and Faith Rubenstein, eds., *Global Business Management* (New York: Southwestern Publishing, 1997); "Renault-Volvo Strategic Alliance (A): March 1993," Case UVA-G-0480, reprinted in Taylor Meloan and John L. Graham, *International Global Marketing Management: Concepts and Cases* (New York: McGraw-Hill, 1997); "Renault-Volvo Strategic Alliance (B): September 1993," Case UVA-G-0481; "Renault-Volvo Strategic Alliance (C): December 1, 1993," Case UVA-G-0482; "Renault-Volvo Strategic Alliance (D): December 2, 1993 and Afterward," Case UVA-G-0483; and "Renault-Volvo Strategic Alliance (B Abridged)," Case UVA-G-0484). Videotapes: "Renault-Volvo Strategic Alliance (A)," Case UVA-F-0480; "Renault-Volvo Strategic Alliance (B)," Cases UVA-G-0481 and -0484; "Renault-Volvo Strategic Alliance (C)," Case UVA-G-0483); Supplement to "Volvo AB/Regie Nationale des Usines Renault," Case UVA-F-1088); and "Volvo/Renault: The Contest for Corporate Control," Case UVA-F-1089.

28. Malcolm Gladwell, *The Tipping Point: How Little Things Can Make a Big Difference* (Boston: Little, Brown, 2000), 89–132.

29. Kristine Kerby Webster, "What's the Benefit of Branding Anyway?" MarketingProfs, October 15, 2002, http://www.marketingprofs.com/homepage/premium_preview.asp?file =/2/webster8.asp.

30. Jon R. Katzenbach, *Peak Performance: Aligning the Hearts and Minds of Your Employees* (Boston: Harvard Business School Press, 2000), 186.

31. "Yahoo! Inc.: Company Report," MSN Money, http://moneycentral.msn.com/ investor/research/profile.asp?Symbol=yhoo.

Chapter 2

1. The SMART goal-setting acronym is widely used in training manuals, Web sites, slide sets, etc. but seems to have no one originator. The words that each letter of the acronym stands for can vary from source to source: for example, R has been said to stand for realistic, reviewable, relative, rewarding, or reasonable, as well as resourced. We have chosen those that we feel are best representative of goal setting within a strategic management context. For a discussion of the variations, see Robert S. Rubin, "Will the Real SMART Goals Please Stand Up?" *The Industrial-Organizational Psychologist* (online journal of SIOP, the Society for Organizational and Industrial Psychology), April 2002, http://siop.org/tip/ backissues/TIPApr02/03rubin.htm.

2. Robert Fritz, *The Path of Least Resistance: Creating What You Want to Create* (Salem, MA: DMA, 1984), 169.

3. Robert Fritz, Shad Helmstetter, and others have pointed out this construct of the way people approach life. See Fritz, *The Path of Least Resistance*; and Shad Helmstetter, *Choices* (New York: Pocket Books, 1989).

4. Victor R. Basili, Gianluigi Caldiera, and H. Dieter Rombach, "The Goal Question Metric Approach," in *Encyclopedia of Software Engineering*, ed. John J. Marciniak (New York: Wiley, 1994).

5. David L. Cooperrider, Diana Whitney, and Jacqueline Stavros, *Appreciative Inquiry Handbook* (Bedford Heights, OH: Lakeshore Communications, and San Francisco: Berrett-Koehler Publishers, 2003).

6. Cooperrider, Whitney, and Stavros, *Appreciative Inquiry Handbook*.

7. See creatingminds.org.

8. Raymond E. Levitt and Nancy M. Samelson, *Construction Safety Management*, 2nd ed. (New York: Wiley, 1993).

9. Rachel Kyte, "The Triple Bottom Line: How Assessing Environmental and Social Sustainability Contributes to Economic Sustainability" presentation to Planet-X symposium, Stanford University, June 2004, http://soe.stanford.edu/alumni/planetx/index.html.

10. In a discussion at Stanford's Planet-X symposium in 2004, Rachel Kyte, IFC's director of environment and social redevelopment, explained that IFC typically takes a longer-term financial position than commercial lenders in its investments, to reduce the risk for the private lenders and thereby render projects fundable. Because it takes a long-term debt or equity position in projects, IFC has to live with all the long-term consequences of not addressing ecological and equity concerns thoroughly at the outset. IFC, she argued, has learned that corporate social responsibility (CSR) pays off handsomely by ensuring stable, long-term returns for its investments.

11. The Leadership in Energy and Environmental Design (LEED) Green Building Rating System is a voluntary, consensus-based national standard for developing high-performance, sustainable buildings. For more information, see http://www.usgbc.org/DisplayPage.aspx?CategoryID=19.

12. The growth in IFC's funds available for investment since it was founded—from about $2.5 billion to over $13 billion in 2006—provides the evidence for this claim. (Rachel Kyte, presentation to Planet-X symposium.) This, together with the concern of any global enterprise about being "named and shamed" for bad behavior by swarms of increasingly vigilant nongovernmental organizations (NGOs) that scrutinize ecological and social justice outcomes of global projects and global business, makes it likely that the move toward triple-bottom-line assessments will stick and even spread for global investors.

13. Clive Crook, "Survey: The World According to CSR—Good Corporate Citizens Believe That Capitalism Is Wicked but Redeemable," *The Economist*, January 22–28, 2005.

Chapter 3

1. Louis V. Gerstner Jr., *Who Says Elephants Can't Dance? Leading a Great Enterprise Through Dramatic Change* (New York: HarperBusiness, 2003), 182.

2. We are indebted to one of our former students, who, as a long-time HP employee, lived through the events described and shared his keen and thoughtful observations with us.

3. Gideon Kunda, *Engineering Culture: Control and Commitment in a High-Tech Corporation* (Philadelphia: Temple University Press, 1992).

4. Michael E. Porter, *Competitive Strategy: Techniques for Analyzing Industries and Competitors* (New York: Free Press, 1998), 4.

5. Alan Murray, "H-P Lost Faith in Fiorina, but Not in Merger," *Wall Street Journal*, May 24, 2006.

6. Edgar Schein, *Organizational Culture and Leadership: A Dynamic View* (San Francisco: Jossey-Bass, 1992).

7. William E. Schneider, *The Reengineering Alternative: A Plan for Making Your Current Culture Work* (Burr Ridge, IL: Irwin Professional Publishing, 1994), 4.

8. Geoffrey A. Moore, *Living on the Fault Line: Managing for Shareholder Value in Any Economy*, rev. ed. (New York: HarperBusiness, 2002).

9. Warren G. Bennis and Joan Goldsmith, *Learning to Lead: A Workbook on Becoming a Leader* (New York: Basic Books, 2003), 25.

10. Larry E. Greiner, "Evolution and Revolution as Companies Grow," *Harvard Business Review*, July–August 1972, 37.

11. Paul R. Lawrence and Jay W. Lorsch, *Organization and Environment: Managing Differentiation and Integration* (Boston: Harvard Business School Press, 1986).

12. See, for example, Clayton M. Christensen, *The Innovator's Dilemma: When New Technologies Cause Great Firms to Fail* (Boston: Harvard Business School Press, 1997); and Clayton M. Christensen and Michael E. Raynor, *The Innovator's Solution: Creating and Sustaining Successful Growth* (Boston: Harvard Business School Press, 2003).

13. Raymond E. Levitt and Nancy M. Samelson, *Construction Safety Management*, 2nd ed. (New York: Wiley, 1993).

Chapter 4

1. Louis V. Gerstner Jr., *Who Says Elephants Can't Dance? Inside IBM's Historic Turnaround* (New York: HarperBusiness, 2002), 226.

2. Michael E. Porter, *Competitive Strategy: Techniques for Analyzing Industries and Competitors* (New York: Free Press, 1998), and "What Is Strategy?" *Harvard Business Review*, February 1, 2000; and Robert S. Kaplan and David P. Norton, *Strategy Maps: Converting Intangible Assets into Tangible Outcomes* (Boston: Harvard Business School Press, 2004). Kaplan and Norton expand on this concept by combining a strategy map with a Balanced Scorecard. Robert S. Kaplan and David P. Norton, *The Strategy-Focused Organization: How Balanced Scorecard Companies Thrive in the New Business Environment* (Boston: Harvard Business School Press, 2001).

3. Sayan Chatterjee, "Core Objectives: Clarity in Designing Strategy," *California Management Review* 47, no. 2 (2005): 33–49.

4. These rough estimates of potential return on organizational effort parallel the Simons and Davila concept of "return on managerial energy" we discussed in the introduction. Robert L. Simons and Antonio Davila, "How High Is Your Return on Management?" *Harvard Business Review*, January–February 1998, 71–80.

5. Robert G. Cooper, Scott J. Edgett, and Elko J. Kleinschmidt, *Portfolio Management for New Products*, 2nd ed. (Cambridge, MA: Perseus Publishing, 2001), 107.

6. R. G. Cooper, "Your NPD Portfolio May Be Harmful to Your Business Health," *PDMA Visions Magazine* 29, no. 2 (2005), http://www.pdma.org/visions/apr05/npd.html.

7. Tom DeMarco and Timothy Lister, *Peopleware: Productive Projects and Teams* (New York: Dorset House, 1987), 66.

8. Leslie A. Perlow, *Finding Time: How Corporations, Individuals, and Families Can Benefit from New Work Practices* (Ithaca, NY: ILR Press, 1997).

9. DeMarco and Lister, *Peopleware*, 45.

10. This might indicate that projects to change hiring or training practices or to enhance the elements of the vision domain are also in order. More on this in chapter 3.

11. Robert Carlson, presentation to Stanford Advanced Project Management executive program, 2002, Slides 17–21.

12. Cathleen Benko and F. Warren McFarlan, *Connecting the Dots: Aligning Projects with Objectives in Unpredictable Times* (Boston: Harvard Business School Press, 2003).

13. Bob Carlson, presentation to Stanford Advanced Project Management, 2002, slides 17–21.

14. Cooper, Edgett, and Kleinschmidt, *Portfolio Management for New Products*, 72–94.

15. Cooper, "Your NPD Portfolio."

16. Tom Geoghan, "Project Portfolio Management @ eBay" (lecture presented at the Stanford Advanced Project Management program, September 2005), slide 3, updated June 2007 via correspondence.

17. Ibid., slides 5–24.

Chapter 5

1. Rich Grimes of AT&T Wireless, interview by author, September 2006.

2. The work process modeling and simulation tool that Rich Grimes used for continuously replanning the Los Angeles regional wireless rollout projects is called SimVision. SimVision is licensed and supported by ePM LLC of Austin, Texas (see http://www.epm.cc). Roughly comparable tools and consulting support for modeling and simulating projects are available from other companies—e.g., Pertmaster Project Risk, from Pertmaster LLC of Houston, Texas, supports Monte Carlo simulation of projects with uncertain task durations (see http://www.pertmaster.com).

3. Raymond E. Levitt, Jan Thomsen, Tore R. Christiansen, John C. Kunz, Yan Jin, and Clifford Nass, "Simulating Project Work Processes and Organizations: Toward a Micro-Contingency Theory of Organizational Design," *Management Science* 45, no. 11 (November 1999): 1479–1495.

4. John C. Kunz, Tore R. Christiansen, Geoff P. Cohen, Yan Jin, and Raymond E. Levitt, "The Virtual Design Team: A Computational Simulation Model of Project Organizations," *Communications of the Association for Computing Machinery* (CACM) 41, no. 11 (November 1998): 84–91.

5. James Oberg, "Why the Mars Probe Went Off Course," *IEEE Spectrum* 36, no. 12 (December 1999).

6. James Thompson, *Organizations in Action* (New York: McGraw-Hill, 1967).

7. Ibid.

8. Henry Petroski's wonderful book *The Evolution of Useful Things* argues that any useful product—even a lowly paper clip—is the result of successive "bug fixes" to multiple generations of failed prototypes. Henry Petroski, *The Evolution of Useful Things* (New York: Vintage Books, 1994).

9. Jay R. Galbraith, "Organization Design: An Information Processing View," *Interfaces* 4, no. 3 (1974): 28–36.

10. Frederick P. Brooks, *The Mythical Man-Month: Essays on Software Engineering* (Reading, MA: Addison-Wesley, 1974).

11. Rich Grimes, interview by author, September 2006.

12. Michael Schrage, *Serious Play: How the World's Best Companies Simulate to Innovate* (Boston: Harvard Business School Press, 2000).

Chapter 6

1. In his 2006 book, *Dealing with Darwin*, Geoffrey Moore provides a model for innovation that sheds considerable light on critical issues of transition. Moore notes that resources tend to get "stuck" at transitions in the innovation cycle, which flows from non-mission-critical "core"—or the birthplace of invention—through mission-critical core, where inventions are deployed at scale, and later to mission-critical context, where mature products are managed through scale processes, to end as non-mission-critical context, when the invention or innovation has run its course as a source of strategic differentiation. Especially at that end, or "offload," stage, when an innovation has run its course, many organizations fail to extract and repurpose the remaining resources to drive the next innovation. (Geoffrey A. Moore, *Dealing with Darwin: How Great Companies Innovate at Every Phase of Their Evolution* (New York: Penguin Books, 2004].)

2. Paul C. Nutt, *Why Decisions Fail: Avoiding the Blunders and Traps That Lead to Debacles* (San Francisco, CA: Berrett-Koehler Publishers, 2002), 61–86.

3. Ibid., 165–196.

4. "The Deep Dive," interview by Ted Koppel, *Nightline*, ABC News, February 1999.

5. Project Management Institute, *A Guide to the Project Management Body of Knowledge* (Newtown Square, PA: Project Management Institute, 2000), 31.

Conclusion

1. Roger Hallowell, Carin-Isabel Knoop, and Neo Boon Siong, "Transforming Singapore's Public Libraries, Case 9-802-009 (Boston: Harvard Business School, 2001), 1–4.

2. Library 2000 Review Committee, *Library 2000: Investing in a Learning Nation: Report of the Library 2000 Review Committee* (Singapore: SNP Publishers, 1994).

3. Ibid., 1

4. Ibid., 2.

5. Ibid., 3.

6. Ibid., 4.

7. Patrick Lambe, Straits Knowledge Research, 2004, 7.

8. Ibid., 8.

9. Lance Armstrong, "Who Says We Can't Do It? Lance Armstrong's Journey," video (Cambridge, MA: Enterprise Media).

10. Lance Armstrong, with Sally Jenkins, *It's Not About the Bike: My Journey Back to Life* (New York: Berkley Books, 2001); and *Every Second Counts* (New York: Broadway Books, 2004).

11. Armstrong, "Who Says We Can't Do It?"

12. Clayton M. Christensen, Scott D. Anthony, and Erik A. Roth, *Seeing What's Next: Using the Theories of Innovation to Predict Industry Change* (Boston: Harvard Business School Press, 2004).

13. "Nordstrom," Wikipedia, http://en.wikipedia.org/wiki/Nordstrom.

Index

accidents and incentives, 130–131
accountability, 109
  championing, 80–81
  sponsorship, 147–148
actions, 2–3
active investors, 171
actively deciding not to undertake wrong
  projects, 7
activities, importance of, 7–8
activity system maps, 150–153
actual portfolio, 181–182
ADP (Automatic Data Processing), 6, 162,
  164
advertising agencies, 100
Airbus, 241–243
  A380 delay, 201–203
  coordination breakdown, 193
Akers, John, 1
aligning portfolios, 184–186
aligning programs, 184–186
  managing white spaces, 191–206
aligning projects, 184–186
  nimble proactive processes, 186–191
alignment, 240, 257–259
Amazon.com, 125
ambivalence, overcoming, 66–67
Anderson, KC, ix
antidote to whack-a-mole execution, 18
APC (American Power Conversion), ix,
  11–14, 36–37, 123, 149
Apple Computer, 1, 126, 218, 220–221
appreciative inquiry versus problem
  solving, 70–73
Armstrong, Lance, 24, 243, 255
  cancer, 250

culture, 251
engagement imperative, 252–253
goals, 251–252
ideation imperative, 249–250
metrics, 251–252
nature imperative, 250–251
Paris-Nice race, 250
portfolio decision, 252–253
sense of purpose, 250
strategy, 251–252
structure, 251
synthesis imperative, 253
Tour de France, 249–254
transition imperative, 253–254
vision imperative, 251–252
AT&T, 92
AT&T Wireless, 157–160
  Los Angeles Wireless Rollout project,
    188–191
  modeling and simulation tools, 203
  no fallback plan for, 184
  Odyssey program, 10, 184–185
  WICIS (Wireless Intercarrier Communi-
    cations Interface Specifications)
    component, 158
Automation Consulting Services, 5–6
avoidance, 65

balanced matrix structure, 114, 123,
  125–126
balancing and optimizing portfolios,
  170–171
Basili, Victor R., 69
Bechtel, 120

Becoming a Category of One (Calloway), 38
belief and balancing desire, 66–67
Bell, Alexander Graham, 35
beneficiary of purpose, 44–45
benefits realization, 218, 230–235
Ben & Jerry's of Vermont, 82
BFI (big fuzzy idea), 217
"Big Dig" (Boston), 233
bilingualism, 182
Biotech Inc.'s strong matrix, 121–123
Blackburn, Darrell, ix
Blue's Clues, 44
Boeing, 201
boutique consultants, 100
boxes, 122
BP (formerly British Petroleum and BP
    Amoco), 29–30, 130–131
BP Alternative Energy, 30
Bradley, R. Todd, 106
branding programs, 150
brands
   attempting to change, 55
   building internal and external, 52–54
   Coca-Cola, 55
   consistent, 51
   cultivating meaning of, 54–56
   customers and stakeholders, 51
   ideation and, 51–54
   identity, 54–55
   loyalty, 51
   market perceptions, 55
   market resistance to change, 56
   meaning customers ascribe to, 55
   Microsoft software services and support,
      55–56
   strong, 51
British Airways baggage loss, 71–73
Browne, John, 30
budgets, assigning ownership, 129–130
Built to Last (Collins and Porras), 46, 132
Bundy, Ann, viii
businesses
   performance innovation, 161
   reviews and optimizing portfolios,
      175–177
   sense of purpose, 37
   working in, 14
   working on, 14
   working to transform, 14

Caldiera, Gianluigi, 69
call center fiasco, 78–79
Calloway, Joe, 38
call time, 79
Capability Maturity Model, 66
capacity
   resources, 164–167
   understanding real, 165–167
Capital Tower Group, viii
Case Western Reserve University, 153
Casio, 96
Cerra, Stephanie, viii
challenges constituting project
   environment, 40–41
Chambers, John, 12
Chandra, Ritu, vii
change, costs of, 224–225
change/rework interdependencies,
   196–197, 200
Chatterjee, Sayan, 153
Chia, Christopher, 244–245, 246–247
choice trumping belief, 67
circumstances, purpose trumping,
   40–43
Cisco Systems, 12, 123
Citibank, 46
Citigroup, 46–47, 106–107
   Dr. Evil trade, 110–111
   Equator Principles, 81
clarifying
   collective why, 38
   identity, 32–37
   long-range intention, 45–47
   purpose, 37–45
clarity, championing, 80–81
clearly articulated strategy, 7
clear statement of desired outcome, 67
closed-loop system, 231–232
closing loop, 231–235
Coca-Cola, 55
Cole, Andrew, ix
collaboration, 99
   companies, 116
   IBM, 106
collaboration culture, 99
collective why, clarifying, 38
Collins, Jim, 46, 132
commissioning, centralized controls
   during, 227–229

commitment and sponsorship, 147
communities of practice, 112
companies
    beginning as simple structures, 110
    boxes, 122
    collaboration, 116
    cost leader, 33
    cultural values of founding team, 98
    customer intimacy, 116
    de facto strategy, 3
    differentiated value provider, 33
    divisional organization, 111
    highly customized solutions, 123
    ideation, 15
    kind of, 33–34
    " make to offer" versus "offer to make,"
        219
    nature, 15
    "offer to make" versus "make to offer,"
        219
    project portfolio, 3
    Skunk Works, 125
    specialized functional inputs or prod-
        uct/customer outcomes, 110
    strategy through project investment
        stream, 4
    sustaining performance, 6
    temporary initiatives, 3
    tiger teams, 125
    transition from "make to offer" to "offer
        to make," 123
    triple-bottom-line goals and metrics,
        82
    virtual communities of practice, 112
    vision, 15
Compaq, 98, 100
competence culture, 99, 116
competitive advantage, 95
competitive objectives, 155
construction workers' motivation, 38
control, 99, 116
control culture, 100, 106
Cooper, R. G., 157, 161
Cooperrider, David, 71
coping rituals, 39
core objectives, translating critical activi-
    ties into, 153–156
corporate culture projects, 108–109
corporate leadership, 104–105

corporate responsibility, measuring, 83–84
corporate strategy, 3–4
corporate values versus executive actions,
    110–111
corporations
    "initiative of the month" syndrome, 18
    projects testing identity strength, 34–36
    whack-a-mole execution, 18
cost leader, 33
cost leadership strategies, 115
Covey, Stephen, 37
creative companies and retaining
    employees, 109
critical activities
    core objectives and execution
        capabilities, 153–156
    identifying, 150–153
critical path, 193
cross-functional project teams, 128
CSR (corporate social responsibility),
    81–84
cultivation, 99
cultivation culture, 99–100, 116
culture, 23
    aligning structure, 108, 116, 257
    anchor of strategic alignment, 97
    assessing organization's, 102–104
    behaviors to value and emphasize, 97
    changing, 93, 97
    collaboration, 99–101
    combining product leadership and
        disruptive innovation, 104
    competence, 99
    control, 99
    create and nurture coherent, 98
    cultivation, 99
    determining strategic fit, 134
    differentiation strategy, 100
    difficulty changing, 93–94
    emphasizing control and competence,
        100
    employees, 101
    environment and, 108
    four Cs of, 99
    guidelines, 97
    identity, 56
    internal carriers, 150
    Lance Armstrong, 251
    linked with identity, 94

culture (*continued*)
  marketing or sales, 99
  nature imperative, 135–136
  operational excellence strategy, 100
  people, activities, and achievements
    celebrated, 100
  power of, 97–98
  primary values, 102
  projects to align, 108–109
  purpose, 56
  research and literature on, 99
  Rolm, 105
  sets of format and informal rules, 93
  single-country, 98
  sources, 98
  strategy aligning with, 102–103
  structural changes, 124
  structure misaligned with, 127–128
  typology of, 99–101
  understanding customer needs, 99
  values cherished by, 100
  valuing technical excellence, 99
  variations in organization, 98
  what executives do versus what they say,
    106–107
culture changes, 104–107, 134
culture egg, 102
culture-strategy misfit, 134
customer intimacy strategies, 33
  companies, 116
  strong matrix, 119–120
customer metric ("customer sat"), 68
  customer emotional response, 68
  customer insistence, 68
  customer loyalty, 68
  customer reference, 68
  customer satisfaction, 68
customer outcomes versus customer
  needs, 153
customer relationship management, 66
customer relationship management
  systems, 150
customers
  ideation, 28
  Internet-enabled global competition
    and, 122
  results for, 218
  serving needs of, 45
custom solution services, 99

Dávila, Antonio, 5
day-to-day activities, 2
DeCastro, Amy, ix
decision-making authority, 109
decision-making rules, 13
decision rules, 5
de facto identity, 33
de facto strategy, 3
delighters, 48
Dell, 96–97
DeMarco, Tom, 165–166
Denver International Airport (DIA), 233,
  235
descriptors, 34
design freeze, 229
desire balancing with belief, 66–67
desired future strategy, 45
Deutsche Bank Equator Principles, 81
differentiated value provider, 33
differentiation strategy, 100
DiPaolo, Andy, vii
disruptive innovation, 33
disruptive innovation strategies, 116, 123,
  125–126
DNV (Det Norske Veritas), 42
doing project right, 181
doing right projects, 181
doing right things, 23, 30
doing right things right, 23, 240
"do it all" mentality, 5
dot-com boom and bust, 48
DPR Construction, 131–133

easyJet, 77
eBay, ix, 123, 125, 176–177, 259
ecological sustainability, 81
economizers, 48
economy, 81
ecosystem services, value of, 83
effective execution, 7
Ellison, Janet, ix
employees
  colocation by function, 128
  retaining, 109
empowerment and sponsorship, 148
engagement, 15–16, 23, 141–142, 241
  effectiveness, 257
  faulty translation in, 9–10

projects for building stronger, 178
strategic execution, 143
engagement domain, 3–4, 13–14, 16, 64, 206
engagement imperative, 23, 143
determining capacity, 164–167
flawed prioritization, 184
handling conflict, 223
identifying potential projects, 149–156
Lance Armstrong, 252–253
linking outputs to strategic outcomes, 155
portfolio governance environment, 144–148
portfolio measurement, 179–180
prioritizing project work, 157–164
project managers, 142
project priority decisions, 143
rating organization on, 178–180
strategists and project sponsors, 142
strategy measurement, 179
strategy to action, 143
transformative projects, 143
engineering innovation, 95
Enron, 42
enterprise resource planning, 66
environment, 82, 108
environmental protection measurement, 82
Equator Principles, 81
equity, 81, 84
European Aeronautic Defence and Space Company (EADS), 201
Every Second Counts (Armstrong and Jenkins), 249
excellence and SEF (strategic execution framework), 255
execution, 9–10, 153–156
executive actions versus corporate values, 110–111
executives
culture and actions, 106–107
defining vision imperative, 85–87
great blind spot, 4–7
where organization will be in two years, 2–4

fairness and equity, 84
fair process, 84

fast-track concurrent development and Lockheed, 198–200
fast-track concurrent engineering, 201–202
fast-track project designs, 196–197, 200
Fault Line: Managing for Shareholder Value in Any Economy (Moore), 49
faulty translation undercutting execution, 9–10
feedback, importance of, 214
Finding Time (Perlow), 166
Fiorina, Carly, 1, 92, 99, 100, 106
first commercial satellite launch vehicle, 198–200
five-Taurus sales call, 124
flashers, 48
flight-simulating projects and programs, 204–205
Florida, Richard, 109
Fluor Corporation, 120–121
fool with a tool, 169–170
Ford, 43
forecasts, more reliable, 207
Forgeard, Noël, 201
forward-looking information and navigation metrics, 74–75
fossil fuels, 29
four Cs of culture, 99
FPIC (free prior informed consent), 81
Frankl, Viktor, 39
Fritz, Robert, 65, 66
functional employees, 119
functional groups and eBay, 123
functional hierarchies and silo mentality, 110–111
functional managers, 117, 119, 128–129
functional organization, 111–112
functional specialists, 118
functional supervisors, 118
future outcomes, best indicator of, 3

GAAP (Generally Accepted Accounting Principles), 223
Galvin, Robert, 172
gap analysis, 71
General Electric, 132
Geoghan, Tom, ix

Gerstner, Louis, 12, 36, 91, 104–105, 123, 143
Gladwell, Malcolm, 44
Global Climate Coalition, 30
goal clarity, 80
goals
  avoidance, 65
  choosing to define, 64–65
  clear, well-communicated, 62–63, 81–82
  customer satisfaction, 78
  defining right, 65
  devising ways to get, 63
  difficult to create, 62
  efficiency, 78
  exacerbated by early success, 63–64
  failing to choose and articulate, 65
  finite and focused, 65
  fundamental questions about, 69
  integrity of investment choices, 62
  issue, 69
  lacking line of sight to, 62
  lack of clarity, 63
  Lance Armstrong, 251–252
  multilevel, 76
  not believing in, 66
  object, 69
  projects to clarify, 69–75
  purpose, 69
  questioning underlying, 70
  setting, 63
  splitting into parts, 69
  spotting misaligned, 77–80
  standards for meeting, 63
  translating intention into, 62, 64–68, 87
  triple-bottom line and, 81–84
  underlying questions relative to, 69
  viewpoint, 69
Goodnight, James, 109
Google, 259
Graffiti input format, 220
great executive blind spot, 4–7
green products and services, 82
Grimes, Rich, viii, 188, 203
The Grove Consultants International, 50
Gyllenhammar, Pehr, 1, 42

handoffs
  right time for, 216–217
  strengthening sponsorship through, 222–223

Harms, Julia, vii
Hewlett, William, 92, 95, 99
hidden language barrier, 7–9
hidden projects of realignment, 13
hidden work, 203–206
Holland, Paul, viii
Holmes, Oliver Wendell Jr., 70
Honda Insight hybrid, 32
honesty reward functions, 207
hot list, 129
"How High Is Your Return on Management?" (Simmons and Dávila), 5
HP (Hewlett-Packard), viii, 1, 69, 92–93, 95–96, 106–107, 124–125
  bottom-up, consensus-driven decision making, 100
  collaboration culture, 99
  combining product leadership and disruptive innovation, 104
  competence, 104
  competence culture, 99
  control culture, 100
  cultivation, 104
  mapping traditional and proposed new strategies, 103–104
  nature domain, 95–97
  operation excellence, 103
  respect for employees, 97
  technological inventiveness emphasis, 97
HP-branded Apple iPod, 106
HP Invent, 96
HP Way, 97, 100
Hrebiniak, Lawrence, 8
HR processes, designing, 149
humanity in workplace, 258–259
human resource capacity, 165–167
Humbert, Gustav, 201
Hurd, Mark, 92–93, 97, 99, 100, 105, 106–107, 124
Hurricane Katrina and sense of purpose, 40
hyperactive portfolio management, 171, 175
hyperpassive portfolio management, 171

IBM, 1, 36, 105–107, 123
  efforts to change strategy, 91
  engagement imperative at, 143
  front-back organization, 124

new strategy, structure, and culture, 91
Project Chess, 126
San Jose assembly team, 43–44
switching context, 166
ultimate power to project managers,
129
IBM Global Services, 105
ideation, 15, 21
Airbus, 241
align all activities to, 30
attracting best employees, 28
BP, 29–30
brand and, 51–54
Citigroup, 46–47
culture linked with identity, 94
customers, 28
deciding what not to do, 35
differentiating organization, 28
elements, 28–29
embedding elements throughout
organization, 50–51
linking external and internal brand,
52
potential investors, 28
power of, 28–32
project list for, 57
strategic execution, 56
strength, 256
without strong, 48
tangible manifestation, 56–57
telling company what not to do, 54
Toyota, 29–30
variations, 57
weak, 57
ideation imperative, 21, 28
average score interpretation, 58
clarifying identity, 32–37
defining beginning and end in strategy
equation, 94
Lance Armstrong, 249–250
long-range intention measurement,
59–60
power of ideation, 28–32
purpose measurement, 58–59
rating organization, 56–60
sustainability through, 48–51
identity
clarifying, 30, 32–37
clarifying purpose, 37–45
consciously chosen shift in, 36
culture and, 56, 94

de facto, 33
external clues, 32–33
out of step with environment, 35
pattern, 35
perceived, 34
projects communicating, 48–50
projects reshaping, 36–37
projects testing strength of, 34–36
strategic, 33–34
strong, 42
system solution provider, 105
too restrictive, 35
too strong, 35
visual mapping, 48–50
wide divergence, 35
IDEO, 231, 259
IFC (International Finance Corporation),
81
immortal-project syndrome, 229–230
incentives, 130–131
information, 127, 134, 169
information technology (IT), 126–127,
176
initiative du jour, 67
"initiative of the month" syndrome, 18
innovation, 161–162
integration test systems, 150
intention
clarifying, 30
strategy, goals, and metrics, 62, 87
interdependencies
change/rework, 196–197, 200
identifying, 195
pooled, 192–193
reciprocal, 194–196
sequential, 193–194
internal branding, 52–54
internal environment, 93
INVEST (ideation, nature, vision, engagement, synthesis, and transition), 16
Investing in a Learning Nation, 245
investments
categories, 157
describing current, 3
engaging strategy through, 23
iPod, 221
IPS (IPSolutions), ix, vii, viii
Iridium LLC, 9–10, 172–174
ISO 900X, 66
It's Not About the Bike (Armstrong and
Jenkins), 249

Japan Private Bank, 46–47
JetBlue, 77
Jin, Yan, x
Jobs, Steve, 126
Johnson, Dave, ix
Johnson, Rob, ix
judgment and optimizing portfolio,
    169–170

Kabai, Bill, ix
Kandarian, Barbara, ix
Katzenbach, Jon R., 54
Kelly, Dave, 231
Kern, Bill, vii
Kunda, Gideon, viii
Kunz, John, x

lagging indicators, 74, 175
large-scale creep, 216
leading indicators, 75
leading rather than lagging metrics,
    73–75
LensCrafters, 38
Levitt, Kathleen Adele Sullivan, x
Levitt, Ray, vii
Lewin, Holly, vii
life cycle management systems, 150
Liker, Jeffrey K., 31
Lister, Timothy, 165
Little, Carissa, vii
Lockheed Martin, 125–126
    launch vehicle, 198–200, 201–203
logo, 54
long-range intentions, 56
    clarifying identity, 45–47
    measuring, 59–60
    projects clarifying, 45–47
    projects communicating, 48–50
    short-term decisions, 45
    translating into goals and metrics, 62,
        64–68
    visual mapping, 48–50
long-term intentions, 46
Los Angeles Wireless Rollout project,
    188–191
low-margin, commoditizing businesses,
    96
Lucent Technologies, 92

Macintosh computer, 126
macro metrics, 75
Maheras, Tom, 111
Man's Search for Meaning (Frankl), 39
"make to offer" world, 12
"make to offer" ("make and offer")
    companies, 219
management by exception, 186–187
management information systems, 150
managers
    costs of preventing accidents, 131
    setting measurable triple-bottom-line
        goals, 82
managing trade-offs, 220–223
Marca, Paul, vii
March, James G., x
market advantage, 48
marketing programs, 150
Mason, Phil, viii
matrix organization, 115
matrix structure
    adjusting strength, 113–115
    combining functional excellence with
        focus on products, 112
    formalizing, 112–113
    new, 149
    projects to tune matrix strength,
        127–131
    taming, 114
mature commodity businesses, 100
mature service industries, 100
media companies, 100
mega metrics, 75
Meier, David, 31
meta metrics, 75
metric clarity, 80
metrics
    aligning with strategic goals, 67–68
    asking fundamental questions about
        goals, 69
    choosing to define, 64–65
    clear, 80–81
    conflicting, 77–78
    conversion rate, 70
    defining, 67–68
    defining right, 65
    doing right things, 72
    Lance Armstrong, 251–252
    leading rather than lagging, 73–75
    levels, 75

multilevel, 76
profit contribution from referrals, 70
projects to clarify, 69–75
referral business, 69
sales cycle time, 70
spotting misaligned, 77–80
total value of referral sale, 70
translating intention to, 62, 87
triple-bottom line and, 81–84
micro metrics, 75, 79
midlevel metrics, 75
milestones, 194
misaligned goals, 77–80
misaligned metrics, 77–80
misses, 75
Moore, Geoffrey, 33, 48, 49, 100
motivation and purpose, 44
Motorola, 69, 172–174, 219
multidimensional matrix organizations, 112–113
multifront strategy, 141

NASA, 69, 191–193
nature, 21, 23, 56, 241
nature domain
HP (Hewlett-Packard), 95–97, 106–107
misalignment of strategy, structure, and culture, 91–92
realigning structure and strategy, 94
nature imperative, 23, 91
aligning strategy, culture, and structure, 93
culture measurement, 135–136
IBM, 105
Lance Armstrong, 250–251
neglecting, 93
project investment list, 134
rating organization on, 135
strategy measurement, 137
structure measurement, 136
navigation metrics, 74–75
new product portfolios, 161
new product releases, 161
Newton, 218, 220
Next Big Thing, 2
Nielsen, Ernie, vii
nimble proactive processes, 186–191
Nokia, 124

Nordstrom, 255
Nutt, Paul C., 227

Odyssey program (AT&T), 158–160, 184–185
"offer to make" world, 12
"offer to make" ("offer and make") companies, 219
open-loop system, 232
operational excellence, 33, 116
operational excellence strategies
culture, 100
traditional hierarchy for, 115, 117
operation excellence, 103
optimizing portfolio
balance, 170–171
business reviews and, 175–177
fool with tool, 169–170
judgment, 169–170
matching projects with resources, 167–171
optimizing projects, 168–169
organizations
assessing culture, 102–104
changes in day-to-day activities, 2
collective who, why, and where, 51
competence culture, 116
continually communicating and reinforcing message, 51
control, 116
cultural gap, 98
descriptors, 34
embedding ideation throughout, 50–51
ideation differentiating, 28
ideation imperative, 56–60
nature, 21, 23
operational excellence, 116
product leadership strategy, 116
sense of purpose, 37
sources of culture, 98
strong sense of purpose and identity, 42
where they will be in two years, 2–4
outcomes
benefits realization, 218
distinguishing from outputs, 217–218, 220
realizing benefits, 230–231
shifting metrics and incentive systems to, 233, 235

outputs
 distinguishing from outcomes,
  217–218, 220
 emphasizing over outcomes, 219
 matching to customer desires, 221
 shifting metrics and incentive systems
  from, 233, 235

Packard, David, 92, 95
Palm Computing, 220
palmOne, 106
Palm Pilot, 220
Paradigm Learning, 50
Paris-Nice race, 250
passive investors, 171
past performance, 65, 74
The Path of Least Resistance (Fritz), 66
PayPal, ix, 125
PDA (personal digital assistant), 220
PDMA (Project Development and Management Association), 161
Peak Performance: Aligning the Hearts and
  Minds of Your Employees (Katzenbach),
  54
perceived identity, 34
performance, 66
 better levels of, 14
 what is not happening, 70
Perlow, Leslie, 166
personal decisions
 purpose driving force behind, 41
 visual mapping, 50
PERT precedence diagrams, 193
Pharma Inc., 118–119
planned portfolios, 181–182, 186
 aligning with real portfolios, 206–209
 unrealistic, 208
plausible deniability, 80
PMO (portfolio or program management
  office), 144
PMO (project or program management
  office), 114
PMT (portfolio management team), 144
pooled interdependencies, 192–193
Porras, Jerry, 46, 132
Porter, Michael, 8, 33, 96, 150
portfolio domains, 157
portfolio governance environment,
  144–148

portfolio management, 14
 hyperpassive and hyperactive, 171, 175
 real-time, 208–209
 small scalable processes, 168–169
portfolio managers' decision making, 225
portfolios
 active investors, 171
 actual, 181–182
 aligning, 184–186
 aligning planned with real, 206–209
 decision processes, 223–225
 failed execution of, 182
 financial criteria, 162
 interdependence, 169
 lagging indicators, 175
 mastering, 171, 175
 more reliable forecasts, 207
 optimizing, 167–171
 passive investors, 171
 planned, 181–182, 186
 planning processes, 169
 PMT (portfolio management team), 144
 realigning, 171, 175
 reviewing, 171, 175
 revising, 171, 175
 senior executive sponsorship, 144
 synthesis measurement, 210–211
 velocity of decisions on projects, 145
positive thinking, 66
potential backlogs, 203–206
power of culture, 97–98
predictable and repeatable results, 66
Premji, Azim, 19
Prince, Chuck, 47, 106, 111
prioritizing
 importance of proper, 158–160
 project work, 157–164
 scoring anchor, 164
 shift away from innovation, 161–162
 weighting and scoring systems,
  162–164
problem-solving mentality, 65, 71–72
problem solving versus appreciative
  inquiry, 70–73
processes, 65–66
 advantages of, 168–169
 gap analysis, 71
 losing credibility, 170
 nimble proactive processes, 186–191
 small scalable, 168–169

process initiative life cycle, 67
product development systems, 150
product excellence, 66
product leadership strategies, 33, 116–118
product line organization, 112
product managers, 118–119, 129
professional services firm, 78
profits, 82, 96
program managers
  advantages of process, 168–169
  information, 134
  negotiation and mutual adjustments
    between, 195
program of the month, 67
programs, 9, 10–11, 23, 191–192
  aligning, 184–186
  new strategy and, 13
  synthesis measurement, 211
  transition measurement, 236–237
Project Chess, 126
project cost engineers, 187
project creep
  managing trade-offs, 220–223
  stakeholders and portfolio decision
    processes, 223–225
  strengthening sponsorship through
    handoffs, 222–223
project investments
  engaging strategy through, 4
  linking evolving strategy to, 11
  necessary to execute strategy, 69
project leaders
  metrics describing specific outputs, 155
  responsibilities, 22
project leadership domains, 15, 23
project management
  critical role, 8
  language of, 7–9
  stages, 234
  technical change logs, 224
Project Management Body of Knowledge
  (PMBOK), 233
"Project Management Manual," viii
project managers
  advantages of process, 168–169
  budgets for deliverables, 119
  buying functional services, 129–130
  costs of preventing accidents, 131
  DPR Construction, 132
  effective sponsors wish list, 148

engagement imperative, 142
  functional resources assignment, 129
  information, 134
  ownership of budgets, 129
  sponsor options, 225–226
  sponsors' wish list, 149
  "yes, if . . ." approach, 225
project outputs, 8–9, 10, 23, 62, 122
  metrics, 68, 155
project portfolio, see also portfolios
  corporate strategy alignment, 3–4,
    13–14
  language of, 9
  leadership, 22
project portfolio management, 5. See also
    portfolios
  leading from middle with support from
    top, 22
  strategic role, 4–7
projects, 3, 23
  actively deciding not to undertake
    wrong, 7
  adjusting evaluation process, 128
  aligning, 184–186
  allocating people to, 129
  BFI (big fuzzy idea), 217
  clarifying goals and metrics, 69–75
  clarifying long-range intentions, 45–47
  clarifying purpose, 43–44
  clearly communicating priorities, 6
  closing out crisply and unambiguously,
    229–331
  commissioning and start-up, 227–229
  communicating identity, purpose, and
    long-range intention, 48–50
  conflict in allocating resources between,
    13
  correctly doing, 10
  criteria, 160–161
  criteria, priority weightings, and scoring
    anchors, 163
  decentralized work, 227–228
  design freeze, 229
  distinguishing outputs from outcomes,
    217–218, 220
  doing right, 7, 181
  engaging in right, 151
  environment challenges constituting,
    40–41
  essential to strategy, 13

projects (*continued*)
  failure and lack of situational awareness, 67
  fast-track designs, 196–197
  fending off chaos, 114
  finite useful life, 214
  highest-priority, 170
  "hot list," 129
  identifying and assigning resources, 144, 164
  identifying potential, 149–156
  impasse, 224
  importance of, 3
  incentive programs, 69
  information about, 168
  interdependencies, 169, 191–192
  internal and external brands, 52–54
  investment decisions, 5
  investment value, 157
  large-scale creep, 216
  life of their own, 229–230
  linking strategic outcomes to outputs, 86
  management by exception, 186–187
  managers, 144
  managing trade-offs, 220–223
  managing well enough to achieve objectives, 10–11
  matching with resources, 167–171
  milestones, 194
  monitoring and aligning work, 181
  multiple, 185
  new product releases, 161
  planned objectives for, 10–11
  planning and replanning intervals, 188–191
  PMO (portfolio or program management office), 144
  pooled interdependencies, 192–193
  portfolio domains, 157
  portfolio governance environment, 144–148
  prioritizing work, 157–164
  priority decisions, 143
  realizing benefits, 230–231
  reshaping identity, 36–37
  sponsors, 144
  strategic buckets, 157
  strategic execution, 3
  strict set of criteria, 6
  stronger engagement, 178
  switching context, 166
  synthesis measurement, 211–212
  synthesizing and integrating work, 23
  tangible things created by, 218
  tasks, 192
  testing identity strength, 34–36
  time to market, 196
  transferring to mainstream, 23
  to transform business, 13
  transform business criteria, 162
  transition measurement, 236–237
  translating strategy-speak into parlance, 7–9
  tuning matrix strength, 127–131
  updating schedule, 187
  victory celebration for completed, 230
  weighting and scoring systems, 162–164
  white spaces between, 183
project schedulers, 187
project scheduling tools, 193–194
project teams, 128
purpose. *See also* sense of purpose
  ambivalence, apathy, and boredom, 37–38
  as basic life force, 39
  beneficiary of, 44–45
  Citigroup, 47
  clarifying, 30, 37–45
  connecting to, 43–44
  coping rituals, 39
  culture, 56
  disconnection to, 41
  DNV (Det Norske Veritas), 42
  driving force behind personal decisions, 41
  goals, 69
  importance, 38–40
  lack of, 39–40
  lack of clarity about, 42
  losing sense of, 39
  matter of life or death, 39
  measuring, 58–59
  motivation and, 44
  need for connection to, 39
  projects clarifying, 43–44
  projects communicating, 48–50
  shared, 41
  Southco Inc., 44

trumping circumstances, 40–43
visual mapping, 48–50
working without, 40

quarterly performance indicators, 73–74
questions, asking right, 70–73

Rassmussen, Neil, ix
reaction becomes management process, 65
real capacity for project execution,
    165–167
realigning portfolios, 171, 175
real portfolios, aligning with planned
    portfolios, 206–209
real skill inventory, 165–167
real-time portfolio management, 208–209
reciprocal interdependencies, 194–196,
    199
Renault, 42
resources
    changes in, 182
    determining capacity, 164–167
    efficient use of, 66
    matching projects with, 167–171
    matching requirements and availability,
        169
    reallocating, 183
reviewing portfolios, 171, 175
revising portfolios, 171, 175
reward systems, 130
Rice, Joyce, vii
Richardson, John A., 219
right things to do, 21
The Rise of the Creative Class (Florida), 109
risk aversion, 71
Rolm and culture, 105
ROM (return on management), 6
Rombach, H. Dieter, 69
Ronberg, Kimm, ix
Roto Corporation (RC), 145–147

sales opportunities, 14
sales training program, 150
sanity checks, 164–167
San Jose Business Journal, 81
SAPM (Stanford Advanced Project Man-
    agement Program), vii

Sartain, Libby, 54
SAS Institute, 108–109
Schneider, William, 99
Schneider culture typology, 101
Schrage, Michael, 204
scope creep and sponsors, 227
scoring anchor, prioritizing, 164
Scott, W. Richard, x
Sculley, John, 1
Seeing What's Next (Christensen, Anthony,
    and Roth), 35
SEF (strategic execution framework), 14,
    17, 241
    from 30,000-foot view, 254–255
    acid test questions, 256–257
    aligning six domains of, 15–18
    critical organizational alignments, 21
    deciding where to start, 254–257
    excellence, 255
    imperatives, 241
    importance of alignment, 240
    intentionally using, 19–21
    making your own miracles, 255–256
    navigating, 16, 18
    project leadership domains, 15
    rethinking stated strategy, 19
    Singapore National Library Board
        (SNLB), 248–249
    strategy-making domains, 15
self-limiting attitudes, 64–67
senior management
    becoming project leaders, 7
    responsibilities, 22
sense of meaning, 40
sense of purpose, 40–42. See also purpose
    Lance Armstrong, 250
sequential interdependencies, 193–194
serious play, 204
service-oriented businesses, 99
Sesame Street, 44
short-term decisions, 45
short-term objectives, 46–47
silo mentality, 110–111
Simons, Robert, 5
simulation tools, 203–206
Singapore National Library Board (SNLB),
    241
    creating right alignments, 244–249
    cultural tone, structure, and strategy,
        247

Singapore National Library Board (SNLB) (*continued*)
  human resources, 246
  ideation domain alignment, 245
  Library 2000 Review Committee, 245
  multimillion-dollar transformation of national library system, 24
  organizational leadership, 246
  portfolios and projects, 248
  SEF (strategic execution framework), 248–249
  significant organizational change, 244
  strategic vision and strategic engagement, 247
  structuring itself, 247
  technology, 246
  transforming user experience, 247
six imperatives
  navigating, 21, 23–24
  strategic execution, 16–19
Six Sigma process, 66
Skunk Works, 116, 123, 125–126
Skype, 125
SMART (specific, measurable, achievable, resourced, time bound) goals, 64
  identifying, 85
  progress and, 65
Southco Inc., 44
Southwest Airlines, 76–77, 150–154, 259
sponsors
  project manager options for, 225–226
  project managers wish list, 148–149
  scope creep, 227
sponsorship
  accountability, 147–148
  combating last-minute blunders, 226–227
  commitment, 147
  critical discipline and support for portfolio management, 145
  empowerment, 148
  guiding portfolio investment decisions, 147
  key characteristics, 147–148
  lack of appropriate, 222
  logjam-breaking decisions, 224
  making tough calls, 170
  project and program managers support, 147

  RC (Roto Corporation), 145–147
  strategic execution, 144–145
  strengthening through handoffs, 222–223
  success or failure executing change, 222
  time to decision, 145
  vision, 147
sponsor trade-off analysis, 225–226
SST (Shared Services Team), 61–62
stakeholders and decision processes, 223–225
start-up, centralized controls during, 227–229
Stavros, Jacqueline, 71
strategic action, importance of, 7–8
strategic buckets, 157
  working in the business, 14
  working on the business, 14
  working to transform the business, 14
strategic clarity, 5
strategic direction, 3
strategic execution, 22
  aligning project portfolio to corporate strategy, 3–4
  compromising, 206–207
  engagement, 9
  engaging strategy through project investment stream, 4, 9
  failures, 247–248
  focusing on past, 65
  ideation, 56
  requiring systemic thinking, 11–14
  six imperatives, 16–19
  sponsorship, 144–145
  success or failure, 144
  unable to define path to, 62
strategic focus, 48
strategic goals, metrics aligning with, 67–68
strategic identity, 33–34, 48–49
strategic intent, clarifying, 13
strategic investments, 239–240
strategic objectives, 131
strategic outcomes, 8–9, 10, 23, 122
  contemporaneous or leading indicators, 155
  finite and focused, 65
  listing, 62
  project output metric, 68

strategic planning office, 150
strategic portfolio management, 5
strategic project investments, 14
strategic project portfolio management, 23
strategic thinking, 7, 11–14
strategy, 23
    acting on referrals creating most value
        to business, 70
    actions and activities to execute, 7–8
    aligning incentives with, 130–131
    aligning structure to, 108–127
    aligning with culture, 102–103
    becoming more clearly defined, 69
    clarifying, 151
    clearly articulated, 7, 134
    cost leader, 33
    cultural and structural adjustments, 97
    customer intimacy, 33
    defining, 93
    differentiated value provider, 33
    disruptive innovation, 33
    engagement domain, 206
    engaging through investment stream, 23
    engaging through project investment
        stream, 4
    failure of, 1–2
    flying in face of organization's culture,
        97
    generating greater dollars per sale, 70
    lacking end points, 62
    Lance Armstrong, 251–252
    language of formulation, 9
    losing grip on project investments
        related to, 6
    multifront, 141
    nature imperative and, 137
    Next Big Thing, 2
    not supported and enabled by its
        structure, 97
    operational excellence, 33
    plan to communicate, 61
    prioritizing referral leads on profit
        potential, 70
    product leadership, 33
    project investments necessary to
        execute, 69
    structure misaligned with, 127–128
    translating intention into, 87
    translating intention to, 62

strategy implementers, 22
strategy makers, 22
strategy making, 15
strategy-making domains, 15, 21
strategy maps
    customer outcomes versus customer
        needs, 153
    identifying critical activities, 150–153
    objectives, metrics, targets, and project
        initiatives, 156
strategy-speak, 7–9
Streiff, Christian, 201, 203
strong ideation companies, 49
strong matrix, 116
    Biotech Inc., 121–123
    cross-discipline coordination, 122
    customer intimacy strategies, 119–120
    Fluor Corporation, 120–121
    functional managers, 122
    nurturing technical communities or
        practice, 123
    project outputs tied to strategic out-
        comes, 116
    responsiveness and agility, 119, 122
    technical expertise and best practices,
        122
    workers' incentives tied to customers'
        values, 122
    workers primary day-to-day direction,
        119
strong matrix structure, 113
    advantages, 122
    authority, 123
    future general managers, 122
    HP sales, 124
    information, 127
    satisfying customer's changing require-
        ments, 121, 123
    systems integration, testing and start-up
        personnel power, 228
structural levers
    adjusting evaluation process, 128
    aligning incentives with strategy and
        structure, 130–131
    allocating people to projects, 129
    assigning budget ownership, 129–130
    cross-functional project teams, 128
    policy and practices changes, 128
structural misfit, 134

structure, 23
  aligned, 108
  changing, 93
  changing long-engrained corporate
    culture, 105
  culture aligned with, 257
  defining, 93
  directing organization toward goals, 109
  incentives aligned with, 130–131
  information technology aligned with,
    126–127
  Lance Armstrong, 251
  misaligned with strategy and culture,
    127–128
  nature imperative, 136
  new layers of culture, 105
  sets of format and informal rules, 93
  strategy aligned with, 108–127
structure-strategy-culture fit, 134
subconscious thought patterns, 67
subgoals, 194–195
success, meaning of, 67–68
sustainability, 81
  Citigroup, 46–47
  ecology and, 83
  through ideation imperative, 48–51
switching context, 166
synthesis, 15, 241, 257
synthesis imperative, 23, 181
  continuous feedback, 182–183
  failed coordination, 184
  Lance Armstrong, 253
  portfolio synthesis measurement,
    210–211
  program synthesis measurement, 211
  project list for building stronger, 209
  project synthesis measurement,
    211–212
  rating organization on, 209
synthesizing and integrating work, 23

target outcome and opposing tensions,
  66–67
tasks
  changes in completion date, 193
  stuck on incomplete, 215
  subgoals, 194–195
technical change logs, 224

Terman, Fred, 95
Texas Instruments, 96
thinking beyond whose job is it, 22
3M and generating disruptive innovations,
  125
tiger teams, 116, 125
time to market, 196
time utilization metric, 79
The Tipping Point (Gladwell), 44
top-level metric of profitability, 79
Total Quality Management, 66
Tour de France, 249–254
Toyoda, Eiji, 31
Toyota, 31–32
  commitment to doing right things and
    doing things right, 19
  ideation, 29–31
  realigning strategic projects around
    change in environment, 29
  strong sense of identity, 34
  Toyota Way, 31
The Toyota Way Fieldbook (Liker and
  Meier), 31
trade-offs
  managing, 220–223
  sponsor trade-off analysis, 225–226
traditional hierarchy
  information, 127
  for operational excellence strategies,
    115, 117
transformation, 14
transformational projects, 19–20
transformative projects, 13
transition, 15, 241
  effectiveness, 257
  project list for building stronger, 235
transition domain, 223
transition imperative, 23, 213
  closing loop, 231–235
  distinguishing outputs from outcomes,
    217–218, 220
  feedback, 214–215
  finite useful life of project, 214
  handoff between strategy carrier and
    ongoing organization, 213–214
  Lance Armstrong, 253–254
  rating organization on, 236–237
  right time for handoffs, 216–217
"triple bottom line" accounting, 81–84

UPS (United Parcel Service), 115, 117, 127
use systems, 164–167

Viabene and real-time portfolio management, 208–209
vision, 15, 56, 241
  clarity, 257
  requiring creative thinking, 71
  sponsorship, 147
vision imperative, 21, 62
  achieving, 85–87
  determining where to start, 85
  inability to articulate outcomes, 85
  Lance Armstrong, 251–252
  long-range goals and metrics alignment with strategy, 130–131
  measuring goals, 88
  measuring measurements, 88–89
  measuring strategy connected to vision, 89–90
  rating organization on, 87–90
  SMART (specific, measurable, achievable, resources, time bound) goals, 64
  starting simple, 85–87
visual mapping, 48–50
Vité Corporation, vii
Volvo, 1, 42–43

Walt Disney Imagineering, 83
Warren, John, ix
Wasserman, Tim, vii
weak matrix, 114, 116–119
Welch, Jack, 132
Western India Vegetable Products Limited, 19
Western Union, 35

wetlands, 83
whack-a-mole execution, 18
"What Is Strategy?" (Porter), 8
white spaces, 183
  identifying, 195
  managing, 191–206
Whitney, Diana, 71
Who Says Elephants Can't Dance? (Gerstner), 36
"Who Says We Can't Do It?," (video) 249
Why Decisions Fail (Nutt), 227
WICIS (Wireless Intercarrier Communications Interface Specifications) component, 158
Wipro Limited, 19–21, 50, 123
worker's compensation (WC) insurance, 130–131
working in the business, 14
working on the business, 14
working to transform the business, 14
workload, calculating, 164–165
work order queue, 129
workplace
  creation of better, 257–259
  energy level, 54
  humanity in, 258–259
The World Bank IFC (International Finance Corporation), 81
WorldCom, 42, 45

Xerox, 36

Yahoo!, 52–54, 259
Yamamoto, Ryoichi, 34
Yeo, George, 245
Yorwerth, Nigel, ix
Yorwerth, Patricia, ix
you accomplish what you measure, 67

About the Authors

MARK MORGAN is the Chief Learning Officer at IPSolutions, Inc. (IPS) and practice director of the Stanford Advanced Project Management curriculum offered by the Stanford Center for Professional Development. He is responsible for the development of learning technology at IPS and has contributed extensively to courses including Converting Strategy into Action, Leadership for Strategic Execution, and Mastering the Integrated Program. He is the lead architect of the strategic execution framework. Mark is a consultant, keynote speaker, educator, and master facilitator for global audiences ranging from the program manager level to the board of directors level. His experience in converting strategy into action stems from twenty-five years of industry experience in project, program, portfolio, and organizational leadership and management. Mark has worked with global teams in top *Fortune* 50 companies to mobilize their strategy. Mark has an undergraduate degree in engineering, a master's degree in business, and is Stanford and PMP certified in project management.

RAYMOND E. LEVITT is Professor of Civil & Environmental Engineering and Coordinator of the Construction Engineering and Management Program at Stanford University. Ray previously served on the faculty of MIT, helping to launch MIT's Construction Engineering and Project Management program. Ray's teaching, research, and consulting focus on designing organizations to execute complex, fast-track projects and service/maintenance work such as IT and health care delivery. His Virtual Design Team (VDT) research group develops new organization design theory and simulation tools to help managers optimize project and matrix organization designs. In 1999 Ray founded the Advanced Project Management

(APM) Executive Program at the Stanford Center for Professional Development, and serves as the program's Academic Director. In 2003, he founded and currently serves as director of Stanford's Collaboratory for Research on Global Projects, a multidisciplinary, multi-university initiative aimed at enhancing the performance of global projects. He has coauthored several books, including *Construction Safety Management*, 2nd ed., and *Knowledge-Based Systems in Engineering*. Ray was a cofounder and has served as a director of Design Power, Inc.; Vité Corporation; and Visual Network Design, Inc.

WILLIAM MALEK is the Strategy Execution Officer for Strategy2Reality LLC and the former program director for the Stanford Advanced Project Management program at Stanford University. William has more than twenty-eight years of corporate experience in strategic planning, management consulting, and organizational alignment, and his focus is on the study of strategy execution and leading a positive organization. William concentrates on effective group planning techniques to generate the leadership required to convert strategy into reality. As a teacher and facilitator, he has earned audience acclaim as an international keynote speaker, workshop leader, and strategic consultant. As one of the instructors in APM, he has presented in the award-winning Stanford courses such as Converting Strategy into Action, Leadership for Strategic Execution, Mastering the Project Portfolio, and Designing Organizations for Execution. William has held executive positions such as CEO of IPSolutions, Inc., as well as facilitating *Fortune* 500 senior management teams in companies such as Qualcomm, Cisco, and McKesson. William holds an MBA in e-commerce from Capella University and a BS in mechanical engineering from the University of California, Santa Barbara. A few of his certifications include the Stanford Certified Project Manager (SCPM), a Project Management Professional (PMP), and a New Product Development Professional (NPDP).